SEMEIA 43

GENRE, NARRATIVITY, AND THEOLOGY

Guest Editors of this Issue:
Mary Gerhart and James G. Williams

©1988
by the Society of Biblical Literature

SEMEIA 43

Copyright © 1988 by the Society of Biblical Literature

All rights reserved. No part of this work may be reproduced or transmitted in any form or by any means, electronic or mechanical, including photocopying and recording, or by means of any information storage or retrieval system, except as may be expressly permitted by the 1976 Copyright Act or in writing from the publisher. Requests for permission should be addressed in writing to the Rights and Permissions Office, Society of Biblical Literature, 825 Houston Mill Road, Atlanta, GA 30329, USA.

ISSN 0095-571X
ISBN 1-58983-180-2

Printed in the United States of America
on acid-free paper

CONTENTS

Contributors to This Issue

Preface
   Mary Gerhart and *James G. Williams* vii

Narrative and Disclosure: Mechanisms of Concealing, Revealing, and Reveiling
   Werner H. Kelber 1

Irony as Hope in Mark's Gospel: A Reply to Werner Kelber
   Dan O. Via 21

Genric Competence in Biblical Hermeneutics
   Mary Gerhart 29

How to Read a Jaguar: A Response to Mary Gerhart
   Robert Detweiler 45

Once Again: Gospel Genre
   Charles H. Talbert 53

And Once Again, What Sort of "Essence"? A Response to Charles Talbert
   David P. Moessner 75

Parable and Chreia: From Q to Narrative Gospel
   James G. Williams 85

Appropriateness in the Form Criticism of the Teaching Source: A Response to James Williams
   Martin J. Buss 115

Aphorism in Discourse and Narrative
   John Dominic Crossan 121

Aphorism and Narrative: A Response to John Dominic Crossan
   Robert C. Tannehill 141

Narrative, History, and Gospel: A General Response
  Adela Yarbro Collins   145

Anteriority, Authority, and Secrecy: A General Comment
  Frank Kermode   155

CONTRIBUTORS TO THIS ISSUE

Martin J. Buss
   Department of Religion
   Emory University
   Atlanta, GA 30322

Adela Yarbro Collins
   Department of Theology
   University of Notre Dame
   Notre Dame, IN 46556

John Dominic Crossan
   155 North Harbor Drive, Apt. 3208
   Chicago, IL 60601

Robert Detweiler
   Graduate Institute of the Liberal Arts
   Emory University
   Atlanta, GA 30322

Mary Gerhart
   Department of Religious Studies
   Hobart and William Smith Colleges
   Geneva, NY 14456

Werner H. Kelber
   Department of Religious Studies
   Rice University, P.O.B. 1892
   Houston, TX 77251

Frank Kermode
   27 Luard Road
   Cambridge, England CB2 2PJ

David P. Moessner
   Columbia Theological Seminary
   701 Columbia Drive
   Decatur, GA 30031

Charles H. Talbert
 Department of Religion, P.O.B. 7212
 Wake Forest University
 Winston-Salem, NC 27109

Robert C. Tannehill
 Methodist Theological School of Ohio, P.O.B. 630
 Delaware, OH 43015

Dan O. Via
 The Divinity School
 Duke University
 Durham, NC 27706

James G. Williams
 Department of Religion
 Syracuse University
 Syracuse, NY 13244-1170

PREFACE

Mary Gerhart and James G. Williams

When we first conceived this issue of *Semeia* in January of 1985, we worked out four questions to be addressed:

(1) What are the roots of narrativity itself? How and why does it function as it does in human existence?
(2) In what ways does generic analysis assist the reader in arriving at a critical interpretation of the text?
(3) What is the genre of the early Christian canonical gospels (if only *one* genre), and what difference does this make theologically?
(4) What role do aphoristic forms play in relation to gospel and story?

We did not expect each contributor to respond in a global way to all four questions, but we asked each one to give the sharpest, most vigorous critical attention to one or more of them. Our expectation was that the product would be a collection of essays and responses that would contribute fruitfully to current critical theory and biblical hermeneutics.

We were not disappointed. All the essays address two or more of the questions, which, as we see them, move from the basic and general to the specific in a more or less continuous spectrum. However, it is possible to identify the contributions in terms of primary focus on one of the questions.

Werner Kelber gives the most attention to the first question in his analysis of "concealing, revealing, and reveiling" as narrative functions that seem to arise out of a concern with secrecy and disclosure that all humans share in their personal relations, traditions, and institutions. He grounds this analysis in a fresh and engaging discussion of the Gospel of Mark.

Mary Gerhart focuses on the second question concerning generic analysis. Preferring the term "genric" to "generic" due to the latter's connotations, she assesses the relation of linguistic and genric competence and performance, and she stresses that genre involves the reader/hearer's production (performance) of a new reading as well as the culturally given classifications that determine how texts are read and heard. She offers six ways in which genre is a productive principle in biblical studies, and she concludes by offering the insight that biblical theologians could understand themselves as mediating between genres.

Robert Detweiler and Martin Buss also concern themselves primarily with genre questions. Detweiler, in responding to Gerhart, continues her discussion of genre and genric competence, but he moves into a "metageneric" question when he asks, "Does genre classification reflect something about the construction of ultimate reality as revealed by interpretation?" Buss, responding to James Williams, argues for the notion of "aptness" in different levels of speech, a notion derived in great part from the chreia form of classical antiquity.

Charles Talbert is concerned chiefly with the third question, the genre of the canonical gospels. He extends and nuances his earlier work on gospel as a form of biography by emphasizing that the ancient biographical genre provided a controlling context of interpretation for the Jesus traditions, and he argues that parable should not be used as a genre term for the gospels.

David Moessner takes issue with Talbert's central tenet that gospel is a form of biography. Moessner argues that Luke especially has predominant features of historiography, with close parallels in the narrative histories of the Hebrew Bible. There is thus, contrary to one of Talbert's theological implications, a great deal of theological significance in the kind of narrative genre developed by the authors of the gospels.

Also in the area of gospel genre, Dan O. Via's response to Werner Kelber is concerned with the genre of Mark and its theological implications. Via stresses that Mark is a parabolic miracle story. The theological import of this is the hope or eschatological new creation that Mark proclaims.

James Williams begins with a variation on the fourth question, the relation of parabolic forms to gospel as narrative and story, in order to shed further light on his earlier conclusion that Mark was a new literary form that emerged out of the interaction of parable and biography. He holds that in Q one can discern an encounter of chreia and parable in which the chreia's biographical impulse tends to turn Jesus into the subject of his own parables, while the dynamic of parable simultaneously affected the chreia from within. There is thus a Q-canonical gospel trajectory that is much different from the social setting, literary forms, and theology of the Gospel of Thomas.

Crossan, remaining primarily within the perimeters of the aphorism-story question (number four), begins with the aphorism *Ask, Seek, Knock* and presents a transmissional analysis that concludes with a comment on its "hermeneutical creativity." He touches also on the theological implications of genre by showing two transmissional tendencies: the *seek* direction in the Gospel of Thomas and Dialogue of the Savior and the *ask* direction in the Johannine tradition.

Robert Tannehill, in his response to Crossan, points to a narrative context in which the triadic aphorism, *Ask, Seek, Knock*, would make sense. He implies that this narrative context has an anterior historical context.

In her general response Adela Yarbro Collins questions Talbert's point concerning the gospels as a form of biographical literature. In entering into general genre questions with her discussion of myth and history, she suggests "that the primary intention of the author of Mark was to write history" in an eschatological or apocalyptic sense. Collins, as a biblical historian, acknowledges her inclination toward making the original historical context of genre normative in reading texts, but she recognizes the legitimacy of other considerations that modify what the ancients said about their texts.

Frank Kermode, taking Kelber's essay as point of departure, offers some interesting comments on anteriority, authority, and secrecy. He wonders whether, contrary to Kelber, it is possible to speak of a narrative *plenum*, or whether "narrative cannot avoid turning its back on us." It is, he suggests, by metacritical reflection that constituent elements of a genre are identified and forms of anteriority are established. The authority of certain forms associated with secrecy, such as aphorisms and parables, becomes paradoxically the greatest when published in the exoteric mode of narrative. Why is this? How, he asks, "does it come about that the attempt to be authoritatively plain creates more secrets and demands more interpretation, including the variety that postulates, in some detail, the existence of anterior secrets?"

There are, of course, other ways of posing that question. Could it be that narrative is a mode of thought and expression which brings into play the violence of founding cultural acts that the human mind unconsciously tries to deny or avoid? This may be one explanation of the dialectic of secrecy and disclosure. (See Williams, Works Consulted, 1985/86 and forthcoming.) In weaving their way through questions such as this one and others raised in this issue, it is crucial both for the academy and human societies that critical interpreters not delude themselves into thinking a "genre-free" position is possible, but that they see themselves as genre mediators.

NARRATIVE AND DISCLOSURE: MECHANISMS OF CONCEALING, REVEALING, AND REVEILING

Werner H. Kelber
Rice University

ABSTRACT

The need to hide and share is manifest in every aspect of the human condition, including that of narrative. This essay continues explorations of secrecy and disclosure in biblical narrative. Mark's gospel which has long been associated with secrecy will serve as a sample for this study.

Based on the premise that narrative seeks to overcome secrecy more than to enforce it, this piece will focus primarily on mechanisms of disclosure. Esoteric secrecy is one form of concealment Mark undertook to deconstruct. An inquiry into the role and genesis of esoteric secrecy sheds new light on the narrator's opposition to it. Identity secrets constitute another form of concealment. At irregular intervals the protagonist's identity is veiled by injunctions not to make it public. These secrets are enjoined only to be revealed. They exert pressure upon the narrative steering it toward final epiphany. Consideration of the role of the reader, finally, reveals a hermeneutical dynamic that is unfriendly toward secrecy. For the reader has access not only to what is communicated to the characters in the narrative, but also to what is concealed from them.

New secrecy arises *inter alia* at the very junctures where disclosure was made. The more the narrative strives to reveal, the more it becomes involved in concealments. Secrecy and disclosure condition each other reciprocally and in complex ways.

For nothing is hidden, except to be revealed; nor has anything been secret, but that it should come to light.
Mark 4:22

> Jesus said: 'I tell my mysteries to those who are worthy of my mysteries.'
> *Gospel of Thomas*, log. 62

> ... they maintain that the Savior privately taught these same things not to all, but to certain only of his disciples who could comprehend them, and who understood what was intended by him through means of arguments, enigmas, and parables.
> Irenaeus, *Adversus Haereses*, II, 27, 2

> We are all, in a sense, experts on secrecy.
> Bok, *Secrets*

> We are most unwilling to accept mystery . . .
> Kermode, *Genesis of Secrecy*

> But the readers have never really been in the dark.
> Magness, *Sense and Absence*

> A 'gospel' is a narrative of a son of god who appears among men as a riddle inviting misunderstanding.
> Smith, "Good News is No News"

0. Since Wrede's classic study on concealment in the gospels (1901 [1971]), narrative and secrecy are thought to be close allies, especially in Mark and John.[1] *Messiasgeheimnis* was the code he had invented to get a significant matter into perspective. To him the term suggested a theological idea which exercised controlling influence upon Mark's narrative, relegating it to "the history of dogma" (1901: 131 [1971: 131]). Today few will give unqualified assent to the term "messianic secret," and fewer still subscribe to Wrede's explanation of its functioning. But the alliance of Mark's narrative with secrecy is not in doubt, and the debate about its genesis and operation continues unabated (Blevins, 1981; Tuckett, 1983). In our generation the issue of narrative secrecy has been revitalized by Kermode's *The Genesis of Secrecy* (1979). For him Mark serves as paradigm for the fundamental secrecy of all narrative. It was less a specific idea that accounts for the gospel's secrecy than the labyrinthian property of narrativity itself which ushers readers along meandering paths into hidden corners and unpromising dead ends. Being an insider in this situation "is only a more elaborate way of being kept outside" (1979: 27). My own work has increasingly moved toward a parabolic reading of Mark's narrative (1983: 117–31). From my perspective, the gospel encourages experimentation with a new logic in defiance of received opinion. Secrecy or, as I prefer to call it, mystery results from a disorienting-reorienting narrative which forestalls closure. Meaning is thereby not allowed to attach itself exclusively to the one, the literal sense. More

recently Williams has asserted that Mark's narrative "stands within the iconoclastic biblical tradition of paradox, irony, and abruptness" (1985: 84). On his reading, the gospel's paratactic style is of a piece with a plot at the center of which stands the mystery of the kingdom of God (1985: 53, 90, 134). Whether one focuses on a central idea or on narrative opaqueness, on parabolic mystery or on mysterious language, narrative and secrecy remain an issue in Mark, and perhaps for all narrative.

0.1   Not all the evidence marshaled on behalf of narrative secrecy is equally persuasive. Perhaps it is primarily to readers schooled on the more densely plotted novel of the 18th and 19th century that fractured surfaces and paratactic style suggest intriguing ambiguities and latent senses. It is well to remember that in the history of story there was no such thing as narrative reticence before we knew what narrative plenum was. As Kermode wisely observed, "Whatever is preserved grows enigmatic" (1979: 64). Distance, both temporal and cultural, produces its own complicities with secrecy. It is thus tempting to suggest that sole emphasis on secrecy and ambiguity draws its principal inspiration from the anxieties of modernity.

0.2   In light of the foregoing it is worth noting that writing, and writing a narrative, is not in the best interest of enforcing secrecy. The best way to keep a secret is not to talk or write about it. Narrative, while inveighing against definitional clarity, seeks to reveal more than to conceal. While it is true that our passion for narrative sequence and propriety, this deep-seated desire to organized fully and finalize, makes us suppress narrative secrets (Kermode, 1983: 133–53), it is also possible that passionate attention to secrets makes us overlook narrative's desire to rid itself of secrecy. Narrative seeks to be a natural ally of disclosure. Notwithstanding the conviction, firmly institutionalized since Wrede, that Mark has entered into a special covenant with secrecy, we shall present the view that the gospel is paradigmatic of narrative's basic urge toward disclosure. The bulk of this piece is about Mark's strenuous efforts at discrediting and disclosing secrecy. To discern the forms and mechanisms of disclosure is a presupposition for understanding secrecy, for the crux of the matter is revealing and reveiling, this dual narrative attention to message and secrecy.

1.0   Mark 4:1–34 narrates what may well be the most intriguing and intractably difficult dramatization of secrecy in the gospel. Despite its traditional label of esoteric secrecy, the passage furnishes a good example both of unlocking and creating secrecy.

1.1   The scene narrates Jesus's public recital of a parable, followed by his withdrawal together with the twelve and a few chosen ones. In response to their question concerning the parables, Jesus volunteers the solemn pronouncement: "To you has been given the mystery of the kingdom of God, but for those outside everything occurs in parables" (4:11). After disclosing additional characteristics of the outsiders (4:12), Jesus entrusts the explication of the "master parable" (Williams, 1985: 4) plus additional parables and parabolic sayings to the circle of select ones around him. The speech is formally concluded with a narrative aside to the effect that Jesus spoke exclusively in parables which he privately explained to his disciples (4:34).

1.2 When taken by itself this narrative scenario enacts a tightly deterministic world. The number of insiders is a limited one, restricted to the chosen few. There is no indication that newcomers might join the ranks of the insiders. Indeed, explication of the parabolic mystery appears to preclude its propagation to the outside world. Public parable and private instruction have set apart the outsiders from the insiders. The rationale for being an outsider is to remain outside and be damned so as to never get the benefit of the inside information. That is the force of what Kermode has termed "the *hina* doctrine of narrative" (1979: 33). Parable, or rather entrustment of its mystery to the chosen few, banishes all others to the outside "*so that* [=in order that] seeing they see but do not perceive, and hearing they hear but do not understand, *lest* they should turn around and be forgiven" (4:12). Inasmuch as this scenario ostracizes the outsiders, it works entirely for the benefit of the insiders. For not only are the latter favored to receive the mystery and interpretation, but they are also informed of the fate and identity of the outsiders. The insiders are thereby doubly privileged. They have received the inside information which concerns both the kingdom's parabolic mystery and the exclusion of the outsiders. They obtained access both to parable and to its hermeneutical operation. The second feature serves to heighten the first one, and together the two reinforce the status of the insiders.

2.0 It is generally assumed that Mark's narration of esoteric secrecy is not entirely an *ad hoc* composition. The feature is out of line with the canonical disposition toward publicity and proclamation of the gospel. The notion that a circle of insiders is hermetically sealed from irredeemable outsiders was unwelcome news for emergent orthodoxy. What is more, the esoteric scenario constitutes a recognizable feature in the non-canonical tradition. There it had developed a distinctive profile. This brings us to consider secrecy in the tradition, although a detailed reconstruction will forever elude us. For while Mark's esoteric secrecy is quite recognizable as an entity in its own right, it has nevertheless been narrated in keeping with the gospel's ends.

2.1 Technically, Mark 4:10–34 constitutes a sayings gospel or revelation discourse of the kind that has come to light near Nag Hammadi. A string of sayings and parables, suspended from a slim narrative frame, and linked with secrecy, is addressed to a group of privileged recipients. In the *Gospel of Thomas*, for example, "where incidentally much of this material recurs" (Robinson, 1982: 47; Koester, 1980: 114), all sayings and parables are introduced as "secret words" and entrusted to a few disciples and women. The task assigned to these privileged insiders is the interpretation of the precious words of Jesus. Interpretation more than proclamation would seem to be at least one function of the sayings gospel.

2.2 Long before the discovery of the Coptic codices the genre of the sayings gospel was known through the writings of the orthodox Fathers. When, for example, Irenaeus in *Adversus Haereses* exposed what he regarded as intolerable absurdities, he shed unwittingly some light on the profile and function of the sayings model. "They [the heretics] tell us, however, that this knowledge has not been openly divulged, because all are not capable of receiving it, but has been revealed in mystery by the Savior through means of parables to those qualified for understanding it" (I, 3, 1). Accordingly, knowledge of salvation is communicated in mystery *(mystēriōdōs)* via parabolic discourse *(dia parabolōn)* to those capable of comprehending it *(tois syniein dynamenois houtōs)*. Irenaeus, on the contrary, sought to enforce what he called "the rule of truth," whereby "the parables ought not to be adapted to ambiguous expressions" (II, 27, 1). Moreover, "the heretics," according to Irenaeus, declared that "Jesus spoke in a mystery to his disciples and apostles privately" (I, 25, 5: *en mystēriō . . . kat' idian lelalēkenai*). The chosen few are here identified as the disciples and apostles, whereas Irenaeus wanted to ensure that "the parables will receive a like interpretation *from all* . . ." (I, 27, 1). "The heretics," in his view, also taught that it was "after his [=Christ's] resurrection," while he spent eighteen months on earth, and before he ascended to heaven, that he "instructed a few of his disciples, whom he knew to be capable of understanding so great mysteries . . ." (I, 30, 14). For Irenaeus's most explicit repudiation of the sayings model the reader is referred to the third epigraph of this piece. There private instruction, the exclusivity of insiders, the comprehension of certain disciples, and parabolic, riddling discourse all come together in invoking the profile of the sayings gospel. Its resemblance to Mark's esoteric secrecy is evident, and all the more so since the evangelist sums up the significance of Jesus's parabolic revelation in terms remarkably similar to those used by Irenaeus: "and he was not speaking to them without parables, but he was explaining everything privately to his own disciples" (4:34: *kat' idian de tois idiois mathētais epelyen panta*).

2.21 In the tradition esoteric secrecy serves important socio-linguistic functions which give additional clues to the genre of the sayings gospel. There are altogether three factors which contribute to esoteric secrecy.

2.22 In the first place, esoteric secrecy serves to defend and strengthen the identity of a small, distinctive group. The more restricted and distinguishable a group, the more likely is the occurrence of esoteric secrecy. Larger, less controllable groups tend to weaken the esoteric factor (Jansen: 46–47). Esoteric secrecy thrives in and on isolation. The exclusivity, therefore, of an identifiable group of disciples/apostles and women in the sayings gospel is an essential fact of the esoteric tradition. Secondly, esoteric secrecy is closely allied with the possession of special knowledge. There is no secrecy without some information to be kept secret. Knowledge conveyed to a limited number of people becomes privileged information. Held by the few and withheld from all others, it fuels the basic needs of esoteric secrecy. In the sayings gospel the prestige of esoteric secrecy rests on the claim that an extreme minority is in possession of aphoristic and parabolic wisdom. Thirdly, esoteric secrecy is a guarantor of authority. Special knowledge granted to the few directly translates into categories of power and prestige. The notion of apostolic authority, for instance, is far better realized in the sayings gospel than in the narrative gospel. For it is the very nature of the sayings gospel that it links privileged knowledge with apostolic beneficiaries. Access to and comprehension of Jesus' words promote the select few to the ranks of guardians of tradition and apostolic successors. To a considerable degree their power hinges on the fact that they are privy to confidential information. Secrecy and authority feed on each other.

2.3 The factors of isolation, knowledge, and authority, finally, help us determine the rationale behind the enforcement of esoteric secrecy. Promotion of the prestige of insiders, while a significant element in esoteric secrecy, nevertheless falls short of a full explanation. For if apostolic authority were the single most important factor empowering the secrecy model, the genre of the resurrection appearance story would just as well have been suited to the task. Few genres in the oral and literary history of early Christianity enhanced apostolic authority as much as the stories narrating an apostle's (or woman's) encounter with the risen Christ. What is remarkable about the mechanism of esoteric secrecy is its unconcern for proclamation. From the perspective of the more exoteric orthodoxy, the sayings gospel could well be seen as a failure in communication. Esoteric secrecy and orthodoxy's kerygmatic impulse served mutually exclusive interests. Interpretation, we saw, characterizes one hermeneutical function of the sayings gospel. Either Jesus takes it upon himself to explicate his parabolic message to the disciples, or the latter are themselves charged with the task of interpretation. However, the combined factors of isolation, special knowledge, and authority point to an underlying, purely pragmatic rationale. Irenaeus' polemics aside, the mechanism of entrusting confidential information to a privileged few at the exclusion of all others ideally functions in the interest of preservation. In other words, the primary intent of esoteric secrecy and the sayings gospel would appear to be neither proclamation nor interpretation, but preservation.

2.31 The preservative function of the sayings gospel illuminates esoteric secrecy from a different angle. Secrecy operates against the better instincts of dissemination and diffusion. For a mentality attentive to matters of collection and preservation, secrecy serves an important social function. In her magisterial volumes entitled *The Printing Press as an Agent of Change* Elizabeth Eisenstein has drawn persuasive parallels between early forms of information gathering and secrecy:

> To be preserved intact, techniques had to be entrusted to a select group of initiates who were instructed not only in special skills but also in the 'mysteries' associated with them. Special symbols, rituals, and incantations performed the necessary function of organizing data, laying out schedules, and preserving techniques in easily memorized forms (Eisenstein, I: 270).

Secrecy and censorship, in other words, could serve as mechanisms for preserving important data. Eisenstein who is primarily interested in documenting links between secrecy and scribal culture proceeded from the observation of the vulnerable state of scribal life. Deficient storage facilities and the perishability of writing materials, the corruption and dilution of manuscripts, drifting texts and vanishing documents all imposed a condition of discontinuity upon scribal life (113–115). For this reason, "many forms of knowledge had to be esoteric during the age of scribes if they were to survive at all" (270). Before the advent of typographical fixity, therefore, the alliance between secrecy and preservation was a necessary and often natural one as far as human culture was concerned. "The notion that valuable data could be preserved best by being made public, rather than by being kept secret, ran counter to tradition" (116). A good way of preserving the integrity of valuable data was to withhold their publication.

3.0   Eisenstein's observations cast fresh light on the esoteric scenario of the sayings gospel. The clustering of sayings and parables in conjunction with secrecy can now be seen as a natural mechanism for storing crucial information. The precious data are withheld from the public and guarded by the circle of initiates so as to protect them against corruption by dissemination. Knowledge is confided to the inner circle precisely for the purpose of keeping it intact. We have to do with an esoteric brotherhood (or brotherhood and sisterhood) whose plain business it is to preserve what has been imparted to it.

3.1   As far as Mk. 4:1–34 is concerned, we are actually dealing with two senses of secrecy, one reinforcing the other. In one sense parable displays an inherent linguistic potential for mystery. In the tradition parables function as bearers of the mystery of the kingdom. According to the narrative scenario of esoteric secrecy, however, the parabolic mystery is entrusted to the twelve and a few chosen ones. Concealed in parabolic discourse is the mystery of the kingdom, and this mystery of the kingdom in turn attracts secrecy by virtue of the means of its preservation. In different words, the kingdom's mystery is itself hedged in by secrecy which aims at protecting the kingdom's mysterious identity. This amounts to saying that esoteric secrecy in Mark is designed to protect and preserve the mystery of the kingdom by entrusting the latter to a group of insiders. In short, therefore, esoteric secrecy is the hedge built around the mystery of the kingdom.

3.2 There lies much irony in the fact that the preservative intent of the esoteric scenario goes against the grain of parabolic objectives. For according to Crossan's well-known typology of story (57–62), parable mystifies while myth reassures, parable undercuts structures of expectancy while myth mediates structural opposites, and parable inclines toward the culture-subversive while myth genuflects before tradition. In our terms, parable is a paradigmatic instance for the open-endedness of language and signification. But parables that were placed into the scenario of esoteric secrecy have lost their power to shatter basic assumptions and to make us vulnerable to the new logic of the kingdom. Parabolic mystery has become a safe possession in the hands of a few. But again, when parabolic discourse has come to be locked into a chapel for secret rites, and when a social world is immobilized by the irrevocable segregation of insiders versus outsiders, parables have died stillborn.

3.3 Curiously, stability is idolized and closure monumentalized on behalf of parables that were intended to invoke instability and open-endedness. Paradoxically, a world is made obvious again by conserving the very discourse that was meant to invert the obvious. In the last analysis, therefore, esoteric secrecy is a mechanism of preservation which has converted its own conservative hermeneutic into a new myth.

4.0 To point out competing tendencies in the esoteric enclosure of parabolic discourse is not to say that Mark is uncritical toward, let alone unaware of, them. Obviously, Mark has used the esoteric scenario as a source, not as model, for his narrative. The hermeneutical operation of the sayings genre is subject to the larger logic of the narrative gospel, and the latter, we shall see, is less than sympathetic toward the parables' retreat behind the walls of esoteric secrecy.

4.1 The breaking of the secrecy code deserves as much attention as the installation of secrecy itself. In assessing corrosive effects on esoteric secrecy, we turn once again to Eisenstein's work. It was, in her view, the new technology of printing which undermined the old alliance between secrecy and preservation in chirographic culture. The preservative and duplicative powers of print, while at times amplifying and reinforcing secrecy, in the long run lessened reliance on secret knowledge and broke down barriers surrounding the crafts and trades, religious and scientific knowledge. The new reproductive technology operated against the ancient esoteric injunctions to withhold the highest truths from the public. To be sure, both secrecy and openness are integral features of the human condition. "We are all, in a sense, experts on secrecy" (Bok, 1982: xv). The modern electronic technology is used for probing and retrieving knowledge, but also for storing and concealing it. In contemporary western civilization "the right to privacy" or the invocation of "national security" often conflict with "the freedom of inquiry" or "the public's right to know" (Bok, 1982). None of this can diminish the validity of Eisenstein's studies concerning changing attitudes toward secrecy in connection with a shift from chirographic to typographic means of communication. Insistence on concealment seemed perfectly appropriate in reference to the privileged few, but odd and even absurd when printed and disseminated to a rapidly growing readership. Notwithstanding the fact that secrecy remained operational in many guises, typographic means of publication fostered an ethos subversive to the ancient norms of privacy and privilege. Arcana were dismantled or disclosed, and secrecy went underground or realigned itself with different social and political forces (Eisenstein, 272–302).

4.2 Eisenstein's observations, while amply documented with regard to scribality and typography, apply with even greater validity to transitions from orality to textuality. Given the nonmaterial mode of communication and the purely mental storage facilities in orality, the need for limiting information to a select few would seem to be more acute with regard to spoken than to written words. Every word written down has for the time being at least escaped orality's insubstantial existence, while every spoken word runs the risk of being lost unless a mechanism exists that facilitates its preservation. In the Christian tradition, such a mechanism is provided by consigning sayings and parables to an authoritative body of traditionists. Esoteric secrecy in conjunction with the sayings genre may thus well find its most logical explanation in orality's pressing needs for preserving the two basic speech events of the language of Jesus. In this, as in a number of other ways, the sayings genre, while a textual production, still reflects the ethos of an essentially oral state of the tradition (Kelber, 1983: 199–203; 1987: 117–18).

4.3 On Eisenstein's analogy of changing attitudes toward secrecy at the interfaces of scribal and print culture, one may expect a diminution of esoteric secrecy already at strategic transitions from orality to scribality. Even though scribal culture remains beholden to sundry forms of secrecy, it may show signs of relief from the pressing needs for esoteric conservation. The narrative gospel mobilizes textuality in ways that loosen dependency on the clustering management of knowledge. It reabsorbs and transforms the commonplace tradition of the sayings genre, and along with it the secrecy surrounding it. Freed from preoccupation with the sayings material, the narrative gospel extends its imaginative recall across the spatio-temporal scope of Jesus's life and death. The drift of narrative attention is away from conserving what threatens to perish, and toward reclaiming the fuller story. In brief, interpretation begins to prevail over orality's urgent needs for preservation and secrecy.

5.0   Mark's tendency to forsake the canons of esoteric secrecy is evident from the wisdom confided to the insiders (4:14–32). They receive the kind of interpretation that is less than suited for, and in fact remarkably inappropriate to, their status as recipients of esoteric knowledge. Is one to regard it entirely accidental that in the explication of the master parable (4:14–20) the seed is replaced by the *logos*? Accordingly, three types of recipients on whom the *logos* is wasted are contrasted with other recipients for whom the *logos* will bear threefold fruit. On this view, the *logos* is deeply implicated in the dilemmas of its dissemination before it scores a manifest victory. This is the parable's interpretation secretly given to the insiders in reference to the mystery of the kingdom of God. Not only is the *logos* to be sown, i.e., publicized, but the failure of its proclamation signals an essential feature of the mystery of the kingdom. Far from reinforcing the sequestering of the *logoi* behind closed doors, this secret interpretation bursts the conceptual frame of the esoteric sayings genre. Essentially, the esoteric explication of the master parable undermines the very rationale of its secret communication.

5.1   The remaining parables, secretly conveyed to the insiders, invoke the dynamics of secrecy and revelation, of surplus and loss. But rather than strengthening secrecy commensurate with their placement in the esoteric genre, they rationalize hiddenness as premise for revelation. This finds paradigmatic expression in the commentary on the lamp saying (4: 21): "For nothing is hidden, except to be revealed; nor has anything been secret, but that it should come to light" (4:22). Conveyed as secret wisdom to a few, this saying deconstructs the rationale for its own secret operation. The measure for measure saying (4:24b) promises surplus, and the saying on having and not having (4:25) reiterates surplus, while pointing up the reality of loss. Contextually, these sayings suggest that those who have inside knowledge (about concealing and revealing) will be privy to revelation (as the story unfolds), while those who fail to grasp the standards set by the parabolic interpretation can in the end incur a total loss. Imparted as esoteric wisdom to a few, these parabolic sayings not merely confirm the status of the insiders, provided they comprehend the rationale of hiddenness and revelation, but they also threaten the collapse of the insiders, in case they remain deaf to the parabolic interpretation. The two concluding seed parables play variations on the theme of hiddenness and revelation. The parable of the growing seed narrates the inevitable process of growth from seed to harvest (4:26–29), and the parable of the mustard seed emphasizes the sharp disjunction between the embryonic state and the fully grown plant (4:30–32). In each case, the seed's hiddenness in the ground has the objective of manifestly rising above the ground. In both parables the wisdom secretly conveyed to the insiders anticipates a state of openness as opposed to hiddenness. In exposing the mechanism of secrecy and revelation, and in entertaining the possibilities of surplus gain as well as total loss, the parabolic wisdom confided to the insiders relativizes its own confidentiality, unsettles the authority of its privileged recipients, and ruptures esoteric closure. The very parables that have gained admittance into the esoteric scenario contain the seeds of its destruction. In Mark's context, esoteric secrecy is in the process of being exploded from within the confines of the sayings genre.

5.2 The seeds of deconstruction sown in the esoteric scenario (4:10–34) blossom into full life in the remainder of the narrative gospel. For far from reaffirming the prestige of the insiders, the narrative hastens their demise. I have elsewhere shown the mechanism of role reversal (1979, *passim*; 1983: 124–29; 1985: 37–40) whereby the outsider characteristics with respect to lack of understanding, and having eyes but not seeing and ears but not hearing (4:12) are applied to the insiders themselves (6:52; 8:17–18). As the plot quickens to its critical moment, it enlightens retrospectively the parabolic wisdom communicated to the twelve as a matter of grave consequence. For that wisdom, in deconstructing its own secret operation, had strained toward releasing the mystery of the kingdom from its hermetic enclosure. In different words, the secrecy-revelation mechanism conveyed through parabolic wisdom had pointed beyond its own secret mode of communication toward epiphany in the unfolding story of Jesus's life and death. Unable to follow this broader vision of the kingdom, the twelve became outsiders in and to its unfolding dramatization, mistook the transfiguration for epiphany while escaping the cross in fear and unbelief. In thus turning the insiders into outsiders, the narrative has completed the destruction of esoteric secrecy. The notion of a distinct group of insiders in possession of confidential information has been turned inside out. In this sense, the gospel does not at all present itself as a patron of secrecy, but rather as an ardent demythologizer of the myth of esoteric secrecy.

6.0 Outside the esoteric scenario a different type of secrecy unfolds along a longer narrative route. For the purpose of clarifying both difference and affinity between the esoteric and this other sense of secrecy we will have to rehearse the features of the latter once again. At Capernaum Jesus does not allow the demons to speak "because they knew him" (1:34). After having healed a leper Jesus enjoins him not to speak to anyone, but to present himself to the priest; the man, however, disobeys and spreads the news freely (1:45). At a northern lakeside setting Jesus again instructs the demons not to make him known as they paid homage to him (3:11–12). On the other hand, the demon-possessed man whose name was Legion is encouraged by Jesus himself to publicize the news of his spectacular healing (5:19). But then again Jesus gives the order to keep his greatest deed, the raising of Jairus's daughter, under cover (5:43). His journey to the area around Tyre appears to be planned as a secret operation, and yet his presence among the Gentiles becomes public knowledge (7:24). While still in Gentile territory, he forbids the proclamation of the healing of a deaf-mute, but "the more he ordered them [not to speak], the more they proceeded to proclaim" (7:36).[2] Peter's so-called confession is immediately checked by Jesus's injunction to keep it secret (8:29–30). Following his appearance on the high mountain, Jesus orders the three witnesses not to disclose the information "until the son of man should rise from the dead" (9:9). While traveling through Galilee he wishes to remain unrecognized because (*gar*) he taught the disciples about his impending deliverance into the hands of his adversaries (9:30–31).[3] Notably, there are no discernible injunctions in the passion narrative requiring characters to refrain from proclamation.

6.1 The above-mentioned secrets differ from esoteric secrecy in at least a twofold sense. In the first place, these secrets placed upon the narrative route do not specifically cover sayings and parables. They rather relate to the distinctive character of Jesus. The deeds of Jesus and his identity flowing from them are the issue more than his words. Because these secrets relate to the particular character of Jesus I shall henceforth refer to them as identity secrets. Secondly, these identity secrets are not enjoined on a limited number of people, but rather on different individuals at isolated intervals. Preservation and the formation of group identity hardly lie at the root of this secrecy mechanism. Thirdly, and perhaps most importantly, the identity mechanism is remarkably lacking in consistency. It is anything but a doctrine systematically applied to the pre-passion narrative. Not only does Jesus enforce secrecy at irregular points in the narrative, but these identity secrets are frequently leaked. Secrecy and leaking enter into a symbiotic relationship. The leaks contribute to the growing fame of Jesus, which in turn invokes the imposition of new secrecy. The identity secrets are of a kind that cannot really be kept. Far from eclipsing Jesus's identity, they exert pressure upon the narrative toward more disclosure. The objective of this type of secrecy is thus not to remain secret, but to enhance the momentum toward revelation. It is in this basic urge toward revealing, finally, that the identity secrets and esoteric secrecy, as deconstructed by Mark, converge. Despite their stated differences, they have been joined to cooperate in shaping the narrative according to a secrecy-disclosure mechanism: "For nothing is hidden, except to be revealed; nor has anything been secret, but that it should come to light" (4:22).

6.2 Wrede had suggested that the so-called Messianic Secret grew out of two contradictory notions concerning Jesus' identity. On one view Jesus became the Messiah at resurrection, while on the other his messiahship was linked already with his earthly life. Mark, seeking to strike a compromise, concealed the earthly messianic identity so as to bring the focus on the messianic epiphany at resurrection. The disciples' failure was also in keeping with this design, for their blindness in the pre-resurrectional period was the necessary condition for their gaining sight with resurrection (1901: 107 [1971: 106]). Mark 9:9 played the key role in shaping Wrede's view that the narrative had been constructed from the vantage point of resurrection perceived to be the moment of unveiling. This latter "is in fact the crucial idea, the underlying point of Mark's entire approach" (1901: 67 [1971: 68]).

6.21 The immediate question posed by this explanation concerns the absence of a resurrection appearance story. Showing next to no interest in the narrative logic of 16:1–8, Wrede postulated a "lost ending of the Gospel" (1901: 164 [1971: 165]. But work since Wrede has confirmed that the "absence" of a resurrection story is by design, and not a freak of history (Lohmeyer: 352–60; Perrin: 44–45; Magness, 1986). Rather than seeking the key to the narrative in an allegedly lost ending, one has to face up to the question why the risen Christ was not included in the plotted narrative. One must also wonder if discipleship comports squarely with the pattern of concealing and revealing as Wrede had suggested. For to assume that the truth had been concealed from the disciples in order to be revealed to them at resurrection is to miss the narrative logic of discipleship. In point of fact, the disciples did receive all the inside information, including the vitally important one pertaining to the mechanism of secrecy and revelation. But as they were unable to follow the operation of concealment and revealing, they came to play the role of outsiders, depriving themselves of epiphany. Wrede's interpretation of 9:9, finally, poses the question whether the luminous Christ is deferred beyond narrative time so as to strengthen his epiphanic significance, or in order to make room for a rather different epiphany inside narrative.

6.3 If it seems the better course not to align the resurrection with epiphany, one has to look for an alternate incident inside the narrative that qualifies as genuine unveiling. Given the nature of the identity secrets one is directed toward a narrative moment where Jesus publicly and unconditionally declares his own identity. One single verse meets this requirement: Jesus's first passion-resurrection prediction (8:31) which is characterized as a word spoken openly (8:32: *kai parrhēsia ton logon elalei*). The crucially important *parrhēsia*, a *hapax legomenon* in the narrative, signals the dénouement of the secrecy-disclosure mechanism. In the perspectives of the larger narrative, identity secrets alternate with injunctions to publicize, and leaks of secrecy with non-secrecy, leaving Jesus's identity oddly unsettled and in need of clarification. In this broader context, identity secrets and their implied mechanism of secrecy-disclosure both enhance narrative tension and in the end relax it with Jesus's open confession as the crucified one. Identity secrets, therefore, are a narrative device aimed at scoring a dramatic, a theological point. The notable decline of identity secrets after 8:31,[4] the lack of identity secrets in the passion story, and the "absence" of a resurrection story all find their explanation and in the narrative epiphany at crucifixion.

7.0 Thus far we have observed that Mark's narrative, traditionally associated with messianic secrecy and mysterious language, is more interested in disclosure than in secrecy. Esoteric secrecy is demythologized. For Mark, as for Irenaeus, representatives of emergent orthodoxy, esoteric privileging of words and persons is not acceptable. The identity secrets help negotiate the narrative suspense surrounding Jesus's identity to the point of relief that comes with his one and only open proclamation. That the latter expresses Jesus's preferred identity is confirmed by the centurion whose confession in the face of death carries the blessing of the narrator (15:39). At this point, then, the gospel narrative would seem to be more concerned with the demystification and disclosure of secrecy, than with its preservation.

8.0 There is yet another way in which the gospel appears to reveal more than to conceal. If we place it in the larger setting of the communications triangle of narrator, text, and reader, marks of secrecy recede to a degree that imperils the very notion of secrecy.

8.1 While narrative undoubtedly originated in oral story-telling, the technology of writing enhanced control over larger portions of language. Scribality allowed writers to accumulate words, and more words, and to coordinate them into more richly complex configurations. As writers positioned themselves over larger and more circumspectly designed compositions, directing narrative strategies, and presiding over narrative endings, they acquired a posture of knowing. The ancient Hebrew narrators and the gospel authors, both among the pioneers of prose fiction in the western tradition, helped enlarge this bold notion of knowing what only God was supposed to know.

8.2 Narrative omniscience, as we call it today, suggests the prerogative of the storyteller to reveal the inner states of individuals, to motivate changes, to delineate temporality, and to rationalize causality. While the characters inside the narrative have only broken threads to grasp, the narrator from his or her perspective oversees the threads coming together in a more or less purposeful design. To this situation we must now add the reader (McKnight; Fowler, 1983, 1984, 1985a, 1985b) who is invited to share omniscience with the narrator, and who may come to know what the characters in the narrative know only partially, or belatedly, or not at all.[5]

8.3 In the case of Mark's gospel, the narrator has placed the readers in a position of knowing. The very first verse (in most textual versions) registers the "primacy effect" (Perry: 35–64, 311–61; Rimmon-Kenan: 120) conditioning readers from the outset to the protagonist's identity as the Son of God. The subsequent narrative induces them to modify and correct this initial impression, and in the end to comply with a revised version of it. To some extent the readers' journey resembles that of the disciples, the initial insiders in the narrative, who were appointed to follow Jesus in order to have their misconceptions about him overturned. Yet the readers enjoy a distinct advantage. While the disciples participate only in certain parts of the narrative, the readers get the full benefit of it. Beginning with the "primacy effect" they are led down the narrative path all the way to the curiously abrupt ending. The disciples are not privy to the "primacy effect" or to John's appearance; they are not even present at Jesus' inaugural proclamation (1:14–15). For them the inaugural proclamation is constituted by the esoteric communication of the mystery of the kingdom (4:10–34). But even in the case of esoteric secrecy, the disciples are outdistanced by the readers. While the disciples receive the inside information concerning the kingdom's mystery and the fate of the outsiders, the readers receive this same information plus the subsequent enlightenment about the true identity of the outsiders. The readers even are admitted to the epiphany on the cross, the very scene from which the disciples had excluded themselves. In thus observing not only what the disciples could observe but also what had lain outside their reach, the readers progressively take on the role reserved for the disciples. This promotes the readers, together with the elusive narrator, to the status of the new insiders.

8.4 What must be borne in mind is that the readers as insiders have not become accomplices to esoteric secrecy. To be sure, to the extent that they are privileged to learn from the mistakes made by the disciples, they thrive on their exclusion to the outside. But what the readers can learn in the process is that esoteric secrecy has been dismantled and that identity secrets pressure toward epiphany. These are narrative experiences that discourage membership in an esoteric brotherhood. Up to a point everyone who reads (or hears) the gospel is invited to follow and to comprehend.

9.0 Biblical scholarship which has barely begun to explore the narrative world of the gospels remains principally attracted to coherence, proportionality, and lucidity. Yet narrative does not so inevitably carry with it the view that existence is lived as an orderly and meaningful continuum. One need not be a partisan of the latest deconstructionist eccentricities to observe that narrative variously interferes with its own project. In Mark's case, narrative reveils what it was most seriously determined to reveal, leaving at its core something irreducible, a void or a mystery.

9.1 Jesus's esoteric proclamation makes the twelve (and a few chosen ones) the privileged recipients of confidential information (4:10–32). This information pertains to the mystery of the kingdom of God which was given (4:11: *dedotai*) in parables (4:2, 10) and summed up in the master parable. Mystery, parable, and kingdom are thereby correlated. From this one may reasonably infer that the parables, epitomized by the master parable, serve as carriers of the mystery of the kingdom. The parabolic mystery of God's kingdom is at the heart of the esoteric proclamation. In addition, the insiders learn that to outsiders "everything occurs in parables" (4:11). The readers, moreover, are told that to the disciples all parabolic discourse will be explained (4:33–34). From this, and from Jesus's own remark (4:13), one may again draw the conclusion that the revised version of the master parable (4:14–20) constitutes interpretation for the insiders. What is, however, striking about this interpretation is its parabolic character. It narrates a story about differing responses to the *logos*, while withholding explanation of its nexus with the kingdom. *Le travail de l'imagination* (Ricoeur: 339–60) is left to the insiders, be they the disciples or the readers. Designed to interpret the master parable, its interpretation acts rather like a parable itself, withholding at least as much as it makes known. What is more, further parables are added to the parabolic interpretation (4:21–32). Presumably, they function as commentaries on the mystery that was proclaimed by way of parable in the first place. There is, of course, a rationale for explicating parable via parables. If mystery is at the heart of the proclamation, parable is its ideal mode of discourse, and parable naturally asks for more parables.

9.2   We have arrived here at a point in the narrative where the esoteric proclamation exposes an intractability at its core. Precisely at the juncture at which narrative labors valiantly to overcome secrecy and to reveal the inside information, little is revealed beyond the promise of future revelation. For the time being the insiders are left with mystery and more parables. If it be said that to the outsiders "everything occurs in parables," it is only fair to note that the interpretation conveyed to the insiders likewise occurs in parables. Now, but only now, may we endorse Kermode's astute observation that "being an insider is only a more elaborate way of being kept outside" (1979: 27).

9.3   Despite the esoteric revealing and reveiling, the narrative continues to strive toward full disclosure. An obvious moment of unveiling comes when Jesus makes his non-parabolic confession *en parrhēsia* (Bishop: 39–52). Both the disciples and the readers are privy to his self-disclosure as the suffering, rising Son of Man (8:31). Both types of insiders are now groomed to anticipate the acute and fateful moment of epiphany. As for the disciples, they deprive themselves of presence at the crucifixion. It is thus left to the readers to act out their role as new insiders and witness revelation. They are by no means unprepared for much that is to come. But not for all! Having had full access to the narrative information, they cannot be surprised to learn that Jesus is sentenced as blasphemer by the guardians of religion (14:64), and crucified on the charge of having made himself "King of the Jews" (15:2, 26). What does, however, come as terrifying news to us, the readers, is that Jesus dies forsaken by the God whom he had called his father (14:36; 15:34). For it is one thing to die a brutal death at the hands of the authorities, but quite a different matter to suffer the absence of God. The former had been foretold, but the latter had not. What constitutes no less a shocking revelation is the centurion's confession of Jesus's sonship of God in view of death in god-forsakenness. For it is one thing to have death reversed by the epiphany of resurrection, but quite a different matter to locate epiphany at the point of absence. The former had been foretold, but the latter had not. What finally is disclosed at the peak of a laborious narrative buildup is that revelation is not transparent. For what is revealed is not epiphany as reversal of death, but epiphany as the darkness of God's absence. The more the narrative struggles to overcome secrecy and to make disclosure, the more it reveils itself in parabolic mystery.

10.0 We, the new insiders, it was noted, have a natural advantage over the disciples, the old insiders. The narrative mechanism, however, of concealing, revealing, and reveiling plays a role in showing us the limited hold we have on understanding. Granted that we are privileged witnesses of the epiphany, do we comprehend? Can one comprehend? But if one cannot understand, do we really have a "natural" advantage over the disciples?

10.1 In view of parabolic mystery at the peak of the narrative, the role reversal of the disciples from insiders to outsiders should have a chilling effect on us, the new insiders. In thinking that we are inside the narrative, we are perpetually reminded of what happens to insiders. It will not let us stay inside for long, if at all, And if we think we are inside, it is a sure sign that we are already outside.

Notes

[1] Regrettably, the translator chose to truncate the title which in its German original reads as follows: *Das Messiasgeheimnis in den Evangelien: Zugleich ein Beitrag zum Verständnis des Markusevangeliums*. Accordingly, it was Wrede's objective to study secrecy in Mark and in the other three gospels. It is worth remembering that he recognized a close affinity between Mark and John with respect to secrecy. What may be even more significant is that Wrede attributed this commonality not to direct literary relations, but rather to shared ideas current in the tradition (1901: 206 [1971: 207]).

[2] With respect to secrecy, Mk. 8:26 is ambiguous. On the one hand Jesus forbids the healed man to go back to Bethsaida, while on the other he orders him to return to his family.

[3] In Mk. 10.48–49 it is not Jesus but the many who order Bartimaeus to be quiet. Moreover,

the beggar's confession is made in the state of blindness. From the narrator's point of view this confession may be as dubious as that made by the followers who hail Jesus as the inaugurator of "the kingdom of our father David" (11.10).

[4] Despite disclosure at 8.31, the very information disclosed to the disciples is still concealed from the crowds at large. This is the significance of secrecy surrounding the second prediction of suffering and rising (9:30–31). This is also the reason why the third prediction is strictly limited to the twelve (10:32–33). Despite revelation at 8:31 and a notable decline of identity secrets thereafter, the narrative seeks to sustain a posture of concealment so as to secure its ongoing existence, i.e., its momentum toward narrative epiphany.

[5] To be sure, the concept of narrative omniscience has lost much of its usefulness for contemporary hermeneutics. We know that all narrative has properties not directly under the control of the narrator. Inevitably there are aspects, meanings, and connections which hide themselves from even the most scrupulous and self-conscious narrator. But the concept can still serve the purpose of formulating the difference in knowledge and perspective between the narrator and also the readers on one side and the characters in the story on the other.

WORKS CONSULTED

Bishop, Jonathan
    1986   "Parable and *Parrhesia* in Mark." *Int* 40: 39–52.

Blevins, James L.
    1981   *The Messianic Secret in Markan Research, 1901–1976*. Washington, D.C.: University Press of America.

Bok, Sissela
    1982   *Secrets. On the Ethics of Concealment and Revelation*. New York: Pantheon Books.

Cameron, Ron
    1984   *Sayings Traditions in the Apocryphon of James*. HTS 34. Philadelphia: Fortress Press.

Crossan, John Dominic
    1975   *The Dark Interval. Towards a Theology of Story*. Niles, IL: Argus Communications.

Davies, Stevan L.
    1983   *The Gospel of Thomas and Christian Wisdom*. New York: Seabury Press.

Eisenstein, Elizabeth L.
    1979   *The Printing Press as an Agent of Change. Communications and Cultural Transformations in Early-Modern Europe*. 2 Vols. Cambridge: Cambridge University Press.

Fowler, Robert M.
    1983   "Who is 'reader' of Mark's Gospel?" Pp. 31–53 in *SBL 1983 Seminar Papers*. Ed. Kent Harold Richards Chico, CA: Scholars Press.
    1984   "Thoughts on the History of Reading Mark's Gospel." Pp.

	120–30 in *Proceedings: Eastern Great Lakes Biblical Society and Midwest SBL*. Vol. 4.
1985a	"The Rhetoric of Indirection in the Gospel of Mark." Pp. 47–56 in *Proceedings: Eastern Great Lakes Biblical Society and Midwest SBL*. Vol. 5.
1985b	"Who is 'the Reader' in Reader Response Criticism?" *Semeia* 31: 5–23.

Jansen, Wm. Hugh
    1965   "The Esoteric-Exoteric Factor in Folklore." Pp. 43–51 in *The Study of Folklore*. Ed. Alan Dundes. Englewood Cliffs, N.J.: Prentice Hall.

Kelber, Werner H.
    1979   *Mark's Story of Jesus*. Philadelphia: Fortress Press.
    1983   *The Oral and the Written Gospel. The Hermeneutics of Speaking and Writing in the Synoptic Tradition, Mark, Paul, and Q*. Philadelphia: Fortress Press.
    1985   "Apostolic Tradition and the Form of the Gospel." Pp. 24–46 in *Discipleship in the New Testament*. Ed. Fernando F. Segovia. Philadelphia: Fortress Press.
    1987   "Narrative as Interpretation and Interpretation of Narrative: Hermeneutical Reflections on the Gospels." *Semeia* 39: 107–33.

Kermode, Frank
    1979   *The Genesis of Secrecy. On the Interpretation of Narrative*. Cambridge, MA and London: Harvard University Press.
    1983   "Secrets and Narrative Sequence." Pp. 133–55 in *The Art of Telling. Essays on Fiction*. Cambridge, MA: Harvard University Press.

Koester, Helmut
    1980   "Apocryphal and Canonical Gospels." *HTR* 73: 105–30.

Lohmeyer, Ernst
    1967   *Das Evangelium des Markus*. 17th ed. Göttingen: Vandenhoeck & Ruprecht.

Magness, J. Lee
    1986   *Sense and Absence. Structure and Suspension in the Ending of Mark's Gospel*. Atlanta: Scholars Press.

McKnight, Edgar V.
    1985   *The Bible and the Reader. An Introduction to Literary Criticism*. Philadelphia: Fortress Press.

Minette de Tillesse, G.
    1968   *Le Secret Messianique dans l'Évangile de Marc*. LD 47. Paris: Les Éditions du Cerf.

Perkins, Pheme
    1980   *The Gnostic Dialogue. The Early Church and the Crisis of Gnosticism.* New York: Paulist Press.

Perrin, Norman
    1971   "Towards an Interpretation of the Gospel of Mark." In *Christology and a Modern Pilgrimage*, ed. Hans D. Betz. Claremont, CA: The New Testament Colloquium.

Perry, Menakhem
    1979   "Literary dynamics: how the order of a text creates its meaning." *Poetics Today* 1: 35–64, 311–61.

Ricoeur, Paul
    1982   "La Bible et L'Imagination." *RHPR* 62: 339–60.

Rimmon-Kenan, Shlomith
    1983   *Narrative Fiction: Contemporary Poetics.* London and New York: Methuen.

Robinson, James M.
    1982   "Gnosticism and the New Testament." Pp. 40–53 in *The Problem of History in Mark and other Marcan Studies.* Philadelphia: Fortress Press.

Smith, Jonathan Z.
    1978   "Good News is No News: Aretalogy and Gospel." Pp 190–207 in *Map is not Territory.* SJLA 23. Leiden: E.J. Brill.

Tuckett, Christopher, ed.
    1983   *The Messianic Secret.* Philadelphia: Fortress Press.

Williams, James G.
    1985   *Gospel Against Parable. Mark's Language of Mystery.* Bible and Literature Series, 12. Decatur, GA: Almond Press.

Wrede, William
    1901   *Das Messiasgeheimnis in den Evangelien. Zugleich ein Beitrag zum Verständnis des Markusevangeliums.* Göttingen: Vandenhoeck & Ruprecht. Reprinted 1971. [Eng. trans., *The Messianic Secret.* Greenwood, S.C.: The Attic Press, 1979].

IRONY AS HOPE IN MARK'S GOSPEL: A REPLY TO WERNER KELBER

Dan O. Via
Duke Divinity School

Professor Werner Kelber has given us another stimulating and provocative study of the Gospel of Mark, the movement of whose argument to climax is as artful as the development of a good story. His claim that Mark's basic urge to overcome secrecy results in a reveiling and a reinstitution of secrecy I find generally convincing. However, I have questions about certain points, and there are some elements in the text which I would interpret in a different way. It is to these matters that I turn. I will comment briefly on several topics and then make two or three more sustained responses.

1. Given the fact that the secrecy which Eisenstein is talking about is largely a matter of *privacy* while Mark's secret is a *mystery*, which Kelber well knows, I wonder how illuminating her discussion is for interpreting Mark. Mark's new departure vis-à-vis the traditional is more a matter of interpretation than of information, and understanding comes not from the broader dissemination of more information but from penetrating the mystery.

2. Since the Christian tradition did change considerably in the process of oral transmission and apparently without creating great anxiety, I wonder if interpretation was as subordinated to preservation as Kelber claims. Is Mark's freer interpretation that much of a break in *principle*, though it may be a considerable break in content?

3. Despite the differences which Kelber posits between esoteric teaching (Mark 4) and the identity secrets, they have more in common than their convergence in the momentum toward revelation. They are both means of concealing revelation at the source. Moreover, in view of the close connection which Mark establishes between the kingdom (to which the esoteric teaching relates) and Jesus (to whom the identity secrets relate) (see Via, 1975:134) it is really the same revelation. There is for Mark a theological—or philosophical—necessity for the "inconsis-

tency" of leaking the secret, namely, that there cannot be a concealment if there is nothing to conceal, so that knowledge has to be given out in the leaks. But this does not break the coherent paradox of concealed revelation because the leaks really do not dispel the secret. The crowds for the most part take no cognizance of the leaks, really do not get it (1:24, 27; 2:10, 12). Some do—those who come for healing and manifest faith—but then without some response there would be no revelation at all.

4. Are there no identity secrets in the passion story? Does not 14:61–62 belong to the identity secret pattern? The acknowledgement that Jesus is the Son of God-Messiah-Son of Man is a very forthright leak. But it fails to move the authorities positively just as the crowds pay no attention when Jesus is identified as Son of God or Son of Man (1:21–28; 2:10, 28) and as the disciples misunderstand the repeated revelations of the suffering Son of Man. There is a relationship in Mark between concealed revelation and discipleship failure. I recently argued that the concealment of revelation at the source is needed to explain why the disciples failed to grasp eschatological revelation (Via, 1986: 179–181). But beyond that the two motifs have the same pattern: revelation is given but is not received by some of those at hand.

5. According to Kelber the resurrection is not an epiphany, but Jesus' first passion prediction (8:31–32) is a genuine unveiling, an open declaration of Jesus' identity. But the Markan narrative renders this unveiling highly ironical. The disciples have already been given open teaching in the form of interpretation in 4:11a, 14–20, 34b, but the ineffectiveness of these explanations, as seen in 6:52, 8:17–21, makes the explanations ironical. The open teaching of 8:31 may seem to be a new departure, but it is followed by obdurate misunderstanding, and thus the irony is doubled. The explanations do not really explain, and the open teaching is not really open. Therefore, we are directed to read 8:32 in the light of 4:34. However open Jesus' words may be, they are still enigmas. And that continues to be true in part for the church after the resurrection as well. What the disciples fail to understand in 8:31, 9:31, 10:33–34 is the post-resurrection preaching of the church.

6. I should now like to comment somewhat more fully on Mark 4 and in so doing to respond to several points or observations which Kelber made. (1) The *hina* (4:12) doctrine of narrative is that it is intended to keep outsiders out. *But hina* also appears prominently in 4:21–25, which facilitates Mark's move away from secrecy. (2) The sayings of 4:21–25 and the parables in 4:26ff. are addressed to insiders. *But* that is not so clearly the case. (3) Mark 4:14–20 withholds explanation of the connection between the logos and the kingdom. *But* that section has a role in making such a connection in Mark 4 as a whole.

Mark 4:11 shows that the disciples have been given the secret of the *kingdom* in the parable of the Sower (4:1–9). The kingdom is like the sowing of seed, a point that is reenforced by 4:26, 30–31. But the seed *is* the word (4:14). Given this allegorical move plus the idea (to be defended below) that the word is power to create faith, the reader learns that the working of the word is the working of the kingdom. And since in Mark 4 the word is the parabolic word (4:2, 10, 30), the kingdom is the parabolic word or the latter is the vehicle of the kingdom, that in which it occurs.

When Jesus tells the disciples that they have been given the mystery of the kingdom but to outsiders everything is in parables (4:11), that might suggest that the disciples have been given the kingdom independently of the parables. But 4:10 shows that he is speaking to the disciples alone at that point, and he still is speaking to them in the parables of 4:26ff., although at some juncture, as 4:33–34 shows, the crowd—or outsiders—has also come back into the audience. So the parables—the *same* parables—are spoken to both disciples and outsiders, but the disciples are to get the mystery of the kingdom from them while the outsiders hear riddles spoken for the purpose of keeping them out. The difference is that the disciples are given interpretations (4:14–20, 34b) as well as parables. The parables then become effective word (4:20) only through interpretation.

But is not interpretation simply one of Mark's functional concepts for the fact that the word is effective only in certain instances? The word is sometimes effective for the disciples by means of explicit allegorical interpretation (4-11a, 34b)). But it is effective for some others without such explicit interpretation. The report about Jesus' authoritative teaching-exorcism spreads in Galilee (1:28). And the logos of his miraculous activity is preached *(kērussein)* and spread (1:45), the hearing of which brings people thronging to him (3:8). Some who came had been brought to faith by the hearing of Jesus' story (5:34; 10:52). That the disciples are given interpretations and others are not is a way of saying that the word is effective for some but not for others. That some hearing the logos of his miracles are brought to faith while others are not is another way of making the same point. Or is it the same way of making the same point? If Mark 4 implies that (allegorical) interpretation is indispensable, then the miracle stories also, by implication, must have been so interpreted. But I take the latter alternative to be improbable.

If that is correct, since the statements about the revealing intention of the word in 4:21–22 are as much spoken to the crowd (4:33) as to the disciples (4:10), the success of the word here is also disengaged from an explicit—or necessary—connection with allegorical interpretation (which is given to disciples). This brings me briefly to consider the movement of thought in 4:10–25 and to comment on the particular function of 4:21–25.

The word's movement from multiple failure to extravagant success in 4:14–20 mediates between revealed-in-order-to-conceal in 4:11–12 and concealed-in-order-to-make-manifest in 4:21–22. The latter passage contains four purpose *(hina)* clauses. The final purpose of the word is unconcealment. But if that word also contains the purpose to conceal, then revelation must remain ambiguous and faith must be "seeing" beneath the surface.

Kelber has argued that the measure which the hearer brings to hearing (4:24) and the understanding which enables more understanding (4:25) comprise the knowledge which has been given to insiders. To the extent that these sayings are referred to insiders he is right about what they mean. But I do think that the reference is primarily to disciples or insiders. In Matthew the "to him who has will more he given" has been shifted back into the dialogue between Jesus and the disciples about why he speaks in parables (Mt. 13:10–12//Mark 4:10–11); there (in Matthew) it is placed *before* the interpretation of the Sower, and it is clearly applied to the disciples: already having discipleship they will be given greater understanding. But Mark places the measure saying and the "to him who has" *after* the interpretation of the Sower in that ambiguous context where the addressees are the disciples (4:10) or the crowd (4:33) or both. Moreover, these sayings are very general in tone, and the statements about the proper predisposition for hearing are addressed to any person *(tis)*. Thus the preunderstanding which gets more understanding does not refer primarily to the knowledge given to insiders but to the necessary precondition for understanding which is the endowment of human beings as such. This meaning is further reenforced by the image of the earth (4:28), which is a symbol of the hearer (4:13–20), producing grain *of itself*.

One more question in this section: why for Mark is the word not effective for all? It is because, as we have just seen, there is a human contribution to be made if revelation is to be effective. But does not everything in salvation come from God? Yes (10:26–27) and no (4:24–25, 28). Actually the inter-working of revelatory word and human response is a mystery unfathomable even by the revealer (4:27b). It is Mark's belief that the revealer of the seed-word himself cannot say exactly how human pre-understanding and revealing word interact, which makes it possible—or necessary—to say that everything comes from God, but something comes from the human person.

7. Is the ending of Mark as dark in tone as Kelber says, and as tragic in meaning? To be sure there is much irony in the Gospel of Mark, but if the last word and primary word in the story of the good news about Jesus Christ, the Son of God, is the epiphany of the darkness of God's absence, then the irony of the Gospel is more bitter than most have imagined. Undoubtedly Jesus is portrayed as believing that he is abandoned by God. Mark stresses the spiritual suffering of Jesus on the cross. But the one on the cross who believes that he is God-forsaken is also the Son of God on the cross. And unless the reader is somehow intended to throw

away the first half of the Gospel, Jesus, the Son of God, is a figure of power who is the eschatological chosen one of God (1:11, 24, 34; 3:11; 9:7). Therefore, the meaning of the epiphany in the centurion's confession is not the unqualified assertion of God's absence but the paradoxical affirmation that God—Power—is victoriously though hiddenly present where she appears to be absent. To believe this one has to take the risk of believing what is behind the veil—or the reveiling. The risk is compounded by the fact that the possibility of hope is held out only by the fragile human word of the narrator who at this point claims to know more about what God is doing than Jesus does; that is, God still has Jesus as his Son.

Also, the resurrection in Mark, while it is not an epiphany, *is* an ambiguous move beyond death. The resurrection, which is so hopefully anticipated (8:31; 9:31; 10:34; 14:28) and which is to clear up the problem of Jesus' identity (9:9), never occurs as an actual event. It is only proclaimed to the women that it has occurred, and they out of fear do not report it to the disciples, who have abandoned the scene. Thus the suggestion that the resurrection will enable the disciples to tell others about Jesus (9:9) is rendered ironical. Mark's resurrection story joins the times before and after Jesus' death and shows that both of them are qualified by the opposition revealed/concealed. The announcement of the young man that Jesus is risen is concealed revelation: it is revelation in that the resurrection is declared, but the revelation is concealed in that the resurrected Jesus is not there in the story. The fear and silence of the women betrays the concealment—ambiguity—in the church's proclamation of the resurrection. But while I would argue that concealment overbalances revelation during Mark's plot, revelation overbalances—but does not nullify—concealment during the time of the narrative world which extends beyond the plot. This is signalled by the fact that the disciples—or some of them—have been restored to the faithful community beyond the end of the plot (10:38–39; 13:3–5, 9–11, 13).

Kelber observes that the disciples become outsiders and deprive themselves of an epiphany. I do not know whether he intends to maintain in the unqualified way that he did in his earlier works (for example, 1983: 129, 186) that the disciples are eliminated as apostolic witnesses and their rehabilitation is positively excluded. But it seems to me that that is not a probable interpretation. Quite apart from the textual evidence of their restoration (slight but real) Kelber's own—deconstructed—position works against the certainty of the disciples' permanent exclusion. He has argued that in Mark insiders become outsiders and outsiders, insiders. If that is the case, as it seems to be, then the disciples, who as insiders became outsiders, are always poised in the position to become insiders again. This is enforced by Kelber's contention that the Markan narrative as parabolic in nature is not closed but is rather open-ended. On Kelber's view of the Markan narrative it is not possible to argue that the disciples are permanently excluded.

I accept his view of Mark as open-ended but would argue that it is generically not so much parable as parabolic miracle story. The miracle story form, especially as it is employed in Mark, takes us closer to Mark's plot than does parable (which does not prescribe plot). The Markan structure can be seen as: (1) description of the illness—sin as sickness (1:4–8; 2:5, 15–17; 3:28–30); (2) impediment to faith—the suffering of the Son of Man prevents the disciples' understanding of Jesus' identity (8–10); (3) act of healing—Jesus' death has power to ransom by giving insight (10:45, 46–52; 15:24–38); (4) the response of faith—the centurion's confession (15:39). Also the miracle story genre provides the rationale for the unambiguous salvation of some characters—the centurion and some who come in faith for healing. Moreover, the juxtaposition of the negation of the disciples with their eventual salvation enhances the miracle story character of the Gospel: Jesus has power to overcome impossible obstacles which constrict human life. Nor can it be said that miracle stories necessarily support structure and culture. Whatever may be the case with miracle stories in other traditions and cultures, in Mark miracle stories—and the whole narrative as miracle story—effect the *eschatological* new creation (1:15; 3:23–27; 4:35–41).

Finally the ambiguous hope expressed in the resurrection narrative (16:1–8) sends us back to look at those places where both Jesus's death *and* resurrection are predicted with confidence (8–10; 14:28). Allusiveness and certainty balance each other. That the resurrection would be less than a demonstration might have been expected by the reader who knows that Jesus refused to give a sign to those who would not see the reality behind the veil (8:11–12). But the resurrection is tacitly there to undergird the only kind of faith that is possible in Mark's narrative world—I believe; help my unbelief (9:24). Jesus "raised" the boy who has "dead" from the impact of the dumb and deaf spirit (9:25–27). The death-and-resurrection of Jesus (8:31, etc.) is the ground for the disciples' finding life through death (8:34–37). The disciples repeatedly prove that this is not the way in which they want to follow. But at least some of them finally did. What Jesus does for the many that they cannot do for themselves (10:45) is to open the eyes of faith (10:51–52). The reality of Jesus' resurrection is not going to be something to be seen (16:1–8), but it is a reality. That is why the Gerasene demoniac now freed and in his right mind (5:15) can proclaim how much Jesus has done for him (see Via, 1986: 108–9, that the Gerasene Demoniac is a resurrection story). People are enabled to see beneath the veil, or the reveiling, because all things are possible for believers (9:23) as all things are possible for God (10:27). There is no visible demonstration of the resurrected Jesus. But there is enough sight given to follow Jesus on the way to Jerusalem (10:52), to follow in the way of suffering. And whether Jesus is raised or not will be known to those who, walking on that road, discover in the moment of utter human powerlessness and abandonment that the power of God is a reality. The God-forsaken one on the cross is on the cross the Son of God.

WORKS CONSULTED

Kelber, W.
    1983   *The Oral and the Written Gospel*. Philadelphia: Fortress.

Via, Dan O.
    1975   *Kerygma and Comedy in the New Testament*. Philadelphia: Fortress.
    1986   *The Ethics of Mark's Gospel*. Philadelphia: Fortress.

GENERIC COMPETENCE IN BIBLICAL HERMENEUTICS

Mary Gerhart
Hobart and William Smith Colleges

ABSTRACT

Genre has been one of the most widely used literary critical concepts in biblical scholarship. Generic analysis in biblical interpretation has generally been confined, however, to historical judgments or social-critical analysis of the *Sitz-im-Leben* of the text. The claim that textual meaning is always "genre-bound" suggests that there are other than historical purposes for generic analysis.

This paper explores the analogy between linguistic and generic competence to support the claim that reading is always reading as a genre. Six illustrations of this claim illuminate other than historical uses of genre analysis: genre as readability, as multiple hypotheses, as conflicting interpretations, as metaphoric process, as retrieval, as innovation.

Generic analysis can also be applied to explicitly theological reflections on biblical texts. The paper concludes by locating a major difficulty with biblical hermeneutics as it is conventionally understood and by suggesting how the difficulty can be overcome by means of generic analysis.

Genric[1] Competence in Biblical Hermeneutics

The names of Graf, Wellhausen, and Gunkel are familiar to this audience for having opened the door of biblical hermeneutics to literary critical methods. Literary criticism has not always been welcome in the company of theologians and of scholars of scripture. A century and a half ago, notwithstanding his own aesthetically complex style of writing, Soren Kierkegaard (1843) dismissed the aesthete as a dilettante.[2] Nor was Rudolf Bultmann, who demanded the "demythologization" of Christian scriptures, a particular friend of the imaginary, the fictional, or of narrativity in general. Even less distant is the time when the study of the Bible as literature was a highly suspect enterprise, something one might do in an English department but never in religious studies. Now all that has changed.

In the past decade literary critical approaches to the Bible have become acceptable, even commonplace. However, the status of these approaches in biblical studies is not clear. Some of the most widely read and provocative studies of the Bible in recent years—e.g., those by Frank Kermode, Robert Alter, Adele Berlin, and Elisabeth Schüssler Fiorenza—however differently,[3] have made use of literary critical methods. Do the successes of these literary studies suggest that other kinds of literary analysis will also prove fruitful?

One answer to this question may be found by examining a concept which has played an important role in both biblical and literary criticism, the concept of genre. The most explicit use of this concept in form criticism yielded important information in biblical studies and, despite criticism from literary critics like Kenneth Burke and biblical scholars like Gerhard von Rad (see J. J. Collins), the notion of genre continues to be useful in literary studies. In the early 70s, the Society of Biblical Literature Seminar on the Gospels formed a Task Force on Genre. As a member of that group, William G. Doty did a comprehensive review of the then current theories of genre and of the status of the concept. After making various observations, he concluded with this point:

> The main propaedeutic role of generic classification lies in the training of the interpreter to comprehend adequately a) the associational complexes in which a work appears [and] . . . c) the prepercerptions about the type of writing which the interpreter carried forward out of his own context, and which hinder or aid interpretation (58).

What is noteworthy about Doty's concluding comment is that, at a time when genre was known to most scholars as a tool for historical-literary analysis. Doty saw genre as clarifying the horizons of both reader and text.

In the late 70s, the Apocalypse Group of the SBL Genres Project saw the "identification of a genre . . . [as] an attempt to bring some order into a rather chaotic area of study" (Collins:iv). In this study genre was used as a "heuristic device" to show both the distinctive elements and the "recurrent features" encountered in apocalyptic texts. The editor, J. J. Collins, observed that "interpretation already involves an implicit notion of genre" and that although similarities among texts "identify" genres, "similarity does not necessarily imply historical relationships" (1). He acknowledged that there was "widespread opposition to any attempt to define [apocalypse] as a literary genre" and saw the work of the Consultation as restricted "to the initial stage of literary analysis" (4). In 1986, a sequel (edited by Adela Yarbro Collins) to this work on apocalypse continued the attempt to define apocalypse and to extend the definition to the social functions of the genre in various settings. One contributor noticed that until now paradigmatic studies (those which group and hierarchize features) have prevailed over syntagmatic studies (those which use text-linguistic methods to analyze meaning), and that the weakness of paradigmatic studies is the "tendency to remain taxonomic and static . . . ." (Aune:33).

Meanwhile, in literary criticism an even stronger claim regarding genre-analysis had been advanced: namely, that generic considerations are *indispensable* to the interpretation of texts. E. D. Hirsch gave a theoretical basis for that claim in his *Validity in Interpretation*, and although his book stirred controversy and earned criticism for his treatment of the issue of authorial intentionality, his claim about genre—"All understanding of verbal meaning is necessarily genre-bound" (76)—has not been challenged. John Barton repeated the claim for the indispensability of genre for understanding a text in his *Reading the Old Testament* (29).

Barton suggested that generic competence is analogous to linguistic competence in reading biblical literature—an analogy which, although it was not new with Barton, is particularly useful in the sense that it is not bound to any single genre or single understanding of genre. No one has elaborated precisely on how this analogy obtains, however. Nor did Barton address the question, If genre is indispensable to interpretation, why are so many readers oblivious of its role?

In this essay I will explore the notion of genre in terms of generic competence—the ability of readers to construct, identify, compare, test, retrieve, and critique genres. As a concept, generic competence shares some of the difficulties of other concepts—for example, the tendency to be taken for granted. Consider the concept of gravity. Before Newton, people realized that bodies fell to the earth and gave various explanations for such occurrences, but not until Newton's formulation was there an explanation commensurate with the demand for intelligibility of certain invariances in the experience of and the phenomenon of "falling." Similarly, readers have perceived that different kinds of texts give rise to different kinds of expectations. They have offered multiple explanations for the similarities among texts and for the ways similar texts function. But only by applying the concept of generic competence can we achieve an explanation compatible with the demand that the relationships between readers' experiences and textual forms be intelligible.

Generic competence is perhaps best understood in relation to Noam Chomsky's notion of linguistic competence in his general theory of linguistics. Linguistic competence is "the speaker-listener's knowledge of . . . language" (4). Linguistic competence designates the potential of human beings to understand presently existing and future possible expressions constructed in their own language, given that such expressions are structured according to specifiable grammatical principles. By analogy, we may say that generic competence designates a potential of human beings for understanding presently existing and future possible texts, given that such texts are structured according to specifiable genric principles.

These basic definitions pertain only initially to the "native" languages and texts of speakers and hearers, writers and readers. The notion of competence does not preclude the case in which speakers, hearers, writers and readers gain linguistic or genric competence outside their "native" language. Nor does the idea of competence preclude the more complicated instance of reading texts in translation (an issue not treated in this paper). The possibility of surpassing the language and texts of one's native culture is a vexed issue because of the privilege given to the historical dimension of genre. Moreover, in Chomsky's work, the surpassing of the boundaries of individual languages raises the controversial possibility of a theory of language that could be applied universally. In the issue of genre, the same, even more controversial possibility becomes manifest. There is also a sense in which language speaks in human beings as much as human beings choose the words they speak and a parallel sense in which genres overtake human beings as much as human beings choose the genres they understand. We will not explicitly address these further questions here. The further questions arise, however, because of the assumption that neither linguistic nor genric competence is limited to the culture of the original audience of the text.

Before continuing with the analogy between linguistic and genric competence, we must distinguish between competence and performance. According to Chomsky, competence refers to the speaker-listener's knowledge of the language in the ideal sense: Competence presupposes a "homogeneous speech community" and a perfect knowledge of the language (3). Performance refers to "the actual use of language in concrete situations." This distinction allows Chomsky to equate competence with grammar: "A grammar of a language purports to be a description of the ideal speaker-hearer's intrinsic competence." Strictly speaking, Chomsky says, "If the grammar is . . . perfectly explicit—in other words, if it does not rely on the intelligence of the understanding of the [speaker-listener] but rather provides an explicit analysis of [the speaker-listener's] contribution—we may call it a *generative grammar*" (4). Performance, on the other hand, includes such conditions as "memory limitations, distractions, shifts of attention and interest, and errors (random or characteristic)" (3) which occur in the application of the knowledge of language to speech-listening situations. It may seem from this distinction that it could be possible to dispense with the aspect of performance and to treat grammar (or in the case of genre, an anatomy of genre) as a distinct phenomenon. One may do so only at the risk of forgetting that competence is known only through reflection on performance. In other words, competence is a derivative concept dependent on performance. Conversely, since "performance does not *directly* reflect competence" (4, emphasis mine), performance and competence must be understood in relation to each other.

The concept of linguistic competence makes it possible for us to understand a phenomenon which is familiar to us: on the side of the speaker-listener, the ability to handle language in such a way as to generate and to understand sentences, and on the side of the system of language, the principled diversity of spoken expressions. By contrast, the concept of generic competence makes explicit a factor which is largely ignored in learning theory, unfocused in postmodern criticism, and frequently treated as an "it-goes-without-saying" in philosophy and religious studies: on the side of the writer-reader, the ability to read a text, and on the side of literature, the principled diversity of texts. Again, whereas the marvel of speech acquisition is repeated every time a child learns to speak, the marvel of genre acquisition is largely a hidden process. Moreover, because the process is hidden, except in specifically generic inquiry, it is usually left to chance and is deprived of both support and criticism.

The role of genre in relation to any text is more complex than the role of linguistic principles in relation to single sentences. Indeed, in actual performance generic competence encompasses linguistic competence. Notwithstanding this complexity, issues of genre draw less attention than issues of grammar. The phenomenon of generic innovation, for example, is less studied than the phenomenon of linguistic innovation. Until recently, generic studies have been primarily an affair of historical and sociological, as distinct from hermeneutical and philosophical interest. Since historical and sociological inquiry is often conducted by means of categories already historically defined, genre in these studies tends to be treated as only a principle of categorization. The problem of generic innovation is subsumed within the documented shift from one historical genre to another. Alasdair Fowler, the author of a comprehensive study of genre from a traditionalist perspective, for example, claims that individual texts frequently escape their boundaries of origin. However, he adds unequivocally, genres never do (132). We shall see, however, that this issue is far more complicated than Fowler's containment principle suggests. Generic competence includes not only the horizon of the text, but that of the reader as well. For this reason, understanding a text is never a simple matter of discovering its "original" genre.

Genres are not only principles of categorization or identification; they are also principles of production. Understood retrospectively, genres can be said to produce, as well as to identify meanings. In another paper, "The Dilemma of the Text: How to Belong to a Genre," I argued that genric analysis at its best is always in the service of an hypothesis; that is, genre reveals itself to be under the guidance of explicit presuppositions and assumptions which struggle against one another and which change history even as history changes them.

Because the foregoing considerations are both numerous and complex, it is doubtful that they can be illustrated by a single example. I have chosen six examples, therefore, to illustrate the ways in which genric competence is evoked whenever we begin to read a text. The examples will also make explicit the issues that have been introduced in the preceding theoretical discussion. In the light of what we learn about genre from these examples, I will attempt to disentangle some of the confusion regarding the role they may or may not play in theological reflection on biblical texts. To this end, I will review what I take to be the prevailing misunderstanding of hermeneutics in literary criticism and suggest that this misunderstanding has distorted the understanding of biblical theology as well.

Genre as a Principle of Production

Genric competence refers to more than the recognition of specifiable conventions and forms. We do not begin by knowing all the conventions of literature, nor do texts "fit" simply into genres. We have hunches, compose hypotheses, make imaginative guesses as informed minds already at work in an area of inquiry—hypotheses which are found to illuminate new data and used to find confirmation in experimental trials. In this paper, genre (or the German "Gattung," which has become almost as familiar to literary critics and biblical scholars) is used in its most inclusive sense: It includes large "modes of cognition," such as narrative, philosophical argument, history (as particularized, for example, in chronologies, journals, treatises), science (as particularized in laboratory reports, journal articles, data files), as well as the "major" genres, such as drama, the epic, the lyric; "sub-genres," such as tragedy, comedy, dialogue; and components of all of these, such as conversation, aphorism, anacoluthon. The purpose of including all of these "levels" of categorizations is to prevent the taxonomic function of genre from obscuring its productive function.

1. *Genre as readability*

In his treatment of method in reading biblical texts, Barton argued that the act of understanding literature, is necessarily genre-bound. Barton used the following example (13) to illustrate our need of genric, and not only linguistic competence, if we are to interpret appropriately:

Dear Sir:

Re: Acct # 23579D

Since this account continues to show a debit of £559.67, I have no alternative but to inform you that unless it is cleared within seven days from the above date we shall be obliged to take steps to recover the sum in question.

Yours faithfully,
A Clerk

Since "Dear Sir" and "A Clerk" are a pair and appear to frame the remainder of the text, how do we know this is not a lyric poem? How do we know that the convention of "notifying of a debt" and "taking steps" are not "empty forms"? Since these phrases follow what seems to be a term of endearment ("Dear Sir"), why are they "veiled threats" rather than "a joke between friends"? How do we know that "Dear Sir" and "Yours faithfully" *are* empty forms and not to be taken literally? The Chinese, for example, would be apt to misread these forms because terms of endearment in China are reserved for intimacy.

In what sense is this use of genre a process of production as well as categorization? Barton claims that it is the discovery of conventions and the kinds of meanings they are capable of having that makes it possible to read with understanding texts that have been previously misread. Conversely, we may say that if appropriate conventions are not discovered and the problem of reading a difficult text cannot be resolved, the irresolution is evidence of incompetence. Of course, if a text is written by an amnesiac, the incompetence may seem to be on the side of the text rather than of the reader because the text seems not to make even conventional linguistic sense. But even in this marginal instance, we may say that texts written by amnesiacs have potential meaning, and knowing that a text is that *kind* of text, i.e., a text written by an amnesiac, enables us to begin to understand its unconventionality and to be open to the possibility of a new convention.

In Barton's letter, the horizon of the text is the primary but not exclusive consideration. Using the analogy with linguistic competence, we may surmise that we have an instance in which the horizon of the text corresponds to the reader's competence—an "ideal" knowledge of the genres of the historical period, that is, a knowledge ordinarily uncomplicated (for a native reader of English) by elements that call those genres into question—elements from the horizons of either the reader or the text. The lack of complication is further shown in the reader's ability to compare and contrast without remainder the conventions of one culture with those of another—thus revealing the presupposition that the conventions of this text are indigenous to one culture.

2. Genre as multiple hypotheses

Heather Dubrow gave a graphic illustration of how different genric hypotheses change our expectations and interpretations of the same text. In her book entitled *Genre*, she asked the reader to consider the following passage from a hypothetical book:

> The clock on the mantelpiece said ten thirty, but someone had suggested recently that the clock was wrong. As the figure of the dead woman lay on the bed in the front room, a no less silent figure glided from the house. The only sounds to be heard were the ticking of that clock and the loud wailing of an infant. (1)

Dubrow argued that two radically different readings of this paragraph result from our assumptions about the genre of its textual context. If we read the passage as detective fiction, for example, we are likely to assume that the dead woman has been murdered—hypothetically a victim of foul play—and we will notice the time on the clock as evidence to corroborate or to challenge what we know later about the activities of the murder suspects. We are apt to see the doubt about the time as part of the detective game or riddle to be solved. We will ask for empirical reasons to explain the clock's being inaccurate: e.g., that it might have been tampered with. With a chill we regard the "no less silent figure" as the victim's potential murderer and we begin to look for other clues to identify the victim, the murderer, and the motive for the crime.

If, on the other hand, we read the passage as part of a *Bildungsroman*, we will tend to see the baby as the central subject and the "silent figure" as the midwife or the grieving father because the *Bildungsroman* features the fortunes and development of a hero from birth to death. The clock we are apt to interpret symbolically in a *Bildungsroman*, perhaps as an allusion to the disruption of ordinary time in a world about to be changed. At the same time we become alert for other references and ideas about time. Natural causes, rather than foul play, are likely to be invoked in the death of the woman we assume to be the mother.

This example makes explicit the hypothetical aspect of genre as the reader tests alternative readings of the text *as* different genres. Reading is always *reading as*, but this fact of interpretation becomes manifest only in the presence of two alternatives, both of which "make sense" of the text. Genre-testing can be done for different reasons: For example, one might test different genres in order to determine the original genre of the text, or to compare and contrast contemporary understandings of the text.

3. Genre as conflicting interpretations

Not all generic considerations pivot on such clear choices as in the foregoing example. In recent studies of 1 John, for example, we find different interpretations which hinge on at least four possible choices of genre:
1) a letter,
2) a "comment" patterned on the fourth gospel,
3) a "paper" in the modern sense,
4) an "enchiridion" (handbook or manual).

In his review of recent books on the First Letter of John, Fernando Segovia stated that 1 John poses a distinctive problem of genre:

> Whereas the designation of 2 and 3 John as "letters" has never been seriously questioned, given their basic agreement with epistolary conventions of the first century CE, the search for the exact genre of 1 John has remained a topic of considerable debate in the literature. The absence of all such epistolary conventions within it, above all the lack of both a prescription and a postscript, has caused many to question its traditional designation as a "letter" and to look instead for other possible options (1).

Segovia shows how the issue of genre is foregrounded (in all except one of the six authors whose work on 1 John he reviews) and how each interpretation (in the work of all six, whether or not the issue of genre is foregrounded) is consequential upon the generic assumptions of each author.

Two of the generic designations ("paper" in the modern sense, and "enchiridion") are not contemporary with the original audience of the text being studied. Segovia seemed to be ambivalent about the non-contemporaneity between the generic designations and the texts. Although he did not object to the designations being non-contemporaneous, he concluded that

> alternative designations of genre, such as that of "enchiridion" or "paper" should be grounded in and argued on the basis of similar writings roughly contemporaneous with 1 John; otherwise, such designations prove to be of little heuristic value in the end (2).

Moreover, he thought that the choices of genre other than "letter" (whether "comment" on the gospel, "enchiridion," or "paper") were "by no means radically different from earlier proposals made under different appellations." He acknowledged the suggestion that 1 John is a "comment" patterned on the fourth gospel to be the most "novel" of the group under review, but judged that the genre of "comment" was like an earlier explication of the text as an "epilogue" to the gospel. Here Segovia reached toward novelty, as distinct from contemporaneity with historical context, as a decisive factor in his evaluation. The choice of genre that he made appears to turn on both novelty and the power that the genric designation has for illuminating the text, rather than on the genre's contemporaneity with the text.

This example provides two clear instances ("paper" and "enchiridion") of the context of the interpreter augumenting the original context of the text. We notice, in addition, that Segovia is not so much concerned with the correct identification of genre, but rather with how each genre controls the meanings of the text. Segovia's is therefore a syntagmatic type of genric inquiry, for it focuses on possible meanings of the text.

4. Genre as metaphoric process

James G. Williams called into question the traditional designation of "gospel." Like 1 John, the texts now known as "gospel" do not readily "belong" to any of the genres contemporary to it, and so Williams (1985) employed a theory of metaphor to account for the singular character of the genre, gospel. Williams suggested that by understanding gospel as the conjunction of Hellenistic biography and biblical parable, we can better understand how Jesus in the gospels becomes the subject of his own parables. Here we have an instance of an attempt to understand a genric innovation by introducing a theory of metaphor (Gerhart and Russell, 1984). Williams used the theory of metaphor to show how the insistence that biography *is* parable best explicates the singularity of gospel. The premise here is that since the texts traditionally referred to as being of this genre are significantly different from other genres contemporary to it, the most important point to be made about it is that it is a genric innovation. Gospel, according to Williams, is functionally similar to and different from both ancient biography and parable, the two most likely candidates for "parenting" gospel as a new genre. His inquiry is paradigmatic insofar as it accounts for the origins of gospel and syntagmatic insofar as it interprets the meanings of texts.

Methodologically, this example is important for bringing into view the historicity of the understandings of genre as a concept. We are somewhat familiar with the historicality of individual genres, especially of those which have become dated or obsolete, but in this example we are invited to a new understanding of genre in addition to understanding a genre as new. By employing a theory of genre that emphasizes the creation of new meaning, Williams opened the door to a new understanding of the role of genre in biblical studies as well as a new understanding of the genre that is called "gospel."

5. Genre as retrieval

Rosemary Ruether has illustrated the way in which the retrieval of genres can provide new stories in old genric skins to call into question the reified interpretations of traditional stories. In her *Sexism and God-talk*, for example, Ruether used the traditional theological sense of myth, as a story that is "false" or which mystifies. But to replace the myth of a god whose primary characteristic is male dominance, she told a new story in the rubric of midrash (a haggadic or halakic exposition and embellishment of the underlying significance of a biblical text—the exposition itself, in this case, in story form). Her book begins with "The Kenosis of the Father: A Midrash in Three Acts," which presents a God who calls into question his own patriarchal authoritarianism, recalls that he has "known other ways of being God" and extends them to others: "to slaves, to Gentiles, perhaps even to women" (Ruether:3). This example, which is situated in the context of a systematic theology, illustrates the transposition of the genre of midrash—historically concerned with androcentric interpretation of specific biblical texts—into a contemporary setting. The result is an effective reinterpretation of the original text, the meaning of which is frequently called into question but more starkly by Ruether's alternative narrative.

6. Genre as innovation

Genres themselves can change as well as be retrieved. Genres are invented for many reasons, and Stanley Kauffmann gives one instance of the need for genric innovation in his column in *The New Republic*. Kauffmann defines a "genre film" as one that "wants the viewer to place it in a certain line of films, to remember its antecedents, and to admire it for either its fidelity to its forebears or its innovations or both" (1987:24). But when any genre is perceived as "too infantile a form" of what the audience believes, the genre must be made more "complicated" if it is to continue being effective. One might point to *A Day in the Life of America* as an example of such complication: in the film the genre, mafia movie, is complicated by making the subject Jewish instead of Italian and the context neighborhood instead of family.

If the genre is changed sufficiently, the problem of identifying the genre in order to be able to read the text may arise. What follows is an excerpt from a complex genre. Unlike the example of a dun letter in "Genre as readability" above, most readers are likely to be frustrated by their inability to make sense of the passage, precisely because its genre is not apparent on a first, perhaps not even upon repeated readings.

The point of this example will best be made if readers conceal from themselves the identification of its source (given below) until they have struggled a few minutes to make sense of the passage:

> What's needed is a way to examine the parts of a string. Well, you can always look at the display—but that invites human error and judgment. You might be tempted to accept certain four-letter words simply because they are neither obscene, uncouth, inflam-

matory, nor abusive. That won't do at all, since, by design, the Automatic Censor must be autocratic and arbitrary to a fault (Stewart).

Most readers will need to be informed that this passage was taken from a computer manual and is an excerpt from instruction for examining the parts of a string (sequence of characters) in Basic memory. The complicated genre, however, is derived from combining instruction with espionage fiction.

This example is similar to the fourth example, gospel, in the sense that both pose the problem of reading a new genre. The examples differ in the sense that gospel, although a new genre at the time of its composition, has acquired a tradition of interpretation, and a new theory of genre is employed to produce a new understanding of the now traditional genre of gospel. By contrast, the combination of instruction and espionage does not have a tradition of interpretation in computer manuals and therefore poses a problem of readability rather than one of adequate interpretation.

Genre and Theology

We are now prepared, on the basis of the foregoing explication of the multiple functions of genre, to suggest the possibility of a long-term gain in explicitly theological reflection on biblical texts. One of the problems with biblical theology as currently practiced and understood is the suspicion, by both literary critics and biblical scholars, that theology *substitutes* itself as self-evident meaning in place of the biblical text. Paul de Man made this suspicion explicit when he located hermeneutics traditionally in the "sphere of theology" and "its secular prolongation in the various historical disciplines." He went on to say that "unlike poetics, which is concerned with the taxonomy and the interaction of poetic structures, hermeneutics is concerned with the meaning of specific texts." Then he made the following claim: "In a hermeneutical enterprise, reading necessarily intervenes but, like computation in an algebraic proof, it is a means toward an end . . . ; the ultimate aim of a hermeneutically successful reading is to do away with reading altogether" (1982:ix–x). For this claim, de Man cited Heidegger's *Being and Time* as a reference.

However, the foregoing analysis of genre in this paper suggests that the necessity of reading can be done away with only if one fails to pay attention to genre. With genric analysis, on the other hand, there is no temptation to translate genred discourse (such as narratives, liturgical hymns, aphorisms) into non-genred discourse (as philosophy and theology are misunderstood to be). With genric analysis, biblical theologians will understand themselves to mediate between genres. They recognize philosophy and theology as also embodied in genres, for example, those of argument, analogy and treatise—genres which require "reading," i.e., genric analysis, no less than the genres of biblical texts.

The recognition of the necessity to take genre seriously—in this case, the genre of narrative—can be seen in the "religion as story" discussions of the last two decades (see Wiggins). Not so helpful was the frequent proposal, found in the same discussions, to *replace* theology by narrative.

Genric analysis also discloses to readers their own predilection for one or another genre, analogous to the ways in which biblical scholars construct a "working canon" by privileging one or another genre (see, for example, J. D. Crossan's use of parable as the key to understanding the gospels). In the middle of this century, one could find theological arguments that the genre of comedy (understood as the harmonious resolution of conflicts introduced in plots) was more appropriate to the "Christian vision" per se than the genre of tragedy (understood as the demise of a character though hamartia, or tragic flaw). One also found arguments that some genres were singularly "christian"—for example, Sallie Mac-Fague's treatment of autobiography in her book on the parables.

There are gains and losses with every generic choice and interpretation. There would seem to be more room in biblical hermeneutics for genre-testing and analysis than is permitted by the present emphasis on doing genre-analysis for the purpose of verifying the historical background or the social-cultural milieu of the text. For the historical is a constructed configuration of elements and, like authorial intention, is not normative for an adequate understanding of the text. Genric analysis would seem to be important, then, for opening up alternative versions and visions of the text for the penultimate[4] purpose of understanding it better.

We can conclude from the preceding genric analysis that it is better to be aware of one's predilections than to be unaware of them, to be aware as well of the limitations of the genres one constructs and employs. This is not to agree completely with the deconstructionists, who have taught us that philosophical and theological discourse is not non-genric as it sometimes pretends to be (see de Man, 1979). Where the deconstructionist posits absence at the heart of meaning, the theologian who does genric analysis can see both presence and absence—for conceptual limits disclose possibility as well as boundary, ambiguity[5] as well as illusion, and always the need for interpretation.

NOTES

[1] I use the adjectival form "genric" to emphasize the functions of the concept of genre in interpretation. The conventional form "generic" has come to connote aspects such as non-specificity and common variety, aspects unrelated to the process of interpretation. The term

"generic" recalls only the taxonomic function of genre whereas the term "genric" points also to its productive function.

[2] As Kierkegaardian scholarship of the last ten years have demonstrated so well, Kierkegaard was a master of rhetoric and used several genres expertly—so well, indeed, that his rhetorical skill was frequently underestimated by earlier scholarship.

[3] The titles of Alter and Berlin indicate that these works are literary critical. Kermode illustrated similarities in the processes of literary interpretation for both sacred and secular texts. Schüssler Fiorenza distinguished between two applications of form critical method: one, which "stresses the 'word' component of a story or tradition, often favoring it as more original than the narrative", the other, which focuses on the "narrative text and the historical actors involved." Although hers is the second emphasis, it does not preclude attention to the word component. Her emphasis on narrative is also intended to modify "the view so widely held . . . that a miracle story or a controversy-dialogue setting is just an illustration or exemplification of the relevatory [sic] "word" or pronouncement of Jesus" (p. 152).

[4] The ultimate purpose is appropriation of the text—a purpose beyond the limits of hermeneutical inquiry.

[5] On ambiguity in genre, see Sternberg (222–26). On ambiguity in relation to theological reflection, see Tracy.

WORKS CONSULTED

Alter, R.
    1981   *The Art of Biblical Narrative*. New York: Basic.

Aune, D.
    1986   "The Apocalypse of John and the Problem of Genre." *Semeia* 31: 65–96.

Barton, John
    1984   *Reading the Old Testament*. London: Darton, Longman, Todd.

Berlin, A.
    1983   *Poetics and Interpretation of Biblical Narrative*. Sheffield: Almond.

Birch, B.C.
    1984   "Biblical Hermeneutics in Recent Discussion: Old Testament," *RSR* 10: 1–7.

Bultmann, R.
    1941   "Kerygma und Mythos." In *Offenbarung und Heilsgeschehen*. Munich: A. Lempp.

Buss, M.
    1979   "Understanding Communication." Pp. 3–34 in *Encounter with the Text: Form and History in the Hebrew Bible*. Philadelphia and Missoula: Fortress and Scholars Press.

Chomsky, N.
    1965   *Aspects of the Theory of Syntax*. Cambridge: MIT.

Collins, A.Y., ed.
    1986   *Early Christian Apocalypticism: Genre and Social Setting.* *Semeia* 36.

Collins, J.J.
    1979   "Preface" and "Introduction: Morphology of a Genre." *Semeia* 14, iii–iv, 1–19.

Crossan, J.D.
    1973   *In Parables: The Challenge of the Historical Jesus.* New York: Harper & Row.

de Man, P.
    1979   *Allegories of Reading.* New Haven: Yale University Press.
    1982   "Introduction." Pp. vii–xxv in Hans Robert Jauss, *Toward an Aesthetic of Reception,* Vol. 2. Minneapolis: University of Minnesota Press.

Doty, W.G.
    1972   "The Concept of Genre in Literary Analysis." Pp. 29–64 in *The Genre of the Gospels: Studies in Methodology, Comparative Research and Compositional Analysis.* Missoula: Society of Biblical Literature.

Dubrow, H.
    1982   *Genre.* London and New York: Metheun.

Fowler, A.
    1982   *Kinds of Literature: An Introduction to the Theory of Genres and Modes.* Cambridge: Harvard University Press.

Gerhart, M. and A. Russell
    1984   *Metaphoric Process: The Creation of Scientific and Religious Understanding.* Fort Worth: Texas Christian University Press.

Gerhart, M.
    Forthcoming   "The Dilemma of the Text: How to 'Belong' to a Genre." In *Empiricism and Hermeneutics: The Invention of "Facts" in the Study of Literature.* Ed. by David Bleich. Bloomington: Indiana University Press.

Gunkel, H.
    1964   *The Legends of Genesis.* Trans. W.H. Carruth. New York: Schocken.

Harrington, D.J.
    1984   "Biblical Hermeneutics in Recent Discussion: New Testament," *RSR* 10: 7–10.

Helmholm, D.
    1986   "The Problem of Apocalyptic Genre and the Apocalypse of John." *Semeia* 36: 13–64.

Hirsch, E.D.
    1967   *Validity in Interpretation*. New Haven: Yale University Press.

Kauffmann, S.
    1987   "Stanley Kauffmann on Films: The Same, Only Different." *The New Republic* 196: 24–25.

Kermode, F.
    1979   *The Genesis of Secrecy: On the Interpretation of Narrative*. Cambridge: Harvard University Press.

Kierkegaard, S.
    1941, 1944   *Either/Or*. Vol. 1. Trans. D.F. and L.M. Swenson. Vol. 2. Trans. W. Lowrie. Princeton: Princeton University Press.

McFague, S.
    1975   *Speaking in Parables*. Philadelphia: Fortress.

Ruether, R.
    1983   *Sexism and God-Talk: Toward a Feminist Theology*. Boston: Beacon.

Schüssler Fiorenza, E.
    1983   *In Memory of Her: A Feminist Theological Reconstruction of Christian Origins*. New York: Crossroad.

Segovia, F.
    1987   "Recent Research in the Johannine Letters." *RSR* 13: 1–8.

Sternberg, M.
    1985   *The Poetics of Biblical Narrative: Ideological Literature and the Drama of Reading*. Bloomington: Indiana University Press.

Stewart, G.
    1981   *Getting Started With TRS-80 Basic*. Fort Worth: Radio Shack.

Tracy, D.
    1987   *Plurality and Ambiguity: Religion as a Test-case for Hermeneutics*. New York: Harper & Row.

Wiggins, J., ed.
    1975   *Religion as Story*. New York: Harper & Row.

Williams, J.G.
    1985   *Gospel Against Parable: Mark's Language of Mystery*. Sheffield: Almond.

HOW TO READ A JAGUAR: A RESPONSE TO MARY GERHART

Robert Detweiler
Emory University

I find Mary Gerhart's essay lucid and instructive and will offer my response as a critical supplement rather than as a rejoinder that argues with her in any important way. However, in the spirit of such supplementarity, I will develop my comments out of a text that itself plays with the problems of genre.

In a fiction entitled "The God's Script," the great Argentine writer Jorge Luis Borges has Tzinacán, an Aztec priest, relate the story of his imprisonment. Tzinacán, who practiced rituals of human sacrifice, has been captured by conquistadores and condemned to life-long incarceration in a dungeon. In the other half of the dungeon he occupies, which is a hemisphere divided vertically, is a jaguar, and for a few seconds each day the priest can see the animal through a grate between the two cells when a trapdoor above them is opened to let down food and water and a brief ray of light. Tzinacán recalls that somewhere in the world is a hidden, magical message of a god and becomes convinced that this message is concealed in the pattern of the jaguar's spots. After many years of studying the animal's skin he deciphers the message in a moment of epiphany. It is a fourteen-word formula, the knowledge of which makes him omnipotent. But he does not utter the phrase that would free him. The experience has been so powerful, so self-obliterating, that he is no longer concerned about worldly things, and he remains in the cell's darkness, awaiting death.

At one point in Tzinacán's struggle to find and read the divine message he asks a fascinating linguistic/theological question that has implications for the latter part of Gerhart's paper on genre and theology. Pondering "the generic enigma of a sentence written by a god," he says:

> What type of sentence (I asked myself) will an absolute mind construct? I considered that even in the human languages there is

> no proposition that does not imply the entire universe, to say *the tiger* is to say the tigers that begot it, the deer and the turtles devoured by it, the grass on which the deer fed, the earth that was mother to the grass, the heaven that gave birth to the earth. I considered that in the language of a god every word would enunciate that infinite concatenation of facts, and not in an implicit but in an explicit manner, and not progressively but instantaneously. In time, the notion of a divine sentence seemed puerile or blasphemous. A god, I reflected, ought to utter only a single word and in that word absolute fullness. (171)

This passage seems to be a fine instance of Paul de Man's Heidegger-inspired comment quoted by Gerhart: "the ultimate aim of a hermeneutically successful reading is to do away with reading altogether." Borges' Aztec priest has accomplished a spectacularly successful reading. He has, in fact, produced the perfect reading by locating and interpreting the text that makes him omniscient and omnipotent ("to utter it in a loud voice would suffice to make me all powerful"—173), so that he would no longer need to read. Here is also the sense in which the deconstructionists refer to interpretation as a nihilating activity: it wishes to get everything under control in order to achieve a condition of stasis, a state of non-effort and equilibrium that would paralyze selfhood and community.

But in Borges' story the perfect reading depends on a perfect text—one so forceful that it can transform all existence—and it is a text that subsumes genre because it contains all generic possibility. Indeed, in the priest's theology of language all human terminology reflects poorly (the Platonic term "simulacrum" is used) the ultimate pure and undifferentiated plenitude of divinity, and he comes to view even "the notion of a divine sentence" as "puerile and blasphemous." That would be so because that sentence could still be generically classified—for instance as a magic formula. (Had Tzinacán been acquainted with speech act theory, he might have labelled it a perlocutionary act.)

Is it the mythology of genre theory that it derives from a hierarchy emanating from such a perfect totalizing word? Gerhart's study does not imply this. She argues, to the contrary, that awareness of genre distinctions helps to keep biblical texts open to interpretation, hinders the substitution of theology and philosophy for interpretation, and extends (perhaps indefinitely) the play of meaning in the treatment of biblical texts. Nevertheless, I am not persuaded that, as Gerhart says, "The foregoing analysis [i.e., the major part of her study] of genres in this paper suggests that the necessity of reading can be done away with only if one fails to pay attention to genre" (40). Her "foregoing analysis" devotes itself (very impressively) to arguments about generic competence, but these arguments do not address squarely the question of "a hermeneutically successful reading" that she brings up via the de Man quotation. Certainly genre literacy is crucial to a knowledgeable theological interpretation of biblical texts, but I do not see that such literacy gives the theologian (or philosopher) any particular hermeneutical edge. Thus I do not understand why it is specifically the biblical theologians who, "With genric analysis . . . will understand themselves to mediate between genres" (40). The implication here is that competency in recognizing, shaping, and employing genres is a sort of ideologically neutral skill that can be learned by the theologian in order to make his/her interpretation less immediately biased (less of a substitute as self-evident meaning, in Gerhart's terms) and therefore somehow more valid. I would argue that the very recognition and creation of genres—the developing of generic competency—is, like everything else, already bound up in ideology, or at least in the network of assumptions and biases that permeates our thinking and acting, and hence that genre literacy is already a central aspect of the hermeneutical enterprise. In that sense, then, the interpreter, theologian or otherwise, of biblical (or other) texts must, like Borges' Aztec priest, always be ready to reflect on "the generic enigma of a sentence written by a god." In other words, he/she must be willing to deal with the "metaphysics" of genre argumentation. Does genre classification reflect something about the construction of ultimate reality as revealed by interpretation? If so, one should be ready to theologize on it more expansively than Gerhart does here (although I would guess that she does so elsewhere). If not, then one should not overestimate what genre theory can do for the theologians.

Tzinacán's genre competency is born out of desperation. Sentenced to a life imprisonment in a dark dungeon, he invents both a text and a "scene of writing" for that text on the jaguar's pelt. All that he has not invented is the genre of the magic divine formula. Combining that literacy with his fugitive text and its suspected location, he gives himself something significant to do as the decades pass. All this is, of course, the effort of a mind so radically isolated and turned inward that it imagines an intense new reality. One sees here a fictional illustration of what Gerhart describes as a "sense in which genres overtake human beings," just as we have been taught by Heidegger that language speaks us and speaks in us. But I am more interested in using the example of the mad priest to ask the question of how much *we* invent not only the genres themselves but also the interpretive conditions to reinforce the validity of the genres. In her section on "Genre as readibility," Gerhart, after presenting Barton's example of the dun letter, asks the question, "In what sense is this use of genre a process of production as well as categorization?" but never answers it directly. I think her point here is that we work creatively with difficult texts to locate them generically and thus interpret them more "correctly." I believe, though, that she is too categorical herself when she argues "that if appropriate conventions are not discovered and the problem of reading a difficult text cannot be resolved, the irresolution is evidence of incompetence" (35). What if irresolution (Derrida calls it undecidability; it is related to Jean-François Lyotard's concept of paralogy) is the intention of the text? Does this mean, as Gerhart remarks of the hypothetical text composed by an amnesiac, that such an undecidable text can still be understood, via our genre sophistication, as unconventional and hence renders us "open to the possibility of a new convention" (35)? This strikes me as too easy an answer. I believe that a good number of creative (more on these later) as well as critical texts composed nowadays are designed to generate in the reader a sense of irresolution that is more than mere ambiguity, and that this design is produced by an intentional confusion and conflation of genres that we find pointless, if not impossible, to try to sort out. To recognize this strategy is not, of course, to denigrate genre literacy and inventiveness. Quite to the contrary, we need all the help we can get to absorb and respond to such texts, and our competence with genres remains an important guide. But one should not claim that irresolution in such cases is the result of incompetence on the part of either text or reader.

Furthermore, there are degrees of irresolution in the undecidable texts being written these days. It is not uncommon to argue of late that Freud is most profitably read as a creative writer and the later Heidegger (a bit more specifically) as a poet. This means, among other things, that Freud has lost credibility as a scientist and Heidegger as a philosopher, yet one finds their texts so compelling nonetheless that one wishes to protect and nurture them under other auspices. Yet because neither one *really* writes fiction or poetry as such—which is to say in any conventional sense—one would have to argue that, say, *Moses and Monotheism* is a blend of quasi-scientific speculation and historical fantasy (perhaps too harsh a judgment), while the essays in *On the Way to Language* are a blend of philosophy, literary criticism, and Heidegger's own poetizing (I am thinking especially of the Trakl essay, "Language in the Poem").

Such texts are, however, far less undecidable than the bulk of Derrida's writing. How is one to classify *Glas*, for example, or *Margins of Philosophy*? These are texts that project undecidability in the process of writing about it. Many philosophers deny that this is philosophy, or at least *proper* philosophy, while the literary theorists are hard-pressed to identify it (let alone define it) as any sort of poetics. Yet even Derrida seems approachable in comparison with the writing of Jacques Lacan, whose *Écrits* one can classify as psychoanalytic theory, yet which designation does very little in helping one to penetrate the willfully obscure prose.

My point is that there are kinds of writing in our midst (kinds that are proliferating at what to some is an alarming rate) that use our genre competency precisely to frustrate it—and not out of mere mischief but in order to argue for the recognition of epistemological and hermeneutical conditions that no longer respond to the sort of mind-set (of which genre classification is a part) in which systematizing is dominant. Gerhart might reply here that such a situation still opens up to a concept of genre as metaphoric process, "a theory of genre that emphasizes the creation of new meaning" (18). I would grant this role of genre but would repeat that in the context of contemporary writing of and on undecidability, it is a role that confirms irresolution more than helping to "explain" it.

The fascination of a number of biblical scholars with the genre of parables indicates, not incidentally, their involvement in the deconstructive mode and mood, with its stress on (and stresses of) undecidability. Some of them, surely, are intrigued by the New Testament parables as instances of a kind of text within their own field that tends toward irresolution—that has, in its way, irresolution as its goal. Although this is not identical with the necessary undecidability of interpretation that Derrida promulgates, it comes close enough to inspire instructive comparisons. There is even the suggestion in James Williams' essay in this issue that recent gospel studies undermine the definition of the parable genre and thus allow us to imagine productive redefinitions of these texts as something more than parable, an imaginative and tentative re-classification not unlike our attempts to accommodate the influential but problematic texts of a Freud or Heidegger by "metaphorically" labelling them as something other than what they once were.

Borges himself is acknowledged as a pioneering composer of "meta-fictions," a term denoting a generic hybrid or crossbreed and a kind of creative writing that has great significance for genre studies. "The God's Script" is an example of Borges' strategy of conducting playful theological and philosophical investigations in the form (one should not say in the guise, for it is more than that) of narrative fiction. His stories dramatize the efforts of various characters to confront and resolve the major perplexing questions of metaphysics and epistemology (appearance, illusion, and reality; the nature of time; randomness, chance, coincidence; etc.). Even more compelling is that in many of the stories the problems are in fact resolved. Borges employs the tactics of narrative fiction to pretend that the grand problems of western thought (at least) can have solutions, and his strategy involves as crucial a confusion of genres as the writing of the deconstructive critics. Thus in "The God's Script" a problem addressed and "resolved" concerns natural theology: what would happen if one could find God perfectly revealed in creation?

Borges is only one of a growing number of writers who exploit genre and turn it against itself not only by employing fiction to write self-consciously about the problems of writing fiction (and thus merging fiction and poetics) but also by teasing fiction (and the reader) into relationships with autobiography, biography, history, reportage, psychology, religion, and a host of other fields. Examples of others are Samuel Beckett, John Barth, Robert Coover, Italo Calvino, Christine Brooke-Rose, Vladimir Nabokov, and G. Cabrera Infante. This is predominantly a kind of writing that plays with the forms as well as the content of the western literary-cultural tradition and engages the reader in what has been labelled "intertextuality," the study of the network of dependencies on older texts and alterations of them that a particular work develops. Examples are Donald Barthelme's *Snow White*, which retells the fairy tale in a modern Greenwich Village setting and interrupts the narration at midpoint to give the reader a multiple-choice quiz; D. M. Thomas' *The White Hotel*, which invents correspondence by Freud and his colleagues as part of the case history of a (fictive) patient of Freud; Julian Barnes' *Flaubert's Parrot*, which merges the informal essay in unique ways with narrative; and Maxine Hong Kingston's *The Woman Warrior*, which draws on Chinese myth and legend, autobiography, and narrative fiction. Such writing, one way or another, erodes the generic designation of the novel by forcing the genre to accommodate more than it has traditionally done. Since some of these texts are no longer recognizable as novels, generic classification of them breaks down, as becomes evident by the make-shift labels we give to them. Along with the term metafiction, we speak of fabulation, the non-fiction novel, the anti-novel, surfiction, etc.

Here is, then, the creative writer's equivalent of the hermeneut's irresolution or undecidability. It needs the concept of genre and in fact relies heavily on the reader's sophisticated genre knowledge, but at the same time it is intent on confusing its generic heritage and in liberating itself from it. Since it undermines its own foundations, it can be viewed as a deconstructive literature that contributes to a deconstruction of genre.

This is not to say that genre studies are any less crucial than Gerhart claims, only that our writing itself, creative and critical (the difference between which is often—significantly—not easy to tell), interacts with genre theory to shape it as much as the theory shapes the scene of writing. Hugo Kuhn reminds us that "each instance of genre naming, of literary types, forms, subforms, etc. can be effectively understood and utilized only when, explicitly or implicitly, the whole horizon of theoretical and historical conditions is taken into consideration."[1] Theories of irresolution now belong to that horizon and must be involved in any serious genre study.

NOTES

[1] Kuhn's sentence in German reads: "Jeder Einzelfall literarischer Gattungsnamen, literarischer Typen-Arten-Unterarten usw. kann nur dann zutreffend verstanden und gebraucht werden, wenn explizit oder implizit der ganze Horizont seiner theoretischen und historischen Bedingungen mitgedacht ist" (151). My translation.

WORKS CONSULTED

Borges, Jorge Luis
    1964   "The God's Script." Trans. L. A. Murillo. In *Labyrinths*. New York: New Directions.

Kuhn, Hugo
    1974   "Gattung," in Diether Krywalski, ed., *Handlexikon zur Literaturwissenschaft*. Reinbek bei Hamburg: Rowohlt.

ONCE AGAIN: GOSPEL GENRE

Charles H. Talbert
Wake Forest University

ABSTRACT

Ancient biography depicts the essence of a significant person. Since all of the Christian gospels have as their subject a significant person and since some have as their aim to indicate what sort of person Jesus was, it is difficult to believe that on first acquaintance the canonical gospels, and certain others, would not have been considered biographical by Mediterranean hearers.

Early Christians utilized the ancient biographical genre in order to provide a controlling context for the Jesus traditions. Thereby they hoped to protect both against the subversion of the gospel and against reductionism.

Ramifications of this viewpoint are three. First, there is no special theological significance to early Christian use of a narrative genre. Second, the theological stance reflected in the use of a biographical genre by the canonical gospels remains relevant today. Third, although it is impossible to use parable as a genre term for the gospels, it is significant that the canonical gospels in their present form are thought to function with parabolic shock.

The basic rule for all reading is: a text is to be interpreted in light of its context. For example, a word means what it means in its sentence; a sentence means what it means in its paragraph; a paragraph means what it means in its section; a section means what it means in the document as a whole. But what does the document as a whole mean? What is its context? It is at this point that genre criticism enters the picture. By locating the individual text within the context of those documents of a similar literary type and by noting both likenesses and differences, one has a handle on at least a primary dimension of the meaning of the individual text as a whole. It is, therefore, important to ask about the genre of the early Christian gospels if one wants to understand them as wholes.

In the current discussion there are two very different conceptions of what is meant by genre. On the one hand, there are those who use genre for classifications that have no necessary ties to a particular social matrix that is limited by time and space: e.g., tragicomedy, parable, fantasy. On the other hand, others speak of genre in the sense of a literary grouping tied to a particular time, place, and cultural milieu: e.g., romance, aretalogy, Greco-Roman history, ancient Mediterranean biography. It is within the latter view of genre that this paper unfolds. Let us begin with the ancient Mediterranean biographies and make our way from there.

Ancient Biographies and Early Christian Gospels

A discussion of ancient biography must begin with those writings that call themselves "lives" (*bioi*, Greek; *vitae*, Latin) and seek to discern what it is that holds them together as a literary group. Modern study of ancient biography may take its cue from what the ancients said about the distinction between history and biography (Polybius 10:21:8; 16:14:6; Cornelius Nepos, "Pelopidas," 16:1:1; Plutarch, "Alexander," 1:2–3; "Pompey," 8), but its conclusions cannot be based upon that alone. Genre is a descriptive, not a prescriptive category (Perry, 1967: 20). Furthermore, ancient theorists are notoriously unreliable. They did not discuss entire genres, like romance, and when they did theorize, they often violated their theory in practice (e.g., Horace). At the same time, therefore, that one is sensitized by the ancients, one must test their descriptive efforts against one's own inductive approach from the extant texts (Vivas, 1968:97–105).

References in ancient literatures to biographies not now extant as well as fragments of numerous "lives" found among the Oxrhynchus and Herculaneum papyri show the paucity of the extant remains of the Mediterranean biographical tradition. Nevertheless, a sizeable body of such material is available, including Greco-Roman, Jewish, and Christian "lives." Some of these biographies circulated singly, others in collections.

Greco-Roman "lives" circulating alone that are extant in significant portions include: Satyrus, *Life of Euripides* (3rd cent B.C.E.); Andronicus, *Life of Aristotle* (ca. 70 B.C.E.), the substance of which is probably to be found in the *Vitae Aristotelis Marciana* (Momigliano 1971: 86–87); Nicolaus of Damascus, *Life of Augustus (1st* cent *B.C.E.);* Tacitus, *Life of Agricola* (98 C.E.); the anonymous *Life of Aesop* (2nd cent C.E.); the anonymous *Life of Secundus* (2nd cent C.E.); Lucian's *Life of Demonax, Life of Alexander,* and *Passing of Peregrinus* (ca. 180 C.E.); Philostratus, *Life of Apollonius of Tyana* (216 C.E.); Porphyry's *Life of Pythagoras* and *Life of Plotinus* (3rd cent C.E.); Ps-Callisthenes, *Life of Alexander* (ca. 300 C.E.).

Certain Jewish and Christian "lives" also circulated alone. Philo's *Life of Moses* and his *On Abraham* and *On Joseph* (ca. 25 B.C.E.) are Jewish biographies circulating outside a collection of "lives." Examples from the numerous Christian "lives" circulating individually include: Pontius, *Life of Cyprian* (259 C.E.); Eusebius, *Life of Constantine* (early 4th cent C.E.); the anonymous, *Life of Pachomius* (4th cent C.E.); Athanasius, *Life of Anthony* (357 C.E.); Jerome's *Life of Paul, the Hermit* (376 C.E.), and *Life of Malchus* (386 C.E.); *Life of Hilarion* (391 C.E.); Sulpicius Severus, *Life of Martin of Tours* (397 C.E.); Paulinus of Milan, *Life of Ambrose* (400 C.E.); Palladius, *Life of Chrysostom* (408 C.E.); Hilary, Life of Honoratus (431 C.E.): Ennodius, *Life of Epiphanius* (503 C.E.).

Greco-Roman collections of "lives" include: Cornelius Nepos, *Lives of Great Generals* (1st cent B.C.E.); Plutarch, *Parallel Lives* (100 C.E.); Suetonius, *Lives of the Twelve Caesars* (120 C.E.) and *Lives of Illustrious Men* (110 C.E.); Diogenes Laertius, *Lives of Eminent Philosophers* (3rd cent C.E.); *Scriptores Historiae Augustae* (3rd–4th cents C.E.). The anonymous *The Lives of the Prophets* (1st cent C.E.) is a Jewish collection of brief sketches of the "lives" of the prophets. Jerome's *Lives of Illustrious Men* (4th cent C.E.) offers an example of a Christian collection.

Although there is no great uniformity in these writings that designate themselves "lives," it is still possible to discern what is essential and what is accidental to ancient biography. It is constitutive of ancient biography that the subject be a distinguished or notorious figure (kings, generals, philosophers, literary figures, lawgivers, saints) and that the aim be to expose the essence of the person. Lucian, *Demonax*, 67, puts it succinctly: "These are a very few things out of the many which I might have mentioned, but they will suffice to give my readers a notion of the sort of man he was." This constitutive feature becomes clear when biography is compared with history in antiquity. Whereas history focuses on the distinguished and significant acts of great men in the political and social spheres, biography is concerned with the essence of the individual. This difference may be seen at two points where history most nearly approaches biography. The first is the historical monograph which concentrates primarily on one individual. In Sallust's *Catiline* and *Jugurtha*, for example, the aim is not to set forth the individuals' essence but to narrate political events with which these two individuals were associated. The second is the incorporation of biographical material into a historical record. In Dio Cassius' *Roman History*, 45–56, for example, biographical material about Augustus is incorporated into a history of Rome. The very inclusion of this material into a historical context changes its aim from concern with Augustus' individual essence to his place in a social and political process. The same thing happens when Eusebius incorporates material from his earlier *Apology for the Life of Origen* into his *Ecclesiastical History*, VI. Biography is interested in what sort of person the individual is, his involvement in the historical process being important only insofar as it reveals his essence. Whereas history attempts to give a detailed account in terms of causes and effects of events, biography presents a highly selective, often anecdotal account of an individual's life with everything chosen to illuminate his essential being. Ancient biography consists of information about a significant person, selected so as to reveal what sort of person he really is.

Having stated what is essential to ancient biography, it remains to describe what is accidental to it. First, it is incorrect to describe ancient biography as an account of the life of a man from birth to death. Some biographies begin with the hero's mature life (e.g., Nepos, "Miltiades," "Aristides," "Pausanias," etc.); others may begin with the subject's birth and stop before his death (e.g., Nicolaus of Damascus, *Life of Augustus*, which ends with Augustus' entrance into the Civil War). How much of a subject's life is described varies. All that is necessary is that enough be given to satisfy the author that the essence of the person is revealed.

Second, the sort of person the hero is was assumed to appear not only in his deeds but also in insignificant gestures or passing utterance (e.g., Plutarch, "Alexander," 1; "Demosthenes," 11:7). Given this fact, it is difficult to exclude Plutarch's collections of sayings, like "Sayings of Kings and Commanders," from the *bios/vita* genre. Indeed, in D, Plutarch says: "their pronouncements and unpremediated utterance . . . afford an opportunity to observe . . . the working of the mind of each man." In this and his other three collections of sayings one finds a series of materials that look like pronouncement stories, a brief narrative framework within which is set a saying. There is just enough of an event to allow the saying to reveal who the speaker really is.

Third, there is virtually no interest in tracing development. The essence of the person was not examined in its chronological development but only as a fixed constituent in a "life" (Stuart 1928: 178). Consequently, many ancient "lives" are only loosely chronological, being more often than not largely topical or logical in their arrangement (Russell 1973: 115).

Fourth, some biographies have as their aim to affect the behavior or opinions of their readers either positively (e.g., Plutarch) or negatively (e.g., Lucian, "Alexander"); others seem to have no overt propaganda aim (e.g., Laertius). When such "lives" seek to affect the readers' behavior positively, this is often described in terms of imitation (Plutarch, "Pericles," 21:4; Tacitus, *Agricola*, 46). The imitation of noble examples as understood in ancient biography is not to be regarded as a blind and unthinking repetition of acts performed by some great man in the past. It meant learning from a great example the way to order one's life and then, without necessarily performing the same actions, to emulate what sort of man he was (e.g., Plutarch, "Aemulius Paullus," 1; "Cimon," 2:3–5) (Gossage 1967: 49).

Fifth, the "life" of a subject may be described in mythical terms (e.g., Plutarch, "Romulus"; Suetonius, "Augustus"; Philostratus, *Apollonius;* Ps-Callisthenes, *Alexander*) or may be devoid of myth. Most biographies that employ myth in the description of their hero treat founders of cities, empires, religions, schools.

Sixth, the literary form in which "lives" are presented varies. The dominant form is a prose narrative similar to history except that it is anecdotal and unconcerned about cause and effect. Most Greco-Roman, Jewish, and Christian biographies fit into this category. Its root seems to be in Xenophon's *Memorabilia,* or memoirs of Socrates. This, however, cannot be considered the only form of ancient biography. Satyrus, *Life of Euripides,* is in the form of a dialogue with at least three speakers, of whom Diodorus and a woman, Eucleia, are named. The roots of this form of biography seem to be in the Platonic dialogues that deal with Socrates (e.g., *Phaedo*). Christian adaptations of the same form may be found in Palladius' *Dialogue on the Life of Chrysostom* and in Sulpicius Severus' *Dialogues on the Life of St. Martin* in which a two day conversation among three friends centers on Martin's life. Yet another form in which biography appears in antiquity is the encomium, a speech praising its subject (e.g., Eusebius, *Life of Constantine;* Gregory Thaumaturgos, *Panegyric to Origen;* Hilary, *Sermon on the Life of Honoratus*). The roots of this form may be found in Isocrates, *Evagoras,* and Xenophon, *Agesilaus*. If the collections of sayings like Plutarch's "Sayings of Kings and Commanders," are also granted a place in the ancient biographical tradition, then one finds at least four literary forms in which biography may appear in the Mediterranean world.

Seventh, ancient biographies perform a multiplicity of social functions. Some apparently had only a literary aim (e.g., Laertius). Others seemed to serve a propaganda purpose of some sort. Within this overall didactic aim a number of more specific functions can be identified. (1) Certain "lives" portray the subject as an ideal figure so the readers will accept his authority (Nicolaus of Damascus, *Life of Augustus*) or imitate his way of life (e.g., Nepos, "Epaminondas," "Agesilaus"; Lucian, *Demonax;* Pontius, *Life of Cyprian;* Athanasius, *Life of Anthony;* Paulinus of Milan, *Life of Ambrose*). Lucian, *Demonax,* 2, states it in an exemplary fashion: "It is now fitting to tell of Demonax . . . that young men of good instincts who aspire to philosophy may not have to shape themselves by ancient precedents alone, but may be able to set themselves a pattern from our modern world and to copy that man, the best of all the philosophers whom I know about." Although the form is that of a history-like narrative, the spirit of the encomium is felt in these "lives."

(2) Other "lives" aim to defend the subject against misunderstanding either by his followers or by outsiders so that his true self may be seen and his influence exerted (e.g., Tacitus, *Agricola;* Philostratus, *Life of Apollonius;* Palladius, *Life of Chrysostom;* Jerome, *Life of Malchus*). Here three of the examples employ the history-like narrative form while the fourth, Palladius, uses the form of a dialogue. The spirit in all four examples is akin to that in Xenophon's *Memorabilia* where Socrates is defended and in Isocrates' *Busiris* where the king is defended against calumny.

(3) Still other ancient biographies intend to discredit the subject by means of exposé (e.g., Lucian's *Alexander the False Prophet* and his *Peregrinus;* also in Suetonius' *Lives of the Twelve Caesars* one finds profound critiques of men who far from measuring up to the ideal exemplify its opposite).

(4) Another social function of didactic biographies in antiquity seems to be to indicate where the true tradition is in the present (Bickerman 1952:49). This is found first of all in "lives" of founders of philosophical schools that contained within themselves not only a life of the founder but also a list or a brief narrative of his successors and selected other disciples, an (a+b) form. In Diogenes Laertius certain "lives" of philosophers reflect this pattern. There is (a) the life of the founder, followed by (b) a brief list or narrative of his sucessors and selected other disciples, followed by (c) an extensive statement of the teaching of the philosopher (e.g., Aristippus—Life: 2:65–84; Pupils: 2:85–86; Teaching: 2:86–104; Plato—Life: 3:1–45; Pupils: 3:46–47; Teachings: 3:47–109; Zeno—Life: 7:1–35; Successors and other disciples: 7:36–36; Teaching: 7:38–160; Pythagoras—Life: 8:1–44; Successors: 8:45–46; Teachings: 8:48–50; Epicurus—Life: 10:1–21; Successors and other disciples: 10:22–28; Teachings: 10:29–154). Examination of Laertius' references to the sources for these "lives" shows that the material in (c) comes from a different origin than that in (a+b). This permits the inference that Laertius took over individual biographies that were written in terms of the (a+b) pattern and added the (c) component himself. Such an inference is supported by three strands of early evidence. First, one of the four different works of Aristoxenos, all of which dealt with Pythagoreanism, was "The Life of Pythagoras and His Associates" which contained a biography of Pythagoras and a history of the Pythagoreans in chronological order (Fritz 1940: 22, n.35). Second, Herculaneum papyrus 1018 treats the Stoic succession. At four points the life of a teacher (e.g., Zeno) is followed by a discussion of his disciples. This is sometimes just a list of names, sometimes it consists of anecdotes about them (Traversa 1952: xiii–xiv). Third, a pre-Christian biography of Aristotle included within itself both a claim that Aristotle was the successor of Plato and an anecdote about Aristotle's selection of a successor to himself (Düring,

1957: 465–66; 345–46). Taken together, this evidence establishes the existence of individual "lives" of founders of philosophical schools that contained within themselves not only the biography of the founder but also a narrative, however brief, about his successors and selected other disciples. Just as Christian biography went to the Classical period for its models in other cases, so here as well. In the *Life of Pachomius* one finds a Christian appropriation of this type of ancient biography. It is fitting because this "life" deals with the founder of coenobitic monasticism and with his successors in the community. The early part of the biography deals with the career of Pachomius. In 117 he appoints Orsisius to succeed him, using language that may be regarded as the technical terminology of succession. In the sections that follow the narrative tells what Orsisus did and said (118–129), zealously emulating the life of Pachomius (119). Then Orsisius appoints Theodore (130). In the sections that follow one learns what Theodore did and said. A second Christian example of this type of biography is Hilary of Arles' *Sermon on the Life of St. Honoratus*. Here is an encomium praising the founder of the monastery that fits into the (a + b) type of "life." In chapter 8, Hilary says he is Honoratus' successor and that his task is to do what the founder had done. In all of these examples, the purpose is to say where the true tradition is in the period after the founder.

(5) Yet another social function performed by some ancient didactic biographies is to serve as a hermeneutical tool, either to legitimate the teaching of the subject by showing that his life corresponded with his profession (e.g., *Life of Secundus the Silent Philosopher*) or to furnish an interpretative clue for the reading of his works (e.g., Andronicus' *Life of Aristotle* which served to introduce his edition of Aristotle; Philo, *Life of Moses*, which served as an introduction to Philo's *Exposition of the Law* (Goodenough 1933: 109–25); Porphyry's *Life of Plotinus*, which served to introduce the *Enneads*).

If our description of what is essential and what is accidental in ancient biography holds, then it is possible to say that we are dealing with the biographical tradition in antiquity wherever we meet the concern to depict the essence of a significant person, that is, to expose what sort of person he really is. The infinite variety of the ancient "lives" results from the multiple combinations of what is accidental to the genre: (1) the extent of coverage—whether from birth to death, from birth to mature life, from mature life to death; (2) the types of material used to expose the soul of the subject—whether preponderently deeds or words or some balanced combination of them; (3) the kind of organizing principle utilized—whether chronology or logic or some combination of both; (4) the degree of detachment or involvement of the author with his readers—whether detached and descriptive or involved and evaluative; (5) the use or disuse of myth—whether the subject is described in divine terms or is depicted without recourse to language about the gods; (6) the literary form employed—whether a prose narrative akin to history or a dialogue or a speech of praise or a collection of sayings; (7) the social function of the "life"—whether didactic or non-didactic, and if the former, whether to hold the hero up as an authority or an example, to defend him against misunderstanding, to ridicule him by means of exposé, to show where the true tradition is to be found in the present, or to furnish a hermeneutical key for proper interpretation. It is crucial that what is essential and what is accidental be clearly understood. When this is done, it is possible both to sense what is shared and what is distinctive in each case. For example, it is possible to say about Hilary's *Life of Honoratus* that it is biographical in its aim to set forth what sort of person this noteworthy Christian was, but that it does so by using the form of an encomium, or speech of praise, shaped in such a way that it serves the social function of saying where the true tradition is in the speaker's present.

One of the most vexed areas of discussion in the study of ancient biography is the relation of the early Christian gospels, canonical and apocryphal, to this genre. To date, reluctance to view the gospels as a part of the biographical tradition of antiquity has been largely due to misunderstanding, either of the gospels or of ancient biography. If, for example, the gospels are viewed as *Kleinliteratur*, not productions of individual authors, as Schmidt (76) and Bultmann (cols. 418–22) proposed, then obviously they are different from biographies produced by self-conscious authors. This view of the gospels, however, has been discarded ever since the emergence of redaction criticism by which the Evangelists as self-conscious authors is assumed. Or if ancient biography is taken as identical with modern biography, then obviously the gospels are different. The gospels, like ancient "lives," however, do not set their hero against the wider historical background of the time as modern biographies do; like many ancient "lives," the gospels do not adhere to a strict chronological order; like ancient "lives," the gospels are not concerned to trace the personality development of the hero; like many ancient "lives," the gospels do not describe the personal appearance of their subject. The gospels, like some ancient biographies, do tell their story in terms of myth. This tendency to impose upon ancient biographies the qualities of modern ones has been disavowed by all who have worked extensively with ancient "lives." If such misunderstandings are cleared away, then it is possible to view at least some of the early Christian gospels as part of the larger literary scene of antiquity.

Since all of the Christian gospels have as their subject a significant individual and since some have as their aim to indicate what sort of person Jesus is, it is difficult to believe that on first acquaintance the canonical gospels, at least, would not have been considered biographical by Mediterranean readers/hearers (Stanton: 135). What is revealed in the narratives about Apollonius, or Pythagoras, or Moses, or Jesus is the same—their distinctive nature (Smith: 35). Some of the gospels share with the ancient biographies that which is constitutive for them—to set forth the essence of the subject, that is, what sort of person he is. Some gospels, canonical and apocryphal, manifest a biographical interest in depicting what sort of person Jesus was: the canonical four and apocryphal gospels like the Gospel of Peter and the Childhood Gospel of Thomas. The Protevangelium Jacobi has a biographical concern but it is for Mary, not Jesus. Parts of the Epistle of the Apostles also manifest a biographical interest. Other gospels' concern is not biographical: e.g., the Gnostic dialogues like the Sophia of Jesus Christ, the Dialogue of the Savior, the first part of the Gospel of Mary, the Apocryphon of James, the Book of Thomas the Contender, and the sayings collection, the Coptic Gospel of Thomas.

The infinite variety among the gospels with a biographical interest matches that of the ancient "lives" and for the same reason. It is due to the multiple ways those things that are accidental to biography are combined. For example, as to form, all of the gospels that possess a biographical character are history-like narratives, not dialogues, encomiums, or collections of pronouncement stories. As to the extent of coverage, the biographical gospels vary greatly. Some, like Matthew and Luke, cover Jesus' life from birth to death; others, like Mark, treat Jesus' life from mature manhood to death; still others, like the Childhood Gospel of Thomas and the Gospel of Peter, deal with more limited periods of Jesus' life. As to social function, all four canonical gospels and the Gospel of Peter find it necessary to correct misunderstanding about Jesus at the same time that they set him forth as the expression and the norm of the community's values. In addition, Luke-Acts shares with certain biographies a concern to say where the true tradition is in the present, even if his sense of the radical difference between apostolic and post-apostolic times caused him to eschew use of the typical succession vocabulary. Matthew, moreover, has in common with some "lives" the interest in the hermeneutical relationship of the hero's life and teaching. Only the Childhood Gospel of Thomas seems straightforward in its praise of the lad in order to reinforce his authority. Regarding the employment of myth, all tell the story of Jesus in mythical terms, although the specific myth may vary: the Synoptics and the Gospel of Peter utilize the myth of immortals, John employs the myth of a descending-ascending redeemer, and the Childhood Gospel of Thomas expands the traditional theme of the precocious youth so that Jesus becomes a playful divine boy. Like most of the other ancient biographies that utilize myth, the Christian hero of the gospels is a founder. As with them, sacred time is focused around those events which first brought the community or cult into being. Myth becomes the means of designating this sacred time. In this regard, the Christian biographies of Jesus manifest a distinctive difference from all other "lives," Greco-Roman, Jewish, or Christian, that are not constructed in terms of myth and a remarkable kinship with those other biographies, Greco-Roman and Jewish, that do employ myth in their depiction of their hero's life (e.g., Moses, Romulus, Augustus, Apollonius, Pythagoras, Alexander). Given these rather obvious links between certain early Christian gospels and the ancient biographical genre, a growing consensus regards certain ancient "lives" as the closest analogy to the canonical four and perhaps a few other early Christian gospels as well (e.g., Cartlidge and Dungan; Farmer; Du Pleissis; Robbins; Schneider; Shuler; Suggs; Talbert 1977; Toews).

Reasons for Christian Appropriation of the Biographical Genre

If early Christians did, in fact, utilize the ancient biographical genre in many instances to tell the good news, why did they do so? It was not, I think, due to some alleged problem faced by Mark (so Crossan) or by Mark and John together (so Robinson) but because of a larger issue. Biographical narration was employed because it provided a controlling context not only for individual traditions but also for various types of traditions. In so doing, it served to protect both against the subversion of the gospel and against reductionism.

By subversion of the gospel is meant an interpretation of the Jesus traditions that altered what mainstream Christians regarded as their true meaning. This happened in the early church both before and after the writing of the canonical gospels (Talbert, 1970). For the period after the composition of the canonical gospels, Irenaeus and Tertullian offer evidence. In his *Against Heresies*, Irenaeus complains about Gnostics who try to adapt the Jesus tradition to their own position by disregarding the order and connection of the gospels, thereby dismembering and destroying the text. "By transferring passages and dressing them up anew . . . they succeed in deluding many through their wicked art in adapting the oracles of the Lord to their opinions." They "endeavor by violently drawing away from their proper connection, words, expressions, and parables whenever found, to adapt the oracles of God to their baseless fiction" (1.8.1). Irenaeus' argument against the heretical violations of context is to appeal to the proper order (1.9.1). In contrast to the heretics, the orthodox Christian "when he has restored every one of the expressions quoted to its proper position, and has fitted it to the body of the truth, will lay bare and prove to be without foundation, the figment of these heretics" (1.9.4).

Tertullian, in his *Prescription Against Heretics*, reflects a similar position. Analogous to the way the heretics treat the Jesus tradition is the

Once Again: Gospel Genre 63

handling of Homer and Vergil in Tertullian's time. "You see in our own day, composed out of Vergil, a story of a wholly different character." In like manner, certain collectors of Homeric odds and ends, "stitch into one piece, patchwork fashion, works of their own from the lines of Homer out of many scraps put together from this passage and from that (in miscellaneous confusion)" (chap. 39). The Gospels offer an even better opportunity for this sort of perverse effort. In response, Tertullian contends that "no divine saying is so unconnected and diffuse, that its words only are to be insisted on, and their connection left undetermined" (chap. 9). Context or order is important. When, therefore, the Valentinians appeal to Matthew 7:7, "Seek and you shall find," Tertullian answers: "But when was this said? At the outset when there was still doubt whether he was the Christ" (chap. 8). The logion is, therefore, not properly used when it is interpreted to mean that Christians, who know Jesus to be the Christ, should continue to seek, that is, for the secret Gnosis the Valentinians offer (chap. 9). The argument from order or context is, therefore, a major weapon in the arsenal of the anti-heretical writers of the early church in order to prevent Gnostic subversion of the individual parts of the Jesus tradition.

In the period before the writing of our canonical gospels, Paul's second letter to Corinth, our 1 Corinthians, offers evidence. In this letter, the apostle carries on a running battle with problem children in Corinth who misinterpret the kerygma (1 Cor 15), a creedal statement (8:6), and Jesus' words (e.g., 4:2 which is a Corinthian assertion directed against Paul and using as an authority tradition like that now found in Luke 12:42–43 and 16:1–15), all in light of their overrealized eschatology. In each case, the individual tradition was subverted by a reading controlled by an alien posture. When Paul responded in each of the three cases mentioned, he used a variety of arguments to give a proper context for understanding the tradition aright.

Given the later tendency of heretics to take material out of its canonical context in order to give it a meaning other than what it had within the gospel narrative and given the practice before the writing of the canonical gospels to interpret individual traditions in line with a point of view other than the apostolic one, it seems a reasonable hypothesis that the canonical gospels were written to give a controlling context to individual Jesus traditions so they could not be misinterpreted as easily as was possible without such a context. Paul Achtemeier says regarding the writing of Mark:

> the composition of such a narrative in itself represents a significant attempt to achieve a new way of interpreting the Jesus traditions. Up to that time, these tradition could . . . be . . . interpreted by adapting and readapting them individually. Mark,

on the other hand, apparently felt that method was no longer adequate to insure the kind of interpretation of the Jesus traditions he now saw to be necessary. The time had come for the individual traditions to be placed under the control of an overall interpretation of the career of Jesus of Nazareth. For that, Mark apparently felt a narrative framework was necessary, within which those traditions could be used in the service of that larger interpretation (Achtemeier: 22).

The narrative framework was employed to provide a controlling context for the interpretation of individual traditions. The individual traditions were thereby not capable of an infinite number of interpretations but only those which were appropriate to the larger context. What has been said of Mark could also be said of the other canonical gospels. Examples could be multiplied almost indefinitely to illustrate the procedure (Talbert 1970:178–180; Talbert 1982:20–21).

By reductionism is meant an interpretation of the Jesus tradition that absolutizes a part of the gospel and treats it as though it were the whole. This also happened in the early church both before and after the writing of the canonical gospels. The seminal work of H. Koester has shown that there were at least four types of collections of Jesus material in early Christianity. *One* type of collection consisted of miracle material. The Childhood Gospel of Thomas, for example, tells the story of Jesus as a boy in which Jesus is depicted as a god walking around in a little boy's body, performing one miracle after another. This second century collection of miracle stories had a first century prototype. Although scholars disagree about the sources used by the Fourth Evangelist, there is a consensus that one source behind the Gospel of John was a Signs Source composed of seven or eight miracles and climaxed by the statement, "Now Jesus did many other signs in the presence of the disciples, which are not written in this book; but these are written that you may believe that Jesus is the Christ, the Son of God. . . ." (John 20:30–31). The collection of miracles seems to have been one way of speaking about Jesus in the early church. In doing so, the Christians were appropriating and using for their own purposes the genre "aretalogy," which existed independently in the Mediterranean world.

A *second type* of collection of Jesus material in the ancient church was that which grouped the sayings of Jesus together. The second century Coptic Gospel of Thomas is an example. Here, after an introduction which says, "These are the secret words which the living Jesus spoke," we find a series of sayings of Jesus strung together without any narrative framework. That such a collection should not be regarded as unique is called to mind by the presence of Q in the first century. Q consists almost exclusively of sayings without a narrative framework. In speaking of Jesus in this way, the church was appropriating the genre "words of the wise" from its Mediterranean milieu (Robinson).

A *third type* of collection of Jesus material found in early Christianity was one which portrayed Jesus as a revealer, as one who makes a revelation to some disciple or disciples. The Apocryphon of John is representative of most of the apocryphal gospels which have Gnostic links. It presents the risen Christ who appears to John to give him a mystery which he could pass on to his fellow disciples. In the first century, the Revelation to John resembles this type of collection. In the Book of Revelation the risen Lord appears to the prophet John to give him a prophecy of the last days. In depicting Jesus in this way, the early Christians were making use of the genre "apocalypse" for their own purposes.

A *fourth type* of collection of Jesus material found in the ancient church is a composite narrative which includes miracles, sayings, and revelation matter, and in addition has a passion narrative. The four canonical gospels, of course, belong to this variety. In depicting Jesus in this way, the Christians were appropriating the genre "biography" for their own use.

What was the significance of early Christians' speaking about Jesus in these different ways? The importance of the collections lies in the fact that they point to distinctive understandings of the nature of the *divine presence* made manifest in Jesus and to the views of *discipleship* associated with those particular ways of seeing God's acts in Jesus. If, for example, a Christian presented Jesus in terms of a collection of miracle stories, how would s/he understand the nature of God's presence in Jesus? The presence of God would be regarded as manifest in an extraordinary display of power. Furthermore, a disciple's response of faith would then be understood as receiving the benefits of the power for himself/herself and subsequently becoming a channel of this power to others. If, however, one presented Jesus in terms of a collection of sayings which gave instructions about how to live and reasons for living that way, the implicit view of God's nature would be different. Such a collection would say that God's presence is manifest in moral guidance for living. A disciple, moreover, would be understood as one who follows the guidance for living set forth. If, furthermore, one depicted Jesus as a revealer making a disclosure of divine secrets, there would be yet another view of God's presence operative. In a revelation collection, God's presence is assumed to be manifest where there is a disclosure of the secrets of one's ultimate origin or destiny. In such a structure, discipleship would mean to receive the disclosed secrets, to repent, and to be ready for the ultimate outcome of history.

The composite gospels with a passion narrative would also point to a particular understanding of the divine presence and to a distinctive view of discipleship (Talbert, 1979). In three of the four canonical gospels, the passion narrative has soteriological significance. Matthew, Mark, and John all view Jesus' death as in some sense connected with the forgiveness of sins. In these three gospels, then, the passion narrative functions to say that God is present where sins are forgiven and that faith is receiving God's forgiveness. Neither Matthew, Mark, nor John, however, tells his story of Jesus as just a passion narrative and nothing more. Each one has, in addition to the passion narrative, miracles, sayings, and a revelation section. This, in effect, says that God's presence in Jesus is manifest in the forgiveness of sins but that it also involves power, guidance for living, and the disclosure of our ultimate destiny. Discipleship, then, involves not only the experience of God's forgiveness but also the experience of God's power, the following of God's guidance, and the hope and readiness that a disclosure of one's ultimate destiny evokes.

Only Luke fails to speak of the connection between Jesus' death and the forgiveness of sins. His passion narrative is mainly a grand rejection story. The death of Jesus is the human NO to God's messenger. This picture of Jesus' death in Luke is tied to a particular *Sitz im Leben*. Confronted with an over-realized eschatology which viewed life in the Spirit as taking one out of the vicissitudes of this life, Luke designed a picture of Jesus that would show him not only in terms of power, morality, and knowledge—all of which emphasize authority over the world—but also in terms of suffering and death. He enters into his glory only *after* experiencing his suffering (Luke 24:26). The one anointed with the Spirit lived out his life within the structures of this world, as evidenced by the fact that he was rejected, he suffered, and he died. Correspondingly it is through many tribulations that his disciples must enter the Kingdom of God (Acts 14:22). For Luke, the significance of the passion narrative was that it said that when God's presence is experienced as power, morality, and knowledge of our ultimate destiny, it is experienced *within the world* and does not take one immediately out of the world. It is significant, however, that Luke, just as the other three canonical Evangelists, does not tell his story of Jesus merely as a passion narrative. Rejection, suffering, and death are not the essence of the Christian's life, even though a Christian still experiences them.

The early Christians agreed that the gospel was the good news that God was present in Jesus for our salvation. It is clear, however, that there was a considerable difference among the believers about the nature of the divine presence manifest in Jesus. Consequently, the gospel was both preached and written down in different ways. There were written collections which focused on miracle, morality, and knowledge of our ultimate origins and destiny, as well as the stance represented in our canonical gospels. Viewed in this light, the canonical gospels appear to be attempts to avoid the reductionism of seeing the presence of God in Jesus in only one way and attempts to set forth a comprehensive and balanced understanding of both the divine presence and the discipleship it evokes. The canonical gospels are not so much kerygma as reflections of the controversies about the legitimacy of the various forms of proclamation in the ancient church. They come to their present form as a result of conscious and deliberate composition related to a clear-cut theological stance about the nature of God and the nature of discipleship. They assume the various types of kerygma and function as parenesis.

Ramifications of the Proposed Thesis about Gospel Genre

The line of reasoning pursued in this paper so far has lead to the conclusion that a significant number of early Christian gospels belong to the biographical genre of antiquity. This number includes all four of the canonical gospels. In their case, at least, the purpose of the Christian appropriation of the biographical tradition was to supply a controlling context for the interpretation of the Jesus traditions that would avoid both the subversion of the gospel and reductionism.

(1) One ought not, I think, to try to find profound theological significance in the early Christian appropriation of this particular narrative genre. The Christians reflected their culture in using biographies and letters alike. This echoed the standard distinction between teaching by precepts and by *exempla*. Seneca, *Epistle* 6.5–6, says the way to wisdom is long if one follows precepts but short if one follows patterns *(exempla)*. Quintilian, *Institutio Oratorio* 12.29–30, argues that one should not restrict one's study to the precepts of philosophy alone. Rather it is important to know both the noble sayings and deeds that have been handed down.

It is true that narrativity has its roots in the fact that the individual self has a developmental history, that the individual is part of multiple communities that have histories, and that both individuals and communities are intertwined with an environment that also has a developmental history (Crites, 1971). But it is an overstatement to say that human experience can be brought to language *only* as narrativity (Ricoeur:195). The same faculty that enables humans to experience and express the world as duration also enables us to abstract, to generalize, to isolate images, all for the purpose of creating formal structures of life in the present (Lischer:34).

If narrative is analogous to a motion picture, then abstract thought is analogous to stopping a movie to analyze one frame. It allows careful attention to detail but is distorting in its effects unless it gives way once again to the movement of the story. All of this is to say that the early

Christian's choice of precept and *exempla*, of epistle and biography, reflected not only their culture's preferences but also the nature of things. Both genres were used to guard the wholeness and balance of the gospel.

It was not the choice of a particular narrative genre that was theologically significant. Narrative was not more conducive to the expression of faith than the epistle. Both could serve the gospel. Both could also serve error, and did so. For example, the Protoevangelium Jacobi, the Childhood Gospel of Thomas, and the Gospel of Peter are biographical narratives that were used in the service of error from the standpoint of the canonical tradition. At the same time, it is true that a certain type of biographical narrative (composite plus passion narrative) was admirably suited to express the wholeness and balance of the good news about Jesus.

(2) Viewed in light of the current argument, the canonical gospels have theological relevance in the present, not because they are biographical in genre, but because of what their particular type of appropriation of the biographical tradition represents theologically. (a) They stand against all attempts to understand God, Jesus, and discipleship in ways that lose the wholeness and balance present in the narratives taken as wholes. The early miracle gospels have their modern counterpart in the type of proclamation one finds, for example, in Kathryn Kuhlman's *I Believe in Miracles*, a collection of twenty-one miracle stories which are intended to evoke faith in the Jesus who lives. The early collections of Jesus' sayings have a modern counterpart in the varieties of modern proclamation that present Jesus as primarily a moral teacher. The early revelation gospels have their modern counterpart in the proclamation of Jesus in terms of prophecy, as in the case with Hal Lindsey's *The Late Great Planet Earth*. Most mainline denominations operate as though the gospel were expressed solely in terms of a passion narrative, as with the apocryphal Gospel of Nicodemus. The canonical gospels as theological statements, which happen to be ancient biographies, stand against such reductionism. They assert that the God who was manifest in Jesus is known in terms of power, morality, mystery, and forgiveness of sin. A response to him calls for a faith that relates to all that has been revealed.

(b) The canonical biographies of Jesus also stand against all attempts to take individual traditions out of their narrative contexts in order to interpret them in light of some other context. The early errorists combatted by Irenaeus and Tertullian have their modern counterparts in tendencies of which Robert Funk is an example. In the first issue of *Forum* he calls for a new quest of the historical Jesus. Its motivation lies in the conviction that Christian faith is rooted in the language of Jesus rather than in the kerygma of the church. The language of Jesus—parable, aphorism, and parabolic act—is the ground of faith. This language constitutes a fantasy by which a new world arrives. The language of Jesus is not self-referential (Funk's usage which is not that of literary criticism); nor is God immanent to the fantasy. In the transmission of the Jesus tradition, Jesus' language had superimposed upon it a tradition of interpretation that was alien to it: e.g., the material becomes self-referential, diverting attention from the kingdom as fantasy to Jesus. In so doing, the original meaning was lost. In the gospel form, there is a framework reflecting the church's life-world in which is embedded the original language of Jesus that contradicts it. The Jesus tradition contravenes the tradition of interpretation that was superimposed upon it. What is needed, therefore, is to detach the original language of Jesus from its alien overlay in the gospels so that its life-world may generate faith. One does not need to continue to be misled by a gospel's setting.

If one were to follow the lead of the canonical gospels and of the early anti-heretical writers' use of them, a response to Funk would contain at least the following. On the one hand, like the Gnostics opposed by Irenaeus and Tertullian, Funk wants to detach the Jesus materials from their context in the canonical gospels in order to find their true meaning. That meaning is a secondary life-world, a way of looking at life that is different from the that of the received world. In examples given, this secondary world or kingdom is essentially a moral order at odds with the received world. So the kingdom is essentially a different moral order. Further, it has no reference to Jesus except as he is the revealer of the fantasy in which one may participate. Here is a new version of Jesus the teacher of a higher morality.

On the other hand, like Irenaeus and Tertullian one would respond by affirming the order and connection of the gospel story. For example, if one reads the narrative of Luke-Acts, it comes clear that the disciples who heard Jesus' language glimpsed something. But whatever it was that they glimpsed caused them to attach themselves to *him*. Whatever the intent, the effects of Jesus' fantasy were self-referential. Furthermore, their attachment to him was not really effective as a result of hearing him. It was not until after Jesus' death-resurrection-ascension-exaltation-gift of the Spirit that the disciples were effectively attached to him and the kingdom. From the order and connection of Luke's biographical narrative one sees first that the kingdom is not so much a moral as a christological reality (one is involved not so much in a new moral vision as in a new personal relationship) and second that the experience of the kingdom mediated through this new personal relationship is not really effective until after Pentecost (it is mediated not so much by the language of Jesus as by what happened to him—death, resurrection, ascension, exaltation, receipt of the promise from the Father—and as a consequence of what happened to him). The canonical gospels as theological constructs, which happen to be biographical narratives, stand against the subversion of the gospel by all efforts to interpret the Jesus tradition in a way alien to that dictated by the order and connection of the canonical gospels' framework.

(3) What is the relation between the type of genre criticism espoused in this paper and the other type referred to at the beginning of the argument? For example, if the canonical gospels are biographies of an ancient Mediterranean variety, can they also be parable (Kelber; Williams)? When the gospels are called parable, I take this to mean that the gospels function as parables are alleged to function, that is, with parabolic shock, reversal, provocation, and the shattering of one's old world. My reservation about this position, if I understand it correctly, is that it is not really a genre matter. Most of the different types of Jesus tradition have or can have a provocative function: parables, proverbs, ethical teachings, miracle stories (e.g., by providing divine legitimation for violation of religious customs, as in Mark 2:1–12; 2:23–28; 3:1–6; 5:17), the Lord's prayer (e.g., by focusing the objects of prayer so narrowly and thereby raising the question why the one who prays cannot pray in this way). If they *all* can have a shock function, then the shattering of one's old world is not a prerogative of parable. It is a language function shared by multiple *Gattungen*. If, therefore, one wants to contend that Mark functions as language in a provocative way, fine. That may be debated on its merits. To claim, however, that because Mark allegedly functions in a shocking way it is to be classified generically as parable is a breakdown in elementary logic. It is significant, nevertheless, that scholars are saying that the gospels *in their present form* have this same type of provocative function that has been claimed for the pre-gospel traditions when isolated from their present context. It means that the Jesus traditions in their present gospel order and connection have not been domesticated (Funk's term) but still retain their revitalizing function for the reader. It is, therefore, not necessary to detach the individual traditions from their present order and connection in order to hear a life-giving word.

WORKS CONSULTED

Achtemeier, Paul J.
    1975   *Mark: Proclamation Commentaries*. Philadelphia: Fortress Press.

Bickermann, E.
    1952   "La chaîne de la tradition Pharisienne." *RB* 59: 44–54.

Bultmann, R.
    1928   "Evangelien." Cols. 418–22 in 2d ed vol. 2 of *Die Religion Geschichte und Gegenwart*. Ed. H. Gunkel. Tübingen: J. C. B. Mohr-Paul Siebeck.

Cartlidge, D. R., and D. L. Dungan
    1980   *Documents for the Study of the Gospels.* Cleveland: Collins.

Cox, P.
    1983   *Biography in Late Antiquity.* Berkeley: University of California.

Crites, Stephen
    1971   "The Narrative Quality of Experience." *JAAR* 39:291–311.

Crossan, John Dominic
    1978   "A Form for Absence: The Markan Creation of Gospel." *Semeia* 12:41–56.

Du Pleissis, I. J.
    1982   "Die genre van Lukas se evangelie." *Theologia Evangelica* 15: 19–28.

Düring, I.
    1957   *Aristotle in the Ancient Biographical Tradition.* Göteborg: Göteborgs Universitets Arsskrift.

Farmer, W. R.
    1967   "The Problem of Christian Origins: A Programmatic Essay." in *Studies in the History and Text of the New Testament,* ed. B. L. Daniels and M. J. Suggs. Salt Lake City: University of Utah: 81–88.

Fritz, K. von
    1940   *Pythagorean Politics in Southern Italy: An Analysis of the Sources.* New York: Columbia University.

Funk, Robert W.
    1985   "From Parable to Gospel: Domesticating the Tradition." *Forum* 1:3–24.

Gigon, O.
    1962   *Vita Aristotelis Marciana.* Berlin: Walter de Gruyter.

Goodenough, E. R.
    1933   "Philo's Exposition of the Law and His *de Vita Mosis.*" *HTR* 16: 109–25.

Gossage, A. J.
    1967   "Plutarch." Pp. 45–77 in *Latin Biography.* Ed. T. A. Dorey. London: Routledge and Kegan Paul.

Hirsch, E. D., Jr.
    1967   *Validity in Interpretation.* New Haven: Yale University.

Kelber, Werner
    1983   *The Oral and the Written Gospel.* Philadelphia: Fortress.

Koester, Helmut
    1971   "One Jesus and Four Primitive Gospels." Pp. 158–204 in

Kuhlman, Kathryn
  1969 *Trajectories Through Early Christianity*, by J. M. Robinson and H. Koester. Philadelphia: Fortress.

Kuhlman, Kathryn
  1969 *I Believe in Miracles*. Old Tappan, N.J.: Flemming H. Revell.

Lindsey, Hal
  1970 *The Late Great Planet Earth*. Grand Rapids: Zondervan.

Lischer, Richard
  1984 "The Limits of Story." *Int* 38: 26–38.

Leo, F.
  1901 *Griechisch-Römische Biographie nach Ihrer Literarischen Form*. Leipzig: Teubner.

Lesky, A.
  1966 *A History of Greek Literature*. London: Methuen and Company.

Momigliano, A.
  1971 *The Development of Greek Biography*. Cambridge, Mass: Harvard University.

Perry, B. E.
  1967 *The Ancient Romances*. Berkeley: University of California.

Ricoeur, Paul
  1978 "The Narrative Function." *Semeia* 13:177–202.

Robbins, V.
  1984 *Jesus the Teacher: A Socio-Rhetorical Interpretation of Mark*. Philadelphia: Fortress.

Robinson, James M.
  1970 "On the *Gattung* of Mark (and John)." Pp. 99–130 in *Jesus and Man's Hope*. Ed. Dikran Y. Hadidian. Pittsburgh: Pittsburgh Theological Seminary.
  1971 "On the Gattung of Q." Pp. 71–113 in *Trajectories Through Early Christianity*. Philadelphia: Fortress.

Russell, D. A.
  1973 *Plutarch*. London: Duckworth.

Schmidt, K. L.
  1923 "Die Stellung der Evangelien in der allgemeinen Literaturgeschichte." Pp. 50–140 in *Eucharisterion: Gunkel Festschrift*. Ed. H. Schmidt. Göttingen: Vandenhoeck and Ruprecht.

Schneider, G.
  1977 "Der Zweck des Lukanischen Doppelwerks." *BZ* 21: 45–66.

Shuler, P. L., Jr.
  1982 *A Genre for the Gospels*. Philadelphia: Fortress.

Smith, J. Z.
  1975 "Good News is No News: Aretalogy and Gospel." Pp. 21–38 in *Christianity, Judaism, and other Greco-Roman Cults: Part One—New Testament*. Ed. J. Neusner. Leiden: Brill.

Stanton, G. N.
  1974 *Jesus of Nazareth in New Testament Preaching*. Cambridge: Cambridge University.

Stuart, D. R.
  1928 *Epochs of Greek and Roman Biography*. Berkeley: University of California.

Suggs, M. J.
  1976 "Gospel, Genre." Pp. 370–372 in *Interpreter's Dictionary of the Bible, Supplementary Volume*. Ed. K. Crim. Nashville: Abingdon.

Talbert, C. H.
  1970 "The Redaction Critical Quest for Luke the Theologian." Pp. 171–222 in *Jesus and Man's Hope*. Ed. Dikran Y. Hadidian. Pittsburgh: Pittsburgh Theological Seminary.
  1977 *What Is A Gospel?* Philadelphia: Fortress.
  1979 "The Gospel and the Gospels." *Int* 33:351–62.
  1982 *Reading Luke*. New York: Crossroad.

Toews, J. E.
  1981 "The Synoptic Problem and the Genre Question." *Direction* 10:11–18.

Traversa, A.
  1952 *Index Stoicorum Herculanensis*. Genova: Instituto di Filologia Classica.

Vivas, E.
  1968 "Literary Classes: Some Problems." *Genre* 1: 97–105.

Williams, James G.
  1985 *Gospel Against Parable: Mark's Language of Mystery*. Sheffield, England: Almond.

AND ONCE AGAIN, WHAT SORT OF "ESSENCE?": A RESPONSE TO CHARLES TALBERT

David P. Moessner
Columbia Theological Seminary

Readers who have followed Charles Talbert's discussions of gospel genre have come to expect penetrating challenges of crusted assumptions and fresh and objective insights into old and vexing problems. His present essay is no exception and is to be welcomed as a model of clarity with remarkable depth in surveying a broad and complex body of literature. Scholarship is particularly in his debt for the way he has sharpened the point of comparison for the canonical and certain apocryphal gospels with the Greco-Roman biographical tradition: These "gospels share with the ancient biographies that which is constitutive for them—to set forth the essence of the subject, that is, what sort of person he is (61)." Because Talbert has shown how this "essential" mark of biography combines with a number of "accidental" features in varying ways to produce the wide diversity in both formal and material aspects of the "lives," and—moreover—because most of the Christian gospels focus on one central subject and within their own diversity clearly display distinctive biographical interests and similarities to these lives, it is tempting to agree with Talbert and leave the discussion at that. What is especially appealing about his thesis is the way he is able to explain the rich variety among the Christian gospels with respect, e.g., to the extent of the life of Jesus covered or the type of narration or their "social function" or their use of myth, etc. by analogy to the "multiple ways those things that are accidental to biography are combined (61)," it would seem that the genesis and development of Christian gospels are a natural outgrowth of the more pervasive Mediterranean biographical soil.

Yet this writer cannot overcome a sense of unease with Talbert's central tenet. To take, for example, the four canonical gospels, are they "essentially" concerned to present the "essence" of Jesus' character, what "sort of person he is"? Granted the multiple messages and themes and possible social functions of the canonical four and especially the manifold ways that Jesus' *identity* is portrayed or posed—through points of view, titles, sayings, behavior of characters, editorial comments and links, to name but a few—are we still right in detecting a heartthrob of these portraits to be that "what is revealed in the narratives about Apollonius, or Pythagoras, or Moses, or Jesus is the same—their distinctive nature" (61)? Due to limits of space I propose to confine my observations to only a few on the "nature" of Luke's portrait. This restriction would seem to commend itself since: (i) only Luke provides a proem in which his work is related to conventions of Greco-Roman literary production; (ii) like Matthew Luke gives a fuller profile of Jesus' "life" including birth and resurrection narratives. This "order" follows Theon's advice (*Progymnasmata* 8) for the beginning of a "life"[1] and provides some material points of comparison with the Infancy Gospel of Thomas which, Talbert argues, along with the Gospel of Peter and the canonical four manifests a "biographical interest in . . . what sort of person Jesus was: (61); (iii) Prof. Talbert's own extensive work on Luke offers a larger context from which certain comparisons with his present contribution may perhaps profitably be made.

I

1) In the way that the narrator (1:5–24:53) ties the figure of Jesus to the story of Israel *from the beginning* of Jesus' "life," the overriding question that emerges both within this narrative world and for the reader is *not*, 'What sort of person is this,?' but rather, 'Who is this person in light of God's dealings with Israel?':

(i) As is not uncommon in the birth accounts of certain figures in Greco-Roman antiquity a divine apparition and/or oracle[2] announces the significance of Jesus' birth (Luke 1:26–38). What is emphasized by the angel Gabriel (v 26; cf. Dan 8:16; 9:21) in two parallel couplets (*houtos estai . . . estai telos*, vv 32–33) is that the "greatness" of this "*Son* of the Most High" (v 32a) will be exhibited in his reign upon the throne of his *father* David and thus over the "house" of Israel (Jacob) in perpetuity. From the outset Jesus' identity is defined primarily in terms of his role in a process of history which is much larger than himself or his own career. Notice how he is "named" 'son' both of an ancestor, David, and of a god, the "Lord God" of Israel (v 32; cf. vv 16, 19, 26, 28, 30);

(ii) Even before this oracle Jesus is introduced through the family and conception of John the Baptist (1:5–25). John too is announced beforehand by the angel/messenger Gabriel, "named" and described with respect to his place in a long priestly line, again, in a larger chain of events: "to turn the children of *Israel* to the Lord their God . . . to make ready for the Lord a *people* prepared" (1:16–17). But unlike the figures

And Once Again, What Sort of "Essence"? 77

paralleled in Plutarch's *Lives*, the narrator carefully engrafts the career of the one into the other in the sinews of the one unfolding *life of Israel*.³ It is true that he deliberately depicts Jesus as greater than the great John in Israel's future (Fitzmyer: 313–21), but more importantly the two lives come together to produce one story of Israel's salvation, as is so vividly illustrated in Mary's journey to Elizabeth (1:39–56). Not only does Elizabeth "bless" Mary for believing that there would be a "fulfillment" of the divine oracle to her, but she also indirectly calls Jesus "my Lord" (1:43), thus giving him the same "name" *(kurios)* as the God of Israel (vv 45!, 46; cf. v 76). As Talbert has observed elsewhere (1984:94), the "idea that history's course fulfills oracles . . . was also a cultural commonplace"⁴ to the Greco-Roman reader. But now this fulfillment is not that of an isolated albeit significant event; rather, the birth and career of Jesus are fused to the primary actor in the narrative, the God of Israel (see "Lord"/"God" as subject/active, 1:25, 26, 28, 32, 37, 45, 58, 66). David's reign and God's reign are merging in unprecedented fashion;

(iii) In inspired prophecies or songs as well as in angelic oracles our narrator presents a passel of hopes and expectations for the royal career of Jesus that calls to mind such stories as the birth of Samuel and the hopes engendered in the reign of David (e.g., Mary: "the Lord God has put down the mighty from their thrones," 1:52a; cf. e.g., I Sam 2:4, 8, 10; or e.g., Zechariah: "that we should be saved from our enemies," v 71a; cf. I Sam 2:1, 4, 10; a reign of "peace" through this "anointed one, the Lord," 2:11; cf. I Sam 2:10 etc.). There is little wonder that these portents and signs elicit a sense of mystery and fear from the families and neighbors of the two children (e.g., 1:12–13, 21, 30, 50, 63, 65; 2:9–10, 18), necessitating a "pondering" or "storing of these things in their heart" (e.g., 1:66; 2:19). Thus it is that when our narrator gives the reaction of the Judean "hill folk" to John's birth—"What then will this child be?!" (1:66)—there is hardly a thought about 'what sort of person' or what 'the essence' of John's nature or character is/will be. In plot and characterization all attention has been placed upon what this child will be or mean for the "people of Israel" whom we meet in the opening scene (1:21) (and never leave throughout the narrative) and for those "pious" of Israel who have pinned their hopes on the "Lord's oath to Abraham and his posterity" (1:55, 73) and uttered "through the mouth of his holy prophets from of old" (v 70). Nor at Jesus' birth is there a passing thought given to the character or nobility or virtues of the one who is a divine Savior-Lord (e.g., 2:17; cf. vv 10-11). Instead the narrator "thickens" the plot by concentrating Jesus' royal career into that of a controversial "sign," a rejected figure who will cause the "rising and falling of many in Israel" (2:34). With Jesus etched in the tones of the suffering figure of Isaiah, all the focus of the narrative is on what this child, this "saving act" (2:30; Isa 40:5; 52:10) of God will be for the nation of Israel, to all those "looking for the redemption/liberation of Jerusalem" (2:38). Rather than extolling the virtues of the child or praising the deity for a beneficent act to humankind, the two (prophet/ess) bless the God of Israel by foretelling at the nation's center, its Temple, what *Israel's* fate through this child shall be ("light of revelation . . . glory to your people Israel," v 32; cf. Isa 42:6, 49:6, 9).[5]

2) The unique mention in the canonical four of Jesus' childhood "education" (2:41–51) would allow, as in certain Greco-Roman "lives," an important glimpse into the formative teachers and principles that were to shape his character or distinctive nature. We do learn 'what sort of person' Jesus is with respect to his greater devotion to "the things of my Father" (2:49) than to obedience to his parents. Or rather, it would be more accurate to say that Jesus' obedience is viewed in line with his growing "wisdom and favor before God and humankind" (vv 40, 52) in a mission of 'dividing' that will eventually climax in a Passover journey to Jerusalem and in "'my' house" as Jesus once again astounds the "teachers" of Israel (20:26; 2:47; cf. 9:51–19:44). How different from the parallel in the Infancy Gospel of Thomas (chap. 19). Coming at the end of a string of 18 anecdotes, the twelve-year old boy Jesus in the Temple is the child prodigy whose unequalled wisdom and knowledge has made fools of the wise teachers of Israel (chaps. 6, 7, 14, 15), and whose vindictive power has brutalized unsuspecting 'offenders' of his superiority (3, 4, 5, 8). Here indeed the string of loosely connected miracles and pronouncements, individually and taken together, demonstrate one main point, Jesus' essential nature: "Truly, this child is either a god or an angel of God!" (17.2; cf. 18.2; 10.2; 7.4).[6]

3) As in certain genealogies of Greco-Roman biography and historiography (Aune: 121–22), Luke's genealogy traces Jesus' ancestry back to a god and thus legitimates the one born in a manger to a servant woman (2:6–7; 1:38, 48). Who this "prince" is, is impressively established by a seventy-seven generation, single linear ascending genealogy (3:23–38; see Kurz). And yet by the way that Luke has sandwiched this list between Jesus' "naming" and commissioning by the divine voice during the ministry of John the Baptist (3:21–22) and Jesus' "testing" in the wilderness (4:1–13) prior to his public activity (4:14–21:38), all the movement of the generations in Israel's past is caught up in the *dunamis* of this "mightier one" who is now "coming" (3:16).[7] What sort of "son of God" this is, what the "essence of his person" is, is almost exclusively described in terms of God's relation to Israel: The one who spans all of humanity back to God's creative act[8] is revealed as the "beloved Son"/"Servant" of Isaiah (3:21; Isa 42:1), the "saving act of God" (3:6 →2:30), the "Lord" (1:43; 2:11→3:6→4:8, 12→7:27) whose coming to Israel brooks the eschatological division of "all flesh" (3:4–6, 16–17).[9]

4) It seems that whenever the identity of Jesus breaks open as a

public issue, our narrator has Jesus "correct" the expectations of his disciples and the crowds with Jesus' understanding of his own *mission to Israel*. For instance, in the opening scene of his public activity (4:16–30) Jesus perceives that the 'fame' that has already preceded him (4:14–15) has framed certain expectations of his identity that do not square at all with the Isaianic promises of the anointed prophet-Servant's role that he has come to fulfill (4:18–19).[10] "Is this not Joseph's son?" is answered by the "beloved Son" (3:22→3:23→4:18) who, like rejected prophets before him, must go "outside" Israel with God's salvation (4:23–27). Or again after a significant amount of the Galilean activity is recounted, the one who served to introduce Jesus to the public as "the Christ" (3:15–17) is now questioning Jesus' identity precisely because of that activity (7:18a, 18b–23).[11] As in Nazareth, Jesus indicates who he is, his "essence," by pointing solely to the nature of his calling *with Israel* and again in the language and demonstration (7:21!) of the Isaianic expectations of the final salvation (7:22; *emoi*, v 23). Moreover, the narrator once again has Jesus define himself in light of Israel's history of the reception of its prophets sent by God/Wisdom, this time by contrast (and continuity) with the mission of John (7:24–35, esp. vv 27–28). Numerous other examples could be cited (e.g., 9:18–36; 10:21–24; 15:1–2, 3–32; 22:66–71, etc.) which illustrate that the "character" that emerges from the Gospel of Luke is totally absorbed in his sending to Israel. It is not by accident that the author organizes much of his plot in the journeying of Jesus to Jerusalem and its Temple, and places Jesus under a divine compulsion to complete the "exodus" of God's salvation to Israel (and to the nations) there (9:31; 24:47).[12] Nor is it by accident that the author in the denouement has Jesus lift the veil of mystery that has enshrouded his own identity among the people from the very beginning by having Jesus point to the whole of Israel's scriptures as the clue to 'what sort of person' he is: the story of Israel has come to its crowning point in its suffering Christ (24:25–27, 44–47; cf. 22:37 and 24:19–21).

It is certainly true that in all of this Lukan sketch of Jesus we do learn a certain amount about the 'sort of person' he was: e.g., his compassion for the ill or grieving (e.g., 5:13; 7:13; 13:12); his predilection for "tax collectors and sinners" (5:27–35; 7:34–35, 36–50; 15:1–2; 19:1–10) and the "poor" (e.g., 6:20; 7:22); or his apparent enjoyment of the company of women and treatment of them as disciples (e.g., 8:1–3; 10:38–42; cf. 24:6–11). But in every instance this "quality" is not linked to a particular moral essence or structure of virtues but rather to the presence or 'reign of God' that gives shape and drive to Jesus' mission to Israel. Even when his "character" vis-à-vis the law is assailed, Jesus' response is "characterized" by his understanding of his presence among Israel (e.g., 5:33–39; 6:1–5, 6–11; 7:29–35; 11:37–52).

Although we have only begun to focus the Lukan portrait of its central figure, it would appear that what the author is primarily interested in presenting is *not* 'what sort of person' Jesus is, but rather what sort of action God is effecting through this person for the salvation of Israel (and the nations) (cf. e.g., the summaries in Acts 2:22–24; 10:36–38).

II

No decision concerning the genre of a specific writing can obviously be based solely on its preface, especially since prose prefaces tended to emulate oratorical prefaces and thus adopted similar conventional vocabulary and style (Callan: 576–77). Analyses of Luke 1:1–4 have yielded diverging judgments as to whether the Third Gospel is history or biography.[13] Yet in light of Luke's particular choice and conjunction of only certain of these stock vocabulary we may have some clues that, when balanced with our observations above, could help to tip the evidence from the prologue in one direction or another:[14]

(i) In the first half of his beautifully balanced periodic sentence it is curious that Luke states that "many have already undertaken to compile a narrative" about "events *(pragmata)* that have come to completion/been fulfilled"; in the second half he indicates that he is doing the same *(kamoi)* in what follows. In biographies, *if* a formal prooemium is present, it invariably includes the notice that a "life" *(bios, vita)* is the subject/theme of the writing.[15] Interesting also is the fact that *pragmata* is a stock term for the subject matter of historians.[16]

(ii) Our author also adds that, like the many, his "method" of writing involves the "compiling/arranging in proper order" a "narrative account" of material stemming from and "passed on" by "eyewitnesses" of the events he is going to relate. This twofold procedure matches Lucian's description of how a good historian, once he has collected his information in the form of a series of notes or aide-mémoire *(hupomnēma)*, should set about to write a smooth narrative *(diēgēsis)* by adding "order" *(taxis*, cf. *kathexēs*, Luke 1:3) and "ornament" and thus "color it with language, give it figures and rhythm" *(How to Write History*, 48, 55).[17] Lucian, as do Greco-Roman historians, also emphasizes that the historian should himself, if at all possible, be an eyewitness of the events and, failing that, should consult those who were in a position to relate the most impartial account possible (ibid., 47).[18] Luke's reference to "eyewitness" traditions in the context of imparting *asphaleia* to the events he will recount could well be another signal that his work is to be aligned with historiography.

(iii) *pasin* (v 3), followed by *akribōs* and *grapsai*, most likely is neuter, referring to "all things," i.e. to the "events" *(pragmata)*. Again a conventional distinction between historiography and biography may be indicated here. According to Plutarch and Nepos, for example, a history

And Once Again, What Sort of "Essence"?   81

involved *complete* accounts of the events of their subjects while biography selected out sayings, insignificant deeds, and even trivial details in order to reveal character.[19] Luke seems intent in giving a full account, motivated *perhaps* by the "many" who he felt had not provided an extensive enough account of the "events fulfilled among us."[20]

None of these or any other features of the prologue, individually or together, is conclusive. Yet with the explicit statements of what Luke intends to write we have found striking resemblance in the scope, plot, and characterization in the work that then follows. The further fact that Luke continues his "volume" on Jesus with a second in which the story of *Israel's* salvation proceeds through the deeds and sayings of significant figures, is redoubled reinforcement of this resonance (see Acts 1:1–5).

III

Finally, it would be interesting to investigate Luke's "omniscient mode" of narration (Alter: 155–77; Sternberg: 84–128) that begins in 1:5 and is sustained throughout until the end, 24:53. After the initial "me" (1:3) and "us" (1:1, 2) in the proem, the author slips behind the narrator in 1:5–24:53 to a consistent third person mode. What is more, from 1:5 he quickly establishes his omniscient 'viewing point' as he freely moves his readers "from above" from one locale to another (e.g., from the Temple to the hill country of Judea to Galilee, etc.), reveals angelic pronouncements in divine visitations (e.g., 1:11–23, 26–38), "quotes" private thoughts and desires (e.g., 1:25; 2:19), and cites prophetic interpretations of "interior" and supraterrestrial events (e.g., 1:41–45, 46–55, 67–79), etc. But what may prove particularly significant for genre questions is the way that the narrator joins his point of view with the omniscient perspective of the "Lord God" of Israel, followed by these two being fused with the omniscient view point of the central character Jesus: e.g., the "word of God" to John (3:2) is declared by the *narrator* (3:4–6) to be summed up by the prophet Isaiah's oracle (Isa 40:3–5), sc. the narrator "speaks" for God (cf. 1:6; 2:25, 40, 52, etc.); the narrator then as omniscient witness fuses the "voice" of God/heaven in 3:22 with Jesus' point of view in 4:1–13 where Jesus now speaks "directly" for the Lord God (4:8, 12) within the narrator's omniscient frame (4:1, 13) (see also e.g., 9:44→45; 10:21a→21b-22!; 18:33→34; etc.). Consequently it appears that the anonymous author of the Third Gospel has adopted a mode of *divine* omniscient discourse similar to the *anonymous* narrative mode of much of the large and often biographically oriented biblical historiography, Genesis—II Kings.[21] It may be that further comparisons of these narrative modes would add greater support to the historiographical bent that we have discerned above and could challenge Talbert's first subpoint of his "Ramifications. . . ." (67–68), viz., that there is no particular theological significance in the kind of narrative genre chosen or developed by the Christian authors of the gospels. A link between the choice of genre and theological significance is certainly possible in the case of the Third Gospel.

In conclusion, given the growing convergence of the historiographical and the biographical genres in the Greco-Roman period and the focus of the gospels on one central character, Jesus of Nazareth, it is to be expected that many elements characteristic of the gospels should be identified as constitutive of biography. Yet our limited survey of just one of the gospels has suggested that in Luke's preponderately theocentric emphasis, his express intent in the introduction, and his use of an omniscient mode of narration, his gospel exhibits rather those features which, on the whole, are more descriptive of historiography, with perhaps the biographically oriented biblical histories as the closest parallels. Certainly more work needs to be done. But if our suggestions for the analysis of Luke provide helpful analogies for the investigation of other gospels, then perhaps we have moved the genre question a bit forward. In any event, it seems clear that Luke composes his "gospel" narrative in a way that guards not only against "subversion" and "reductionism" of the gospel but also against any discussion and distortion of "a comprehensive and balanced understanding of the divine presence (67)" in Jesus that speaks without reference to this divine presence in *the long history of God's dealings with Israel*.

NOTES

[1] Aune: 65: "By adding background material, genealogies and birth narratives . . . and resurrection appearances . . . Matthew and Luke have moved closer toward the biographical and historiographical expectations of pagan readers."

[2] E.g., Diodorus Siculus, *Library of History*, 4.9.1–10 (Heracles), Diogenes Laertius, *Lives of Eminent Philosophers*, 3.1–2 (Plato), Plutarch, *Alexander*, 2.2–4, 3.1–2 (Alexander the Great); Suetonius, *Lives of the Caesars*, 2.94.1–9 (Augustus).

[3] As Plutarch states in his differentiation of biography from history (*Alexander*, 1.1–3), he is concerned in the former to describe the "character" (*ēthos*), often taking advantage of insignificant events, deeds, gestures, etc. in order to reveal the virtues or vices of a famous figure. In his *Parallel Lives* he compares and contrasts two public figures with similar careers (usually a Greek and a Roman), but with an interest to reveal their "private" virtues or "natures", e.g., *Demosthenes*, 3.1: "I shall examine their actions and their political careers to see how their natures (*phusis*) and dispositions compare with one another." (All citations are taken from the LCL translations). A working rationale for Plutarch seems to be that history provides a setting in which transcendent values may be displayed through exemplary individuals, see further A. Dihle.

[4] Talbert is correct to point out that the "promise-fulfillment" schema does not include all the "data," nor every Lukan use of Jewish scriptures (95), nor can it be regarded as the one and only major theme (101). But precisely because it functions, especially in the opening introductions of Jesus and in the concluding summaries (e.g., chap. 24), to organize and focus the *entire* career of Jesus, it must be regarded as a decisive and determinative category for the Lukan portrait.

⁵ Contrast e.g., the "seers" and vision at the birth of Alexander: his mother was pregnant "of a son whose nature *(phusis)* would be bold and lion-like" (Plutarch, *Alexander,* 2.3).

⁶ E. Hennecke and W. Schneemelcher, *New Testament Apocrypha,* I (Philadelphia: Westminster, 1963) 398; notice how differently the "precocious youth" *topos* is used, e.g., in Iamblichus, *The Life of Pythagoras,* 9–10; Plutarch, *Pompey,* 2.1; *Agesilaus,* 1.1 ("he had been educated to obey before he came to command . . . . to the commanding and kingly traits which were his by nature"); *Alexander,* 7, *Caesar,* 3, etc.

⁷ Notice the careful synchronism of the "word of God" to John with Tiberias Caesar et al. in 3:1–2.

⁸ Kurz, 178) mentions Acts 17:27b–29a in interpreting Luke 3:38.

⁹ 3:4–6 is the *narrator's* description of John's preparation for Jesus as the "Christ, the Lord" (2:11) which thus links the angelophany to the Isaianic "coming of the Lord" with respect to both John as the "voice" of the "Lord" (Jesus) (3:4) and to this "coming" Lord as "the Christ" (Jesus) whom John announces (3:15–16).

¹⁰ Note how the narrator's description of the Holy Spirit "upon him" *(ep' auton)* in 3:22a is reaffirmed by Jesus in 4:18 using the words of Isa 61:1. Both "voices" thus attest to the "voice from heaven" (3:22b) that Jesus is the "beloved Son/Servant" in whom God delights (Isa 42:1). See further part III, below.

¹¹ Notice how the narrator conjoins "Lord" with John's "coming one" in 7:19 as in 3.4, 16, see also 7.27–28. Cf. also *prosdokaō* in 3:15 and 7.19, 20, see note 9.

¹² Both Jesus (5:35) and the narrator (6:16) intimate an impending violence/betrayal before Jesus links this fate to Jerusalem and his journey there in 9.22–23, the "passion" predictions (9:44; 12:49–50; 13:33–34, 17.25; 18:31–33) and the journey notices (9:31, 51, 57, 10:1, 38; 11 53; 13.22, 32–33, 14:25; 17:11; 18.31, 35; 19.1, 11, 28–29, 41) continue this link. At certain points Jesus expresses or is compelled by a "divine necessity" *dei* (2:49; 4:43, 9:22, 13:33; 17.25; 19:5; 22:37 [24:7, 26, 44—retrospectively]). Thus by 9:22 and 13:33 all three motifs have been woven together to form a distinctive plot.

¹³ E.g., history, Callan: 577–80, W. C. van Unnik; biography, e.g., V. K. Robbins.

¹⁴ This point is passed over in Talbert's otherwise lucid discussion of 1.1–4 (1982:7–11).

¹⁵ See Callan (581 n. 10) who lists 8 biographies from four authors—Plutarch, Tacitus, Philo, Eunapius.

¹⁶ E.g., Polybius, *The Histories,* 1.3.9; Diodorus, *Library of History,* 1.4; Dio. *Roman History,* 1.2; Dionysius of Halicarnassus, *Roman Antiquities,* 1.3, Lucian, *How to Write History,* 47, 55.

¹⁷ Lucian likens this to a sculptor with given material: "they confine themselves to fashioning it" (50); van Unnik (Prologue, 12–13) comes to the same conclusion regarding Luke's twofold procedure.

¹⁸ Van Unnik (13–14) mentions Heraclitus' famous proverb ("the ears are less trustworthy . . . than the eyes") and discusses five historians' emphasis on eyewitness accounts.

¹⁹ Plutarch, *Alexander,* 1.1–3; Cornelius Nepos, *Pelopidas,* 16 1.1, see further, D. L. Barr and J. L. Wentling ("The Conventions of Classical Biography and the Genre of Luke-Acts. A Preliminary Study," *Luke-Acts, New Perspectives,* 70–71), Aune *(Environment,* 29–31).

²⁰ Cf. Lucian's *(How to Write History)* stress on proportion and balance of structure in chaps. 11 and 55—make each section or topic "complete" (entelē, 55); Diodorus *(Library of History)*— the actions or events of kings and nations should be "complete" (autoteleis, 16.1).

²¹ 1:1–4 then would explain to readers unfamiliar with biblical historiography and *consistent* omniscient narration that his work should be compared or aligned with Greco-Roman histories

MODERN WORKS CITED

Alter, Robert
    1981   *The Art of Biblical Narrative.* New York: Basic Books.

Aune, D. E.
1987 *The New Testament in Its Literary Environment*. Philadelphia: Westminster.

Barr, D. L., and Wentling, J. L.
1984 "The Conventions of Classical Biography and the Genre of Luke-Acts: A Preliminary Study." Pp. 63–88 in *Luke-Acts: New Perspectives from the Society of Biblical Literature Seminar*. Ed. C. H. Talbert. N.Y.: Crossroad.

Callan, Terrance
1985 "The Preface of Luke-Acts and Historiography." NTS 31:576–81.

Dihle, Albrecht
1983 "Die Evangelien und die biographische Tradition der Antike." *ZTK* 80:33–49.

Fitzmyer, J. A.
1981 *The Gospel According to Luke I–IX: Anchor Bible 28*. N.Y.: Doubleday.

Kurz, W. S.
1984 "Luke 3:23–38 and Greco-Roman and Biblical Genealogies." Pp. 169–87 in *Luke-Acts: New Perspectives from the Society of Biblical Literature Seminar*. Ed. C. H. Talbert. N.Y.: Crossroad.

Robbins, V. K.
1978 Prefaces in Greco-Roman Biography and Luke-Acts." Pp. 193–207 in *Society of Biblical Literature Seminar Papers* 2. Ed. P. Achtemeier. Missoula: Scholars.

Sternberg, Meir
1985 *The Poetics of Biblical Narrative*. Bloomington, IN: Indiana University.

Talbert, C. H.
1982 *Reading Luke. A Literary and Theological Commentary on the Third Gospel*. N.Y.: Crossroad.

———
1984 "Promise and Fulfillment in Lucan Theology." Pp. 91–103 in *Luke-Acts: New Perspectives from the Society of Biblical Literature Seminar*. Ed. C. H. Talbert, N.Y.: Crossroad.

Unnik, W. C. van
1973 "Once More St. Luke's Prologue." *Neot* 7:7–26.

PARABLE AND CHREIA: FROM Q TO NARRATIVE GOSPEL

James G. Williams
Syracuse University

ABSTRACT

In *Gospel Against Parable* I argued in cursory fashion that the narrative gospel was the outcome of an interaction of two forms from different worlds of meaning: the Hellenistic *bios* or biography of the divinely gifted man or immortal, and the parable so closely associated with Jesus in the primitive Christian tradition. Here I step back into a prior stage of the tradition and analyze the function and interrelation of two of the three dominant forms of speech in Q: the parable and the chreia. (The third is parenesis, which is not as determinative of the final form of Q and the formation of the narrative gospel.)

In Q the chief characteristic of much of the parabolic material (parables, parabolic sayings, metaphorical sayings, near-parables, and near-parabolic sayings) is *intensification*, both theological (Beardslee) and literary (Alter and Kugel). The "pronouncement story" or chreia is a form that carries with it a biographical impulse. Many of the chreiai identified, of which ten are about Jesus and one about John the Baptist, emphasize the meaning of the kingdom of God as revealed in the divine character and deeds of Jesus.

As for the relation of parable and chreia in Q, the chreiai that contain parables and those closely related to parables have the effect of *making Jesus himself the subject of his own parables*. There is, moreover, a metaphoric vitality in many of the chreiai that shows the literary influence of the parables that were brought into conjunction with the chreiai.

I conclude therefore that Q is neither a collection of the sayings of the wise (Kloppenborg) nor a prophetic document (Boring), but a parable-chreia collection that is well on its way toward the form of the narrative gospel. Q is closer to the canonical narrative gospels than to the Gospel of Thomas. In the Q-

Gospel trajectory Jesus becomes the center of the story and the voice of divine wisdom. In Thomas, Jesus is not the subject of a story but the very Wisdom that stands against all worldly stories and structures. The theology of a tradition according to the Thomas pattern cannot be written but must be formulated in the interaction of a community with the leader who in the instructional situation represents the "living Jesus." In the Q-Gospel pattern the leaders of the community have to accede in principle to the pastness of the biographical aspect of the gospel form, and this pastness is reinforced by the very paradigm of pastness: *writing*. However, both these patterns are modified somewhat in the other direction. In Thomas there is a minimal limit on the contemporizing tendency of the oral situation by virtue of the understanding that Jesus "spoke" to his *alter*, the twin Thomas (the community). In the synoptic gospels the parabolic aspect of the gospel form gives it a certain contemporary, polyvalent potential.

In this essay I am concerned chiefly with the relation of parables and parabolic forms to the emerging narrative gospel. In other words, I begin with a form of the fourth question that we posed for contributors to this issue (see Preface). On the basis of this initial study I move on to the question of gospel as genre and the theological implications that I draw from this discussion.

The process began for me in the interpretive work that resulted in my book *Gospel Against Parable*. There I argued that Mark's peculiar language, which I call a "language of mystery," is in large part determined by the tension between the contextualization involved in creating a larger narrative ("myth," if one wishes) and the lack of contextualization or literary world-making involved in parabolic forms. In an addendum to the main body of the work I maintained that the narrative gospel as we know it from the New Testament synoptic gospels was the result of a metaphoric process, a creative interaction of two forms from different worlds of meaning and different understandings of existence: the Hellenistic *bios* of the divinely gifted man or immortal (see Talbert) and the parable so closely associated with Jesus in the early tradition of the Jesus communities. Here I wish to develop and refine that thesis by stepping back into Q, the so-called sayings source, and looking at the interaction of parabolic forms and a rhetorical form that may well have been the seed of the biography in classical Antiquity, the *chreia* or "pronouncement story."

My procedure will be first to engage in literary analysis of parables and chreiai in Q and take note of how the two are related to each other. I shall simply presuppose a general consensus of what constitutes Q as it can be marked out from Luke and Matthew (and occasionally Mark).

Moreover, in part II of the study I will list its contents for the sake of making a judgment about its overall literary form. That will be the second step, to arrive at a conclusion about Q's literary form and its place in a trajectory that issued in the narrative gospel. The third and final section of the essay will present some of the theological implications of the study. These implications will revolve around the contrast between the Q-Gospel tradition and the Thomas tradition.

1. Parable and Chreia in Q

Recent studies of Q have highlighted its variety of literary forms within the broad category of "sayings." There are parables, pronouncement stories, eschatological utterances, prophetic sayings, and parenetic forms (see Kloppenborg; Edwards; Carlston; Boring). By any accounting, both parables and pronouncement stories are important in Q.

A. Parables

I would identify the following as Q parables:

> 11:24–26, unclean spirit that returns
> 12:36–38, 42–46 (Thom. 21), watchful servants
> 13:18–19 (Thom. 20), the kingdom of God like a mustard seed
> 13:20–21 (Thom. 96), the kingdom of God like leaven
> 13:25–27, householder shuts door
> 14:16–23 (Thom. 64), the great supper
> 15:4–6 (Thom. 107), lost sheep
> 19:12–13, 15–26 (cf. Gospel of Nazoreans 18), entrusted money

There are also parabolic sayings. These are not quite the short narrative forms we associate with the word "parable" in English, yet they exhibit a certain narrativity (Alter:171–72). Narrativity in this case means an action sequence, however compact, and a problem, lack, or conflict that must be remedied. The action sequence and narrative tension could readily become a story if the slightest narrative development occurred. I have found three of these in Q:

> 9:58 (Thom. 86), foxes have holes
> 12:2–3, what is covered and revealed
> 12:6–7, hairs of the head numbered

In addition, there are some passages that are very close to having the features of a parable or parabolic saying. There is a form that is centered in metaphor, as parable necessarily is, but does not exhibit the narrativity of parabolic saying or the narrative development of parable. I locate three of these, which Bultmann called metaphorical sayings: 6:43–45; 6:47–49; 11:33–34. 6:43–45 compares moral intentions and deeds to the fruit of trees. 6:47–49 contains two minute narratives, but the point is really the comparison and contrast of two character types. 11:33–34 compares human insight and moral decision to a lamp.

There are other instances where one can easily imagine an underlying parable or how the passage in question could be formed into a parable. The saying about John the Baptist and the Son of man in Luke 7:33–35 has the vivid metaphors of parable and allow, if not invite, the reader to understand it as a "likely story" or "true fiction" (see Williams, 1985:41) except for the references to John and the Son of man. Matthew's version, with "they say" rather than "you say" (Matt. 11:18–19) may be closer to the original Q wording; in any case the third person form would be more appropriate to a parable, if it was such. The command to the disciples in Matthew 10:16 (Lk. 10:3) would be a parabolic saying except for the "you" of direct address and the narrative setting. It reads: "Behold, I send you out as sheep in the midst of wolves; therefore be wise as serpents and harmless as doves." The second verset is not found in Luke 10:3 and so is not usually considered to be from Q. However, the Matthean version forms a striking chiasm that follows an ancient Judaic poetic pattern:

sheep   wolves

serpents   doves

"Doves and sheep are associated with innocence and are offered in sacrifice. The wolf and the serpent are known as sly hunters" (Williams 1981:61). Finally, Matthew 7:9–10 could be a parabolic saying in the form of a rhetorical question except for the direct address. (Compare Lk. 11:11–12, which by putting the scorpion *after* the serpent softens the effect of the saying.) With a slight shift of wording we have: "What one (*anthrōpos*)—or father (*patēr*)—gives his son a stone if he asks for bread/ or a serpent if he asks for fish?" It is easy to imagine how this saying might become a parable: "The kingdom of God is like a man whose son has worked in the field all morning, and so by noon he's famished; he says to his father, 'Father, I'm about to die with hunger. Let me have my lunch of bread and fish.' The man gives his son not only the son's share, but his lunch also."

A list of all the material:

Parables: Return of the Unclean Spirit, 11:24–26; Faithful Servants, 12:36–38, 42–46; the Mustard Seed, 13:18–19; the Leaven, 13:20–21; Householder Locking Door, 13:25–27; the Banquet, 14:16–23; Lost Sheep, 15:4–6; Entrusted Money, 19:12–13, 15–26.

Parable and Chreia 89

Parabolic Sayings: Foxes Have Holes, 9:58; the Covered and the Revealed, 12:2–3; Hairs of the Head Numbered, 12:6–7.

Metaphorical Sayings: Tree Known by Its Fruit, 6:43–45; Wise and Foolish Builders, 6:47–49; Eye and Light, 11:33–34.

Near-Parables: Wisdom's Different Children, 7:33–35; How a Father Treats His Son, Matt. 7:9–10 (Lk. 11:11–12).

Near-Parabolic Sayings: How a Father Treats His Son, Matt. 7:9–10; Wise As Serpents and Harmless As Doves, Matt. 10:16 (Lk. 10:3).

If all these sayings be accepted as relevant to a consideration of parables in Q, then we find 18 or 19 parabolic forms (one overlap, Matt. 7:9–10). It is interesting to examine them for what is there and what is not there. We find a few instances of metaphor functioning paradoxically (Mustard Seed, Banquet, Serpents and Doves), but only one of these instances, the Banquet, really exhibits what Ricoeur has called "extravagance," an extravagance that "transforms the poetics of the parables into a poetics of faith" (Ricoeur:118). Rhetorical exaggeration or hyperbole is the necessary condition of parabolic extravagance, and there are four instances of hyperbole (Foxes Have Holes, Covered and Revealed, Banquet, and How Father Treats Son). Four occurrences do not make, of course, a higher percentage. The relatively non-paradoxical, inextravagant character of Q becomes even clearer when we note those sayings that may be typified as "ordinary wisdom." That is, those which present typical instances of human behavior and character, and which of themselves do not call any world into question that we could easily determine or imagine for either a Jewish or a Hellenistic setting. These parables are the metaphorical sayings, Tree and Its Fruit, Wise and Foolish Builders, and Eye and Light, and the narrative parables, Return of Unclean Spirit and Entrusted Money. A good tree bears good fruit, etc. A house should be built on solid foundations. Life and character depend on the "light" that one has. The cure can be worse than the disease. Money and property should be used to the profit of the possessor, not put in profitless safekeeping. These sayings are all "proverbial." In a certain setting they could conceivably become radicalized, but in and of themselves they are not remarkable. However, attached to the lamp parable is a saying that reads like a paradox: "So be careful lest the light in you be darkness" (11:35). The Matthean form may not only be a paradox, but an enhancement of the image: "If the light in you is darkness, how great the darkness?" (Matt. 6:23). This enhancement is closely related to *intensification*.

Intensification seems to be the one feature of the Q parables and parabolic sayings that stands out and provides a bridge to some of the non-Q parables which are known for their paradox and hyperbole. "Intensification" is a dynamic that functions as much at the level of content as of form. It was proposed by William Beardslee as a way of understanding the "proverbial insight" of Jesus' sayings. For example, concerning the "Golden Rule," Luke 6:31, he says that

> In its setting in Q the rule takes man's own situation as the presupposition for his understanding of his neighbor's in such a way that what can be a merely prudential rule becomes a complete transposition of the "little history" within which each man lives: one must die to his own little history, and thereby that of his neighbor is exposed as the object of true, free concern (39).

He says further, "The proverb in Q calls one out of his framework of security to be at the disposal of the concrete encounter" (41). For Beardslee, therefore, intensification is a phenomenon that depends on an understanding of the setting, in this case the Q "text" and the community of Q. In parts II and III of this paper I will indicate how I myself view Q as a whole.

I think it is useful also to employ the term "intensification" in a literary manner "as two basic operations of specification and heightening" (Alter: 62; see also Kugel, ch. 1). Alter applies specification and heightening to parallel versets in biblical Hebrew poetry, but with proper qualifications they are also pertinent to the Q material. Some sayings represent literary intensification or certainly lend themselves to such. I have identified seven, of which three are parables, 13:25–27 (Householder Locking Door), 15:4–6 (Lost Sheep), and 7:33–35 (Wisdom's Different Children), and four are parabolic sayings, 9:58 (Foxes Have Holes), 12:2–3 (Covered and Revealed), 12:6–7 (Hairs of the Head Numbered), and Matthew 7:9–10 (reconstructed as How Father Treats Son).

What Alter means by specification is the tendency to move from the general to the specific instance.

> I shall put an end *in the cities of Judah/*
> and *in the streets of Jerusalem//*
> to the sound of gladness and joy,/
> the sound of bridegroom and bride
> (Jer. 7:34; Alter's example: 19).

Alter cites this verse in Jeremiah as an instance of spatial or geographical specification, but it applies also to mood or emotions in the second line. There is a movement from the general assertion of removal of the sound of gladness and joy to an attachment of that sound to the celebration of bridegroom and bride.

Specification and heightening are often interwoven and so must be understood as overlapping terms. Heightening will more often than not employ specification in a dramatic focusing or hyperbolic stepping-up of a key term.

> Face to the dust they *will bow to you,/*
> they *will lick the dust of your feet*
> (Isa. 49:23; Alter's example: 21).

The four parabolic sayings are good examples of the operations of intensification. Q 9:58 in particular could be construed as coming directly out of the stylistic tradition of ancient Hebrew poetry.

> Foxes have holes and birds of the sky nests,/
> but the Son of man has nowhere to lay his head.

This is an antithetical aphorism (Tannehill:88–101), not a line in synonymous parallelism such as Alter's examples. However, the functions are basically the same. The general observation of the first half-line or verset is attached in the second verset to a specific figure in his concrete circumstances, and there is a movement from the image of dwellings to the picture of someone trying to lie down on a bed, mat, or perhaps even the ground. The versets are antithetical, not synonymous because the Son of man has *nowhere* to lay his head. This may be read also as hyperbole, and in actual instances there is often a fine line between hyperbole and intensification.

In 12:2–3 we find these operations somewhat expanded.

> Nothing is covered that will not be revealed/
> or hidden that will not be known.//
> For whatever you have said in the dark
>   in the light shall be heard/
> and what you have whispered in private rooms
>   shall be proclaimed on the housetops.

This is somewhat prolix for an aphorism in the ancient Hebrew style— although my translation has more words than the Greek. I have translated *anth'hōn* at the beginning of the second line "for" rather than "therefore" as in the Revised Standard Version. It sometimes means "because," as in Luke 1:20, 19:44, and Acts 12:23. This line thus reads like the motive clause of Hebrew instruction proverbs that begins with *kî* "for" or "because." The explanatory line, 12:3, not only becomes rather expansive in the use of words, but employs the second person plural address, which is a departure from the biblical proverb tradition. The second person was used in instructions carrying a command or prohibition, but not for an assertion or indicative statement. But even if 12:3 is not a pure form in the Hebrew aphoristic tradition, it certainly exhibits intensification. The general truth of the first line, which could be construed as ordinary or traditional wisdom, is directed to the reader or hearer in the second. Not only that, but what is covered up is specified as "what you have said in the dark," and even more, it is "what you have whispered in private rooms." There is thus a hyperbolic stepping-up in the dramatic contrast between secrets shared in a private room and the denouement of a revelation in full light of day.

Q 12:6–7 is different from the others in that it begins in the form of a rhetorical question.

> Are not five sparrows sold for two pennies?/
> And not one of them is forgotten before God./
> But even the hairs of your head are all numbered./
> Fear not: you are worth more than many sparrows.

This saying is unusual in form, but a close inspection shows the features of Hebrew contrastive parallelism. It is framed as a chiasm:

sparrows	not forgotten
numbered	sparrows

The first line departs from the style of specification in that a general assertion is made in the second verset. (On rarer instances of movement from specific to general see Alter: 22.) However, the second verset of line one expresses reassurance, which is the function in a more intense form of the second verset of line two. And the specification and dramatic heightening in line two as contrasted to line one are obvious. If even the sparrow is not forgotten (=is valuable) before God, how much more valuable are the members of the community addressed, all of whose hairs of the head are numbered (=known and valued) by God!

Matthew 7:9–10 does not contain specification, but it is a good example of dramatic heightening. The parabolic saying as I have reconstructed it:

> What father gives his son a stone if he asks for bread/
> Or a serpent if he asks for fish?

The version of this saying in Luke is wordier and puts the deadly animal (scorpion) in the first verset. Unless one holds that Matthew characteristically improved Q's literary style, I think the Matthean form of the saying should be considered closer to Q. There is an exaggeration of an unlikely situation as one imagines a father giving his son a stone instead of bread to eat—which is bad enough. But then instead of a fish he passes him a serpent!

My comments on the three parables will be briefer. The householder who shuts the door, 13:25–27, presupposes an opening line or two that was presumably in an original form of the parable. Servants or guests have gone away for the evening, apparently in an impolite manner (at least they shouldn't have returned so late!). Those barred from the house knock and call at the door, but the householder pretends not to know them (v. 25). Those outside protest that they even ate and drank with the master of the house (v. 26). The exaggerated intensification of the impasse reaches a climax when the master of the house adds insult to injury by calling those outside "workers of iniquity" (v. 27)!

The parable of the lost sheep, 15:4–6, does not work by specification, but there is a dramatic heightening effect through a series of extreme contrasts: leaving the 99 sheep to go after the lost one; a shepherd pastoring the flock but carrying the lost one on his shoulders; flock in the *wilderness* and shepherd rejoicing *at home* over the sheep that was found. These contrasts lose their heightening effect in Thomas' version of the parable. In Thomas 107 the lost sheep is the *largest*, and the shepherd tells the lost sheep that he cares for it more than for the ninety-nine. Someone hearing the Thomas version of the parable could say, "Well of course, it seemed strange that the shepherd would go to all that trouble and leave the rest of the flock in danger—but if it was his largest sheep and he was more fond of it than of the rest. . . ."

As for Luke 7:33–35 (= Matt. 11:18–19), it is clearly not a parable as it stands, but I would call it "parabolic." It is difficult to tell whether the response to John the Baptist and Jesus was cast in a parabolic mode, or a parable about the public's inability to respond to prophets and teachers of wisdom became attached to John and Jesus. What strikes me about the contrasting images of the two is that the rejection of John is rather general and conventional ("He has a demon!"), whereas the abusive epithets about the Son of man[1] are heaped up. That he would be caricatured as a glutton and "wino" *(oinopotēs)* is bad enough. "A friend of tax-collectors and sinners" (= adulterers, prostitutes, and pimps) is really insulting! "And Wisdom is justified by all her children," i.e., Wisdom may accomplish her ends in ways the public does not expect. As a matter of fact, one could conceive of an original parable in which *Chokmah* or *Sophia*, wisdom personified, sends out two servants, or two of her "children," prophets who are rejected.

To summarize the findings so far, a preliminary survey shows a great deal of parabolic material, in the form both of short narratives and aphorisms. Although any definition of parable would have to include the vital metaphor, some of the other literary characteristics that contemporary interpreters tend to ascribe to parables are not in such prominent display. Although one finds instances of paradox, as well as the sort of hyperbole that may easily move into the "extravagance" perceived by Ricoeur, I cannot conclude that these terms are the best ones for describing parables in Q. *Intensification* is the one feature that is both characteristic and provides a bridge to some of the favorite non-Q parables of modern hermeneuts.[2] Intensification, as defined literarily by Robert Alter in terms of specification and heightening in biblical Hebrew poetry, is nicely exhibited in three parabolic sayings, 9:58, 12:2–3, and 12:6–7. I also detect it in two parables, 13:25–27 (your origins are unknown → workers of iniquity) and Luke 7:33–35 (demon → glutton and drunkard → friend of tax-collectors and sinners). Dramatic heightening is found in the reconstructed parabolic saying, Matt. 7:9–10, as well as in the short parable, Q 15:4–6. We found an intensifying of the picture of the Son of man's homelessness in the world, of the full disclosure of God's judgment, of the divine care for members of the Jesus community, of the confidence children (members of the community) may place in the divine Parent, of the fate of those who do not act as good guests or servants, of the concern of the shepherd for the lost sheep, and of the inability of most humans to perceive and accept true wisdom. Although the focus was on literary analysis, by taking these seven passages together we can already begin to form a picture of Q's theology. We begin, indeed, to construct a continuum between these literary results and Beardslee's point that in the context of Q, the sayings of Jesus call "one out of his framework of security in order to be at the disposal of concrete encounter" with God through Jesus the Son of the man and with God through the neighbor, who is likewise the object of God's care.

B. Pronouncement Stories

Another form of speech in Q almost as common as parable and parenesis is one that exegetes usually call the "pronouncement story" since Taylor coined the term (Taylor: 29–30, 63–87). This refers more or less to the same form that Bultmann called "apophthegm" (Bultmann: 11–69), and it overlaps with Dibelius' "paradigm" (Dibelius: 26, 37–69). In Hellenistic rhetoric it was called *chreia* (see Hock, and Butts on Theon). In the chreia a great personage, usually a sage who is viewed as "divine" or "immortal," teaches by issuing a pronouncement in response to a question or state of affairs in a setting that may be only vaguely described, if at all. The primary interest lies in the *character* of the teacher, whose authority is presupposed. Very often his wit turns the situation into an occasion to display his wisdom or offer his audience a memorably stated insight. His sayings characterize him.

> It is said that Plato, seeing someone playing at dice, rebuked him. And when the other protested that he played only for trifles, he said, "But character *(ethos)* is not a trifle" (Diog. Laert., III. 38, trans. modified).

Here Plato's ethos as a philsopher is shown. He is able to discern the ethos, the character or pattern of behavior that lies behind someone's actions.

The chreia carries with it a biographical impulse and may have been the seed of the *bios*, life or biography. The example given above is, in Tannehill's terminology, an "objection story" (1981a:6–7). Tannehill surveys all the chreiai or pronouncement stories in the synoptic gospels and constructs a typology:

> 1. *Correction stories:* "By action, by outright statement, or by implication from something said, someone has taken a position as to what is right or expedient, and the responder corrects that position" (7).

> 2. *Commendation stories:* ". . . In commendations the responder commends rather than corrects the other person" (7).

> 3. *Objection stories:* "Objection stories, like correction stories, present a situation of conflict. However, in corrections the conflict is first indicated by the response, while in objections it is created by an objection to the behavior or views of the responder [the teacher or great personage] or his followers" (8). I should note in passing that the example given previously in Plato from the *Lives* of Diogenes Laertius is more complex than the classification as stated by Tannehill. Plato first objects to someone's playing at dice, and then when this person objects to the reprimand, Plato makes his pronouncement.

> 4. *Quest stories:* A person on a quest asks a question to which the teacher responds. This response determines the success or failure of the quest. This is a more elaborate pronouncement story, and the person asking the question has a more important role than in most of the chreiai (9).

> 5. *Inquiry stories:* "An inquiry story moves from a question or request for information to the answer to that question or request" (10). The responder does not correct the questioner, nor does the questioner object to the behavior or views of the responder.

> 6. *Description stories:* "Description stories begin with a general indication of the situation to which the pronouncement relates.

This provides the setting for a comment in which the responder describes the situation . . . The speaker is saying, '. . . this is the way it is'" (10–11).

Using Tannehill's survey of the varieties of synoptic pronouncement stories (1981b), I find eleven chreiai in Q. Here is a tabulation thereof, with an indication of the type of story:

3:7–8: John the Baptist's exhortation—correction
7:1–10: The centurion's dying slave—correction (also objection?)
7:18–23: Messengers from the John the Baptist—inquiry
7:24–35: On John the Baptist—correction
9:57–58: On following Jesus—correction
9:59–60: On burying the dead—correction
11:14–26: On exorcism—objection
11:29–32: The sign of Jonah—correction
11:45–52: Against the lawyers—objection
13:22–30: On entering by the narrow door—inquiry
17:5–6: The apostles' request for increased faith—inquiry

The correction story dominates, with six occurrences. There are two (or three?) objection stories and three inquiry stories.

What do these chreiai communicate about the character of Jesus? A considerable number of them emphasize his divine works. His deeds are of God, they display and confirm the good news. Immediately after the great sermon (6:20–49) he accedes to a request a heal a Roman centurion's slave (7:1–10). This episode is followed by the request of John through his messengers that Jesus confirm his divine mission. Luke 7:21 is perhaps Luke's own insertion into the Q pericope (missing in Matthew): "In that hour he cured many of diseases and plagues and evil spirits, and many of the blind he graced with sight." Jesus's response to the messengers is a summary of the good news:

> Go tell John what you have seen and heard: the blind see again, the lame walk, lepers are cleansed, and the deaf hear, the dead are raised, the poor receive good news. And blessed is the one taking no offense at me (7:22–23).

The Beelzebul controversy, 11:14–26, deals with conflict about Jesus' source of power and authority over the demonic. The parable of the unclean spirit that returns to someone with "seven other spirits more evil than himself" (11:26) reads in the Q context as a tale responding to the objection of opponents. To wit, as if to say, "Just as you know a tree by its fruits, you can tell by examining those I have healed whether their health and their deeds show God's work or Satan's." It is interesting that in the same context Matthew uses the Q material differently, placing Jesus' teaching on a tree and its fruits between the Beelzebul controversy and the demand for a sign:

Matt. 12:22–32/Lk. 11:14–23—Beelzebul controversy
Matt. 12:33–37/Lk. 6:43–45—a tree and its fruits
Matt. 12:38–42/Lk. 11:16, 29–32—demand for a sign
Matt. 12:43–45/Lk. 11:24–26—unclean spirit that returns

I would suppose that Luke stays closer to the Q order, but that Matthew, sensing what was at stake in the Beelzebul controversy, placed the teaching on good and bad fruit immediately after it. Jesus is not demonic because his fruits are good, as seen in those he heals and exorcizes.

Q 11:29–32, the demand for a sign, is also a works chreia. Jesus as Son of man is *the* sign because his deeds show that he is wiser than Solomon and a greater proclaimer of repentance than Jonah. As I shall point out in part II on the literary form of Q, this sign chreia could be taken as paradigmatic of Q as a whole.

The focus on the divinely authorized and empowered deeds of Jesus is probably also a concern in the woes against the lawyers, 11:45–52. The implication is that in "this generation" (11:51) Jesus is the last in the line of prophets and apostles sent by the Wisdom of God (11:49). Matthew transforms this implication by having Jesus himself speak as the voice of divine wisdom (Matt. 23:34). As will be indicated in part III on theological implications of this study, Matthew's rendering of Jesus into the divine subject, the divine wisdom *as such*, is what happens in Thomas, but in Thomas Jesus is not contextualized (or made narratively contingent) by being born, growing up, dying, and being raised from the dead.

Q 17:5–6 is by implication a deeds chreia. When the apostles ask that their faith be increased, Jesus gives an answer that stresses the wonders that faith can work. By implication he is an exemplar of such faith.

So five of the ten chreiai about Jesus set his divine character in bold relief by pointing to his deeds. (One of the eleven is about John, 3:7–8). It is also worth noting that Q includes the story of Jesus overcoming the basic temptations that the devil is thought to pose to all humans: the desire for miracles, the desire for power and prestige, and the desire for safety from danger and death. Although the temptation story, 4:1–13, is a real narrative with a beginning moving through engagement and conflict to an end, one can see how each episode of testing could have been built out of a chreia. In any case, in the present form of Q Jesus' character is displayed at the outset, and it undergirds the authority of what he teaches as well as reinforcing the chreiai that follow. If biography is character, as it evidently was in the ancient world, then we can see already in Q a biographical element. Yet it is also "parabolic," so I must next examine the relation of chreiai to parables to Q.

C. The Relation of Chreia and Parable in Q

There are two ways in which parables are related to chreiai in Q: They are included in some chreiai, and there is a close, thematic or consequential relation in other instances. These forms of relationship will be taken up in order.

There are two chreiai that include parables (11:14–26, 13:22–30), and one that includes what I have termed a "near-parable" (7:24–35). There is also a chreia that includes a parabolic saying (9:57–58). In addition to these four instances I want also to note how Luke provides a setting for the Banquet and the Lost Sheep (14:15–24 and 15:1–7).

The parable of the unclean spirit that returns (11:14–26) could just as appropriately have been placed in a warning to the disciples about mechanical or unconcerned exorcism on which the exorcist does not follow through in a proper pastoral manner. Making it part of a controversy implies two things, both very important: (1) The Q community was involved in controversies with opponents about healings and exorcisms. (2) The parables associated with Jesus were of such weight in the primitive tradition that the tendency was already to use them even in settings where the "fit" was not obvious.

We find the same lack of obvious connection to the context in the relation of the parable of the householder that shuts the door, 13:25–27, to the chreia that ends with a pronouncement on the Kingdom in 13:22–30. These dicta at the end assert that the outside audience, presumably the Jews who are hostile, will not enter into the kingdom of God (13:28–30). However, if one focused on the parable itself, its more obvious point could be contrued as the need to act as good guests or servants; not to be slack, but to bear fruit showing faith in God.

The near-parable about Wisdom's Different Children, 7:33–35, is very intriguing in relation to the entire passage, 7:24–35, which could be read as a long chreia. It is intriguing in great part because one has no absolute proof that it is the adaptation of some parable to this context. I would, however, be surprised if there were not some such *mashal* or *parabole* circulating in a Jewish or Hellenistic context. See, for example, the biblical *mashal* about the lovers of Language who eat of her fruits in Proverbs 18:21, a proverb closely related in its imagery and possible meaning to the lovers of Wisdom in Proverbs 8:17, 21. The point I would make about Wisdom's Different Children is that one of two options would best explain the parabolic form in context: (1) A parabolic saying was composed to bring the comparison of Jesus and John to a fitting conclusion. (2) A parable already known was adapted to the needs of the chreia. In any event, one of the primary motifs of Q is that both John and Jesus represent the divine voice. Given the parabolic quality of much of Q, Wisdom's Different Children is an apt climax to the questions that Q presupposes and addresses about the mission and deeds of John and Jesus.

Q 14:16–23 and 15:3–6 are not chreiai in Q. Luke, however, very easily changes them into such by introducing a setting. The parable of the lost sheep thus becomes a moving rejoinder to the Pharisees (15:1–2). Of course, this parable about the good shepherd searching for his sheep does not have to be imagined in a controversy setting. As for the Banquet, 14:16–23, there is some tension between the form of the parable in Luke and the exclamation that occasions it: "Blessed is whoever eats bread in the kingdom of God!" (14:15). The Lukan version emphasizes the mission, the repetition of the effort to bring in people of all sorts from the highways and byways. The parable as it stands in Luke seems to have been revised according to Luke's theology of salvation history, although much of the Q material already represented as kind of "deuteronomistic theology" (Kloppenborg, drawing upon Jacobson). Thomas' version (Thom. 64), which presents only two trips of the servant, may be closer to an earlier form of the parable, even though it reflects the style and theology of Thomas in other respects (Williams, 1985: 164–165).

Concerning the parabolic saying, 9:58, I find it difficult to conceive a better conjunction of occasion and saying. I would say the same about the connection of 9:59 and 9:60, except the latter is parenetic, not parabolic: "Leave the dead to bury their dead."

So in four of these six instances the fit of the parable with the chreia is not tight. It is difficult to arrive at a judgment about Wisdom's Different Children since it is not certain the saying had a prehistory. In all six instances the parable functions to reveal the character of Jesus or his mission—a mission that includes his relation to John's mission in 7:33–35. Indeed, something quite interesting occurs in four of the six: *the effect of the chreia is to make Jesus the subject of the parable.* That "the Son of man has nowhere to lay his head" is something the potential follower of Jesus must understand (9:57; cf. 9:59). Whatever his opponents may charge, Jesus' exorcism is the work of God, not Beelzebul (11:14–26). Jesus, like John, is one of Wisdom's children (or according to Matt. 11:19, does her works). And in the chreia Lukes makes of the Q parable, Jesus, who eats with sinners, is the shepherd who goes out searching for the one sheep that is lost (15:1–7).

In the other two chreia passages, 13:22–30 (Q) and 14:15–24 (Luke), the Kingdom or the preaching of the Kingdom remains the subject of the parable within the chreia.

There are also chreiai that are related in some consequential way to parables not included in the pronouncement stories themselves. Two of these are among the five passages discussed above:

11:14–26 (with 11:29–32)	related to 11:33–34
13:22–30	related to 13:18–21

Also these:

3:7–8	related to 4:1–13; 6:43–49; 12:36–38, 42–46; 19:12–13, 15–26
7:18–23	related to 7:24–35

The parable of the lamp, 11:33–34, bears no apparent connection to the preceding chreia, but placed as it is it functions as part of an exhortation to sound judgment in evaluating what is God's work in the world and what is not. The mustard seed and the leaven that a woman hid in flour read like introductions to 13:22–30, a chreia on exclusion from the Kingdom. Or it could be viewed vice-versa, the episode of the narrow entrance being a kind of commentary on the previous two parables. The work of the Kingdom has small beginnings and not everyone is able or called to participate. This connection between the two parables in 13:18–21 and the chreia is made more explicit by Luke's addition of 13:23: "And some of them said to him, 'Lord, will those who are saved be few?'"

The consecutive chreiai, 7:18–23 and 7:24–35, deal with the works of Jesus, and as already discussed, these are capped with the parable-like saying in 7:33–35. Like 11:33–34, 7:33–35 is an expression of the tendency to identify Jesus as the subject of his own parables.

Of the chreiai related to parables, the episode of John's preaching, 3:7–8, seems to have an internal thematic connection with the greatest number of parables. If it was the beginning of the Q document, the Q writer probably sensed this connection. The saying attributed to John:

> O brood of vipers! Who warned you to flee from the wrath to come? Bear fruits worthy of repentance, and don't begin to say among yourselves, "We have Abraham as our father." For I tell you, God is able from these stones to raise up children to Abraham.

Whatever the intention of the Q writer, doing deeds worthy of repentance seems to be confirmed in various ways in passages that follow. Jesus shows himself to be the one who is to come (3:16–17) by resisting the temptations of the devil (4:1–13). The proclamation of John and the temptation story prepare the way for Jesus' teaching about a tree and its fruit (6:43–45), men building a house (6:46–49), the faithful servant (12:36–38, 42–46), and the money entrusted to servants (19:11–12, 15–26)." To "bear fruit worthy of *metanoias*" ("mind-changing" or repentance) is the parenetic theme of Q, just as the relation of Jesus' sayings and works to himself as the messenger of the Kingdom is Q's proclamatory theme.

The initial stages of a tendency to move Jesus himself into the center of what he teaches is the most significant finding of this examination of chreiai and parables Both the parables within chreiai and the consequential relation of parables and chreiai signify that Jesus is the one who is to come, whose message and works represent the *metanoia* of the rule of God.

A more difficult question is whether the literary form of the parable had a reciprocal effect on the chreia. Can we find a vivid metaphoric pattern and a central element of intensification in the chreiai? Given the biographical impulse of the chreia and the corresponding tendency to make Jesus himself the subject of the parables ascribed to him, are the metaphoric vitality and level of intensification in the chreiai the effect of the biographical impulse that was undoubtedly fed by the centrality of Jesus in the early tradition? Or did the parables themselves help to create this metaphoric vitality? It is hard for either the social or the literary historian to disentangle these factors, which were probably interacting. Let me observe that the Hellenistic biographies that I have read do not maintain either the metaphoric quality or the intensification that the Q chreiai communicate. The Q tales relate a certain unconventional quality and summon the hearer to a radical discipleship. At least six of them deal with how Jesus should be viewed or what discipleship entails. Jesus concludes his reply to John's messengers, "And blessed is the one who takes no offense at me" (7:23). In the next episode he says that even though John is great, "yet the least in the kingdom of God is greater than he" (7:28). Taken in conjunction with 7:27, about John as the messenger "who shall prepare the way before you," the intention of the chreia is to justify the ministry of Jesus. Q 9:57–60 is a combination of two chreiai to which the author of Luke has evidently added a third, 9:61–62. The three pronouncements are noteworthy:

> Foxes have holes, and birds of the sky nests,
> but the Son of man has nowhere to lay his head.
>
> Leave the dead to buy their own dead;
> but as for you, go and proclaim the kingdom of God.
>
> No one putting his hand to the plow and looking back
> is suited for the kingdom of God.

The homeless Son of man—departure from conventional society—not looking back once one has started the task: these form a picture of discipleship centered in Jesus as Son of man that brings together various forms of intensification, sociological, theological, and literary. One might characterize this picture by saying that the Son of man without a place for his head is a literary image giving focus to radical commitment to God and an itinerant ministry.

The parable of the returning unclean spirit, 11:24–26, apparently functions to reinforce the pronouncement at the conclusion of the Beelzebul controversy: "Whoever is not with me is against me, and who does not gather with me scatters" (11:23). The point of the demand for a sign, 11:29–32, is that "a greater than Solomon is here" and "a greater than Jonah is here" (11:31, 32).

The Q pattern we see in these six chreiai is continued by Luke, as in 15:1–2. The Q saying in 15:7, "there will be more joy in heaven over one sinner who repents," etc., justifies Jesus against opponents as Luke has set the frame of reference.

When we consider also the healing of the centurion's servant (7:1–10) and one of Jesus' teachings on faith (17:5–6), a twofold pattern emerges in the Q chreiai: Jesus' deeds are wonderful and marvelous and his teaching is a radical call to commit oneself to service of the Kingdom. Do we find anything comparable in the Hellenistic sources?

Scholars with more expertise in these sources than I will have to speak to the question, but on the basis of what I have read I would say the answer is yes and no. On the one hand, the biographers wanted to present the unusual virtue of their subjects' deeds and teachings. Socrates, according to Diogenes Laertius, was remarkable even in old age. He learned to play the lyre, "declaring that he saw no absurdity in learning a new accomplishment." All his life he was divinely guided:

> He used to say the divine (*to daimonion*) warned him beforehand of what was to come (11.32, trans. modified).

Philostratus describes Apollonius' discourse as wise and oracular:

> "How then," O Apollonius, "should the sage converse?" Again he told him, "Like a law-giver, for it is necessary that the law-giver give to others the instructions of whose truth he is persuaded" (I.XVII, trans. modified).

On the other hand, the tendency of the biographers seems to have been to integrate the sage's teaching into the conventional and ordinary. The literary and social function of the chreia in biographies was not to jar the mind and inculcate any radical notion concerning following the sage, but to explain and instruct in terms of what was commonly known. When Apollonius was asked why he did not write a book, he replied, "I have not yet kept silence" (I.XIV). If left like that, the pronouncement could be a paradox giving rise to thought: in order to write one must first observe silence. However, the effect is dispelled with the biographer's subsequent description of the teacher's five years of silence (I.XIV, XV). In other words, the biographer is not satisfied unless he offers conventional description and explanation.

Diogenes' tales of Socrates are so relaxed—the contrary of the typical quality of intensification in the Jesus tradition—that the reader is bound to assimilate the narratives simply as items of knowledge that are interesting to learn about the great philosopher, not as presentations of a marvelous and inspired model.

> He used to say that he most enjoyed the food which was least in need of condiment, and the drink which made him feel the least hankering for some other drink; and that he was nearest to the gods in that he had the fewest wants (11.27).

To conclude this subsection of the paper, what we find in a study of the relation of parable and chreia are two phenomena which are especially important in this context: (1) The tendency of the chreia is to shift Jesus from parable-speaker to parable-referent. (2) Many of the Q chreiai reveal a degree of metaphoric patterning and a high level of intensification like a number of the parables.

II. The Literary Form of Q

John Kloppenborg has argued in his original and exhaustively documented doctoral thesis that Q is a document presenting a well worked out view of Jesus, and that its earliest stage was a series of sapiential speeches: Q 6:20b-49; 9:57–60 [61–62]; 10:2–11, 16; 11:2–4, 9–13; 12:2–7; 12:22b–31, 33–34; 13:24; 14:26–27; 17:33; 14:34–35. A major redaction introduced prophetic and apocalyptic words and framed many of the sayings as chreiai: Q 3:7–9, 16–17; 7:1–10, 18–35; 10:12, 13–15; 11:14–26, 39–52; 12:8, 9, 10; 12:39–59; 17:23–37. His argument concerning these two stages is basically twofold. (1) The sapiential speeches appear to form a literary whole after the pattern of ancient Near Eastern texts presenting instructions of the wise (see Robinson). In the second stage or stratum Q became a chreia-collection. (2) There is considerable evidence of the interpolation of judgment sayings within and between the wisdom speeches (e.g., 6:23c added to 6:22–23b) by means of thematic association and catchwords. (On the latter note "hear," *akouō*, in 10:16 and 10:21–24.) These interpolations are evidence of the deuteronomistic theology of the prophetic and apocalyptic sayings of the second, non-sapiential stratum.

Finally, Kloppenborg contends that the Temptation was added as the latest development of Q. Its effect was definitely to shift Q towards a biographical forming of the sayings of Jesus.

Kloppenborg's thesis has the merit of trying to establish the literary genre of Q, and this means also its implied readers. It is of interest in this paper to compare his thesis to the diametrically opposed position argued by Eugene Boring.

Boring maintains that the form of Q is the address of the risen Savior to his community (137–182). His "analysis offers concrete support for the often made assertion that Q is a prophetic document from a charismatic community" (180). His examination of Q leads him to the conclusion that many of the Q sayings probably originated as the oracles of Christian prophets: Luke 6:22–23; 10:3; 10:4; 10:5–12; 10:13–15; 10:16; 10:21–22; 11:29b–30; 11:39–52; 12:8–9; 12:10; 12:11–12; 13:34–35; 16:17; 17;22; 22:28–30.

It will be noticed that some of these sayings are ones that Kloppenborg identifies as sapiential. I think that Kloppenborg is right about 6:22–23a, for the macarism is a wisdom form. However, that proves nothing in itself because we know that the ancient Israelite prophets used many different forms of speech, including both macarisms and woes—both of which may have had their original life-setting in the wisdom tradition (see book of Amos and Crenshaw, 1967; bibliography in Crenshaw, 1969). On the other hand, it appears to me that Boring is more correct concerning 10:1–16. This speech on the mission of the disciples clearly has wisdom elements in it (e.g., 10:3), but I find it difficult to follow Kloppenborg's delineation of 10:2–11 as part of a sapiential stratum. That is, unless one could validly picture the seventy sent out as something like Cynic teachers of wisdom, yet simultaneously as proclaimers of the approach of the kingdom of God.

Of course, 10:1–16 is a "community-directed speech," which is characteristic of all the passages that Kloppenborg places in the formative wisdom form of Q. However, the criterion of I-You speeches will not suffice to support the formative character of these so-called sapiential logoi. For one thing, in prophetic works we often find an alternation between community-directed speech and third person proclamation. See, for example, the prophet's command to bind up the testimony in Isaiah 8:16–20 in relation to the oracle of the word against Israel in Isaiah 9:7–17. The latter is, as far as we know, just as integral to the formation of the Isaiah scroll as the former, which is a "community-directed" oracle. Indeed, the first person I-Thou or I-You address may be a fiction that masks other speakers in the persona of the prophet. It may be a way of legitimating what the community believes to be true by seeing it as the prophetic or divine word. The same thing *could* have happened in the formation of Q: Jesus' words, refracted and revised in the primitive tradition, would have been incorporated in order to justify the life-style of those who were beginning to find themselves in bitter conflict with Jewish or non-Jewish contemporaries.

I said that Boring is more correct about the particular pericope 10:2–16. I would say that his total argument is finally untenable because its literary critical grounds are shaky. He devotes a chapter to formal characteristics of prophetic speech (126–135), dicussing the following topics: oracles in poetry, speaking for the risen Lord in the first person, Käsemann's "sentences of holy law" and the "eschatological correlative," the formula "truly I say to you *(amēn legō humin/soi)*, and blessing and curse.

It has already been indicated that blessing and curse are not sure signs of prophetic discourse apart from additional information about the literary and historical context. But the most serious problem with Boring's argument is that we do not have sufficient evidence to know how to determine when a given speech ascribed to Jesus has its origin in the speaking of a prophet in the Jesus tradition who identifies his "I" with the "I" of the risen Lord.

In any case, even if one accepted all the formal features of prophetic speech presented by Boring, it would, I think, be difficult to apply them to Q and arrive at the conclusion that it is a prophetic document. There is indeed a noteworthy prophetic element in Q, both in terms of concern with the function of John, Jesus, or Jesus' followers as prophets and with the relation of this prophetic proclamation to Israel's past rejection of the prophets. However, the prophetic elements do not form a "prophetic document." I have already noted that the number and extent of prophetic oracles in Q is uncertain. Moreover, some of the basic features of the prophet as homo religiosus (81–94) cannot be located in Q with any certainty. A prophetic document in the Jewish tradition would presumably include a narration of the prophet's calling or a reference to it. Is there an allusion to Jesus' vocation in Q 10:21–22 ("All things have been delivered to me by my Father," etc.)? Or is this a concealed reference to the Christian prophet's vocation, the implied logic of which would be the word from Father to Son to prophet? We do not know. Another problem is that prophets do not tend to write.[3] The process of literary formation would have to be dealt with if one were to argue Q is a "prophetic document." In sum, a sharper answer to the question of what constitutes a prophetic document is needed.

Now as for the contrary argument put forth by Kloppenborg, that Q's formative stratum was an instructional genre, there is no doubt that much of Q is made up of wisdom material. There may even be a thematic connection between the opening of some of the speeches and what follows (6:20b–22 in relation to the rest of the great sermon is a good example). It is, however, an imposition of modern assumptions about form and genre to conclude that clusters of an identifiable type in a text represent a different stratum of redaction. Although I find Kloppenborg's thesis attractive in some respects, I tend to the view that there is not a firm basis for delineating redactional strata in Q. It is problematic enough when we have an extant work! For example, catchword associations there clearly are in Q. But the method of catchword association could occur in one and the same compositional process. Let us say that the Q author had at hand some sapiential sayings ascribed to Jesus; perhaps they were already thematized in the manner indicated by Kloppenborg. In any case, the author places them at appropriate points in a work already begun. Where prophetic or deuteronomistic material was added by catchword association, that could have been simply in order to harmonize the wisdom teachings with the rest of the work.

Some such process seems to make more sense than an original wisdom composition, for when one looks at what we have of Q Kloppenborg's easily discernible wisdom blocks do not appear to dominate. Here is an outline, with the sapiential blocks in upper case letters. I shall place a question mark after those units that are not, in my view, dominated by wisdom forms. It will also be useful to indicate whether a given pericope may be marked as a chreia (C) or contains parabolic material (P).

John's Coming and Preaching 3:2–3, 7–9, 15–17 (C) in vv. 7–9
The Temptations 4:1–13
DISCOURSE: Beatitudes 6:20b–23
  Woes 6:24–26
  Love of Enemies 6:27–36
  On judging 6:37–42
  Bearing Fruits 6:43–45 (P)
  House on Rock 6:46–49 (P)
Healing Centurion's Slave 7:1–10 (C)
Jesus Answers John's Question 7:18–23 (C)
Jesus' Witness to John 7:24–35 (C)(P) in vv. 31–35
ON FOLLOWING JESUS 9:57–60 [61–62?] (C)(C) [(C)] (P)
COMMISSIONING THE SEVENTY ? 10:1–12 (P)
WOES ON GALILEAN TOWNS 10:13–15
WHO HEARS YOU, HEARS ME 10:16
Sons Thanks Father, Blessedness of Disciples 10:21–24
HOW TO PRAY (The Our Father)? 11:2–4
PERSISTENCE IN PRAYER 11:9–13 (P)
The Beelzebul Controversy 11:14–23 (C)
Return of Unclean Spirit 11:24–26 (Not identified by Kloppenborg as a wisdom form of speech, but it could be so construed.) (P)
Sign of Jonah 11:29–32 C)
LAMP OF THE BODY 11:33–36 (P)
Against the Pharisees 11:37–54 (C) in vv. 45–52
APOCALYPSE AND FEARLESS CONFESSION? 12:2–12 (P)(P)
ON ANXIETY 12:22–31
TREASURES IN HEAVEN 12:33–34
Watchfulness and Faithfulness 12:35–48 (P)
Troubles and Signs in the Last Times 12:49–59

The Mustard Seed 13:18–19 (This and the following parable are not among Kloppenborg's instructional sayings, but they could be so viewed.) (P)
Kingdom of God Like Leaven 13:20–21
Exclusion from the Kingdom 13:22–30 (C) (P) in vv. 25–27
Lament over Jerusalem 13:34–35
The Great Banquet 14:16–23 (P)
Conditions of Discipleship 14:25–33
Salt 14:34–35 (Wisdom)
The Lost Sheep 15:3–7 (P)
On Having Two Masters 16:13 (Wisdom)
Law and Prophets Till John 16:16–17
On Faith 17:5–6 (C)
When the Son of Man Is Revealed 17:22–37
Parable of the Pounds 19:11–27 (P)
Precedence in the Kingdom 22:28–30

I think that any such glance at the topics and forms in Q should suffice to indicate that "instructions of the wise" played a definite but not formative role in Q. Prophecy too must have had some part, but we should keep in mind the problems and unknown factors I have already mentioned in the presentation of Boring's thesis. What takes form in my view is a tendency to bring parabolic material and chreiai together, as already discussed in part I. The findings were as follows:

(1) There are two chreiai that include parables (11:14–26, 13:22–30), one that includes a "near-parable" (7:24–35), and one that includes a parabolic saying (9:57–58). There are two other Q parables that Luke easily turns into chreiai (14:16–23, 15:3–6). In four of these there is not an obvious fit of parable and chreia. (As indicated, the function of Wisdom's Different Children in the formation of 7:24–35 is uncertain.) The real exception is 9:57–58, where the conjunction of occasion and saying is perfect. In four of the six chreiai the effect is to make Jesus himself the subject of the parable.
(2) There are chreiai closely related to parables (or parabolic material) not included within them. Three of these are instrumental in two complexes that change Jesus into the subject of his own message. The first is simply a sequence: 7:18–23 → 7:24–35 (7:33–35). The second I would term a "network": 3:7–8 with (16–17) ↔ 6:43–49; 12:36–38, 42–46; 19:11–12, 15–26. As previously stated, both sets of relations signify that he is the one to come; his message and works represent the required transformation of heart and mind that happens when God's rule is fulfilled.
(3) There is a metaphoric vitality in many of the chreiai that may well have been literarily influenced by the parables that were brought into

conjunction with them in the tradition. The parable-chreia relation that had perhaps already emerged in the tradition was then exploited by the writer responsible for the final form of Q.

What probably occurred—and I realize this is little more than conjecture concerning the actual proceess of literary formation—was the use of the chreia or pronouncement story by some author in order to delineate Jesus' relation to John the Baptist and to promote a view of Jesus' character and deeds that would have been understandable in a Hellenistic setting.[4] The various parabolic forms that I have discerned as part of a network related to John's preaching of *metanoia* serve to show that Jesus continues this proclamation. The "string" of chreia passages in Luke 7 indicate that in relation to John Jesus is *ho erchomenos*, the Coming One, and these passages are undoubtedly related to Q 11:29–32 and 16:16–17. In fact, the "sign of Jonah" pericope is a kind of mediating passage which may be paradigmatic of the process: in its present form it is a pronouncement story that envinces interest in both the wisdom of Jesus and his prophetic proclamation of repentance. And even though the primary sign is the proclamation of *metanoia*, the "greater than" formula is evidence that the proclaimer himself is becoming the sign of God's reign.[5]

> When the crowds were increasing he began to say,
> "This generation is an evil generation. It seeks a sign, but a sign shall not be given to it except the sign of Jonah. For just as Jonah became a sign to the Ninevites, so the Son of man shall be to this generation. The Queen of the South will arise at the judgment with those of this generation and condemn them, for she came from the ends of the earth to hear the wisdom of Solomon, and behold, a greater than Solomon is here. The Ninevites will arise at the judgment with this generation and condemn it, for they repented at the preaching of Jonah, and behold, a greater than Jonah is here."

In my book *Gospel Against Parable* I included an addendum in which I argued that a metaphoric process lay behind the creation of a new literary form, the narrative gospel. In speaking of "metaphoric process" I drew upon the argument of Gerhart and Russell that metaphor is properly understood as a shorthand term for a process in which two previously separate understandings from different fields of meaning are brought together into a new pattern or "world of meaning." I went on to present the thesis, in a very cursory form, that one can discern this metaphoric process at different literary levels in the gospel tradition: in the parables, in the relations of parables to their settings, and in the formation of the gospel as narrative.

Concerning the formation of the gospel as narrative, I proposed that two literary forms from seemingly incongruous settings were brought together and seen as equivalent in early Christianity: the biography of the great person and the type of parable attributed to Jesus. My conclusion:

> In the resulting form we know as the narrative gospel the [central structuring element of the parable, the likeness] transforms biography so that it functions as an image of God's rule, and the [central structuring element of biography, the life of the immortal] renders parable so that it functions as a kind of "history." Thus gospel as a new genre (213-214).

I believe I was on the right track with this argument, but I would now refine it to a generically prior stage. It was the chreia with its biographical impulse that early Christian interpreters began to play against the various parabolic forms integral to the early Jesus tradition—integral for two reasons: (1) Because Jesus himself surely characteristically taught in parables, parabolic sayings, and metaphorical utterances. (2) Jesus' way of using language and the life-setting of many followers inspired the creation and development of parabolic language. If the relation of parable and chreia in Q is anything approximating what I have concluded in my analysis, then at the heart of the narrative gospel was a process in which parabolic forms, whose distinguishing literary feature is intensification, were drawn into chreiai, whose distinguishing literary feature is the pronouncement of the great man who offers guidance for life. The parabolic forms, in their turn, affected the chreiai from within.

III. Theological Implications

My conclusion about Q is that it is *not* a collection of sayings of the wise but parable-chreia collection that is well on its way toward the form of the narrative gospel. It is still a kind of blend or mixture in a way that the Gospel of Mark, for example, is not. Jesus, particularly through the chreiai, is becoming the referent of his own sayings, and the effect of the chreia is to diminish the contemporizing effect of sayings and speeches that are allowed to stand in their own right. The so-called "sayings source" is thus much less an expression of orality than Werner Kelber contends in *The Oral and the Written Gospel*. However, two aspects of orality remain. One is the fiction of the present Lord addressing his community. Even though that is a fiction, there are fictions that will carry readers into the oral situation if they are persuaded to follow the text.

The other aspect of orality comes from the historical Jesus tradition itself: the parables (including parabolic sayings and metaphorical sayings), which as Kelber has pointed out are a transitional, mediating form between orality and writing. They demand interpretation, yet they are polyvalent and can be narratively contextualized in different ways.

The concrete historical problematic of the community to which Q was addressed must have included two interrelated conditions: frequent, if not persistent persecution, and the need to legitimate the Jesus community in a world requiring license and authority. Q did not develop all the marks required for this validation in the Graeco-Roman world, but the seeds were there. John the Baptist as predecessor, Jesus overcoming the tests of Satan, disciples who are blessed and sent out by the Master, the wise sayings and prophetic pronouncements of the Master—these together make up the seminal form of the narrative gospel. I would say that Q is therefore considerably closer to the canonical narrative gospels, particularly Mark, than to the Gospel of Thomas.

In the Q-Gospel trajectory the protagonist of the text, the prophet, story-teller and sage, becomes the center of the story and the voice of divine wisdom. The story itself becomes the target of attention, as we can see especially in Matthew and Luke. Q does not give a full story, being still a form very much in transition. Mark offers a plotted narrative, but partially undercuts the gospel story through the theme of the mystery of the Kingdom that is conveyed in the parables, above all the parable of the sower.[6]

As for the Gospel of Thomas, it is an interesting fact that not one of the chreiai I have identified in Q is so used for sayings. Indeed, where there are signs of the chreia genre it is nonetheless greatly attenuated. Pheme Perkins has pointed out that the literary and religious context of Thomas "cannot appreciate the dynamic interaction of the synoptic pronouncement story, since it lacks the imaginative realism of the synoptic tradition" (121). The tendency in this trajectory of the Christian tradition is to assimilate sayings material into a larger dialogue form. Whether or not Thomas is "Gnostic," as Perkins holds in her 1981 article, the dialogue rather than full narrative was the vehicle of the later gnostic communities. Even in Thomas Jesus is not made out to be the referent of his own sayings, but the very reality of divine wisdom speaking from "another world," so to say. The sayings spoken by "the living Jesus" to Didymos Judas Thomas will enable the knower or believer not to experience death if he or she finds their interpretation (Thom. Incipit and 1).

Jesus is not a prophet or sage or storyteller in Thomas, but the very Wisdom that stands against all worldly stories and structures. Orality is evidently much more important for the Thomas community than writing because the true wisdom is always contemporary, coming through the living Jesus. In the actual social setting this means the wisdom has to be mediated by the teachers of the community. Its true, esoteric character could be maintained only through oral interpretation. I infer that the problematic of the Thomas community must have centered in justifying the esoteric wisdom of the living Jesus community as it sought liberation from everything involved in worldly license and authority. Its life setting and theological concerns thus took expression in a very different form from the Q-Gospel tradition.

The theology of a tradition according to the Thomas pattern cannot be written but must be formulated in the interaction of a community with the leader who in the instructional situation represents the "living Jesus." However, the understanding that Jesus "spoke," in the past, to his *alter*, the twin Thomas who stands for the community, means that the tradition and the written text place at least a minimal limit on the contemporizing tendency of the oral situation.

By contrast, the theological pattern of those whose canon is the synoptic Gospels leads inevitably to writing the further *logoi theou* of the tradition, inasmuch as the leaders have to accede in principle to the pastness of the biographical aspect of the gospel form. The paradigm of pastness is writing; this pastness is renewed in the present by further writing. Yet in spite of this "historicizing" tendency, the parabolic aspect of the gospel form gives it a certain contemporary, polyvalent potential.

> To you has been given the mystery of the kingdom of God, but for outsiders everything is in parables.

NOTES

[1] On the occurrences of the title "Son of man" in Q, see Edwards. 39–43. There are six references to the Son of man in the future (11.30, 12:8–9, 12.40; 17.24, 26, 28) and three references to his present activity (7:34, 12:10; 9.58). More than likely Q, at every point, assumes Jesus to be the Son of man. See also Boring. 239–250.

[2] E.g., Lk. 10:30–35 (the Samaritan), 16.1–8a (the Unjust Steward), and Mk. 4:25 par (Having and Not-Having).

[3] I do not know a single unarguable instance in the ancient world of a prophet writing as part of his or her vocation. That prophets related and even dictated oracles and other material to disciples is well known. In the Hebrew Scriptures see Isa. 8:1, 16; 30:8 and Jer. 36. Also Muhammad, known in the Muslim tradition as illiterate, dictated the *ayat* or revelations to companions.

[4] I do not intend to imply that Q was composed in a Hellenistic setting outside of Palestine. It may have been, but it remains an open question as far as I am concerned. We know that not only Jerusalem but also "numerous cities throughout Palestine" were subject to Hellenistic influences (Perrin and Duling: 78). It is difficult to determine whether the primitive Jesus tradition would have already begun, say before 50 C.E., to utilize Hellenistic ideas and genres in the Palestinian Jewish context. Some of the recent studies indicate a relative paucity of chreiai in the Jewish literature from the second century B.C.E. to the second century C.E. (see Vanderkam, Greenspoon, Porton; also Neusner on the "biographical apophthegm" in the Pharisaic-rabbinic

literature). But again, there were Hellenistic influences in Palestine, so the possibility of a Palestinian provenance for the literary formation of Q cannot be excluded.

[5] Although "a greater," *pleion*, is neuter, the sign is the work to be associated with the Son of Man, i.e., Jesus.

[6] See Williams, 1985: 10–11 and 196–199.

WORKS CONSULTED

Alter, Robert
    1985   *The Art of Biblical Poetry*. New York: Basic Books

Beardslee, William
    1970   *Literary Criticism of the New Testament*. Philadelphia: Fortress.

Boring, M. Eugene
    1982   *Sayings of the Risen Jesus: Christian Prophecy in the Synoptic Tradition*. SNTSMS 46. Cambridge: Cambridge University.

Bultmann, Rudolph
    1963   *The History of the Synoptic Tradition*. Trans. John Marsh. New York: Harper and Row. (First pub. in German 1929.)

Butts, James R.
    The Progymnasmata of Theon: A New Text with Translation and Commentary. Philadelphia: Fortress, forthcoming.

Carlston, C. E.
    1980   "Proverbs, Maxims, and the Historical Jesus." *JBL* 99: 87–105.

Crenshaw, James L.
    1967   "The Influence of the Wise Upon Amos." *ZAW* 79: 42–52.
    1969   "Method in Determining Wisdom Influence Upon 'Historical' Literature." *JBL* 88: 129–142.

Dibelius, Martin
    1935   *From Tradition to Gospel*. Trans. B. L. Woolf. New York: Scribner's Sons. (First pub. in German 1919.)

Diogenes Laertius
    1950   *Lives of Eminent Philosophers*. 2 Vols. Trans. H. D. Hicks, Loeb Classical Library. Cambridge and London: Harvard University and Heinemann.

Edwards, Richard
    1976   *A Theology of Q: Eschatology, Prophecy, Wisdom*. Philadelphia: Fortress.

Gerhart, Mary and Russell, Allan
    1984   *Metaphoric Process: The Creation of Scientific and Religious Understanding*. Fort Worth: Texas Christian University.

Greenspoon, Leonard
    1981   "The Pronouncement Story in Philo and Josephus." *Semeia* 20: 73–80.

Hock, Ronald F.
    1986   "General Introduction to Volume 1." Pp. 1–60 in *The Chreia in Ancient Rhetoric*, Vol. 1. The *Progymnasmata*, by Ronald F. Hock and E. N. O'Neil. Atlanta: Scholars Press.

Jacobson, Arland D.
    1982   "The Literary Unity of Q." *JBL* 101: 365–389.

Kelber, Werner H.
    1983   *The Oral and the Written Gospel*. Philadelphia: Fortress.

Kloppenborg, John
    1987   *The Formation of Q*. Philadelphia: Fortress.

Kugel, James L.
    1981   *The Idea of Biblical Poetry*. New Haven: Yale.

Neusner, Jacob
    1971–1972   "Types and Forms in Ancient Jewish Literature: Some Comparisons." *HR* 11: 354–390.

Perkins, Pheme
    1981   "Pronouncement Stories in the Gospel of Thomas." *Semeia* 20: 121–132.

Perrin, Norman and Duling, Dennis C.
    1982   *The New Testament: An Introduction*, 2nd ed. New York: Harcourt Brace Jovanovich.

Philostratus
    1917, 1921   *The Life of Apollonius of Tyana*, 2 vols. Trans. F. C. Conybeare. London and NY: Heinemann and Putnam's.

Porton, Gary G.
    1981   "The Pronouncement Story in Tannaitic Literature: A Review of Bultmann's Theory." *Semeia* 20: 81–99.

Ricoeur, Paul
    1975   "Biblical Hermeneutics," *Semeia* 4.

Robinson, James M.
    1971   LOGOI SOPHON: On the Gattung of Q." Pp. 71–113 in *Trajectories Through Early Christianity*. Eds. H. Koester and Robinson. Philadelphia: Fortress

Talbert, Charles H.
    1977   *What Is A Gospel?* Philadelphia: Fortress.

Tannehill, Robert
    1975   *The Sword of His Mouth*. Semeia Supplements 1. Missoula: Scholars Press.
    1981a   "Introduction: The Pronouncement Story and Its Types." *Semeia* 20: 1–13.

	1981b	"Varieties of Synoptic Pronouncement Stories." *Semeia* 20: 101–119.

Taylor, Vincent
    1933   *The Formation of the Gospel Tradition*. London: Macmillan.

Vanderkam, James C.
    1981   "Intertestamental Pronouncement Stories." *Semeia* 20: 75–82.

Williams, James G.
    1981   *Those Who Ponder Proverbs: Aphoristic Thinking and Biblical Literature*. Sheffield: Almond.
    1985   *Gospel Against Parable: Mark's Language of Mystery*. Decatur and Sheffield: Almond.
    1985/1986   "The Sermon on the Mount As A Christian Basis of Altruism." *Humboldt Journal of Social Relations* 13 (Special Issue): 89–112.
    Forthcoming "The Innocent Victim: René Girard on Violence, Sacrifice, and the Sacred." *RSR*.

APPROPRIATENESS IN THE FORM CRITICISM OF THE TEACHING SOURCE
A Response to James Williams

Martin J. Buss
Emory University

It has been noted that much significant advance comes from cross-fertilization between disciplines; it is, of course, a task of *Semeia* to further such a process. The Hebrew Bible and the New Testament are not very far apart, but for each a specialized circle of scholarship has developed. Once in a while it is helpful to look across the borders between these two disciplines. Williams has done that and so does the present writer in responding to him. One can hope that the observations made and questions raised here may prove useful for future analysis. Williams has already made outstanding contributions to the literary study of the Hebrew Bible and, more recently, to that of the New Testament. Now he has shed light upon the structure of the Teaching Source (Q).

On History

In support of his procedure, one can point out that it is entirely appropriate to give literary attention to a reconstructed source. In recent years, the view has been expressed that a synchronic or structural analysis deals with the final shape of the text. This opinion is just as erroneous as the opposite one, widely held at one time, that an analysis of forms, or "form criticism," deals with the prehistory (specifically, the oral prehistory) of a text. The truth of the matter is that a synchronic analysis (which is formal, or structural, insofar as a pattern can be found) or a formal analysis (which is synchronic except insofar as one believes that there are historical patterns) can operate in relation to any stage of a text. In the study of literature, it is often useful to oscillate between the historical and the formal aspects, with strict priority belonging to neither one of these.[1]

While one may agree with Williams' historical orientation in general, certain details of his analysis can be debated. For instance, he believes that the tradition embodied in Luke 13:25-27 (householder shuts door) had at one time a fuller parabolic form than it does now. In principle such an opinion is legitimate, but his reconstructed form does not fit its literary context and is thus irrelevant to his stated purpose, to examine Q, unless he can show that the history of this fable explains an oddity in the text.[2] Furthermore, while all the stories and parables with which he deals undoubtedly have a history, it is difficult to recover any part of that history without reference to other similar texts. One reason why one can have some (even if not full) confidence in the reconstruction of Q as a background for Luke is the fact that it is not hypothesized purely on the basis of Luke itself, but that Matthew and Mark serve as additional reference points. One can say that the extrapolation of a history, with an anchor on only one side of it, is much more risky than the interpolation of a history linking two or more items.

On Form

The historical question concerning the householder's shutting the door is not unrelated to a formal issue. Luke 13:25–27, with its use of the second person, is not a parable, as normally defined, but a metaphor—perhaps what Williams calls a "near-parable." Similarly, it is difficult to see how Luke 11:24–26 (return of the unclean spirit) is a parable, at least in its present context. This text is rather puzzling and has repeatedly been classified by biblical scholars as a parable. It is likely, however, that in Luke and Q it was taken more or less literally as a warning against complacency after exorcism, and it may have meant this for Jesus as well. Like the reference to a householder shutting the door, it is best taken as a text which combines metaphorical with realistic speech.

In regard to chreiai, there is some vagueness in the definition; that is most likely a problem that Williams shares with other scholars. Analyses of the chreia in rhetorical literature describe it in part as the report of an action or of a short statement attributed to a specific person. In addition, they refer to the action or statement as being apt, or aptly attributed, and to its being effective—either by being useful for life generally or by solving a given problem, such as by wit (see the studies by Hock and O'Neill and Butts, listed by Williams). Obviously, there are elements of unclarity built into such a definition. How short is "short"? How "apt" or "effective" does the statement or action need to be? There is in principle nothing wrong with having a somewhat vague definition, but it follows that classification must necessarily reckon with unclear boundaries. One way of solving the problem, of course, is to make the standards fairly precise; in that case, no doubt, some of the texts now counted as chreiai may have to be classified as "chreia-like," just as certain sayings are classified as "near-parabolic."[3] This is not to imply that Williams is wrong in calling certain texts chreiai, but to point out that the category, as it is applied, is a fluid one, just as virtually all literary genres are fluid to a larger or lesser degree.

In generic analysis, more important than the fixing of boundaries is a recognition of the special thrust of a certain way of approaching or expressing existence. Future work on the chreia in Q will need to pay attention to its typical characteristics, such as its interest in the appropriateness of content or attribution; important steps in this direction are taken in the essay under discussion.[4]

On Form and History: Jesus and the Tradition

The author points out that a chreia in Q can include a parable or parabolic saying.[5] That is not at all surprising, for in the gospel tradition the classifications of chreia and parable do not operate on the same level. A chreia is about Jesus, while a parable is by Jesus (assuming accuracy of attribution). In principle, the report of a short and apt parable is a chreia.

With perceptiveness, Williams recognizes the "biographical impulse" of Q's chreiai, together with a tendency to make Jesus himself the subject of the parables ascribed to him. This tendency represents a shift in focus from Jesus' orientation to that of his followers, but there are, as Williams well observes, important literary continuities between the two levels. These include, in general, metaphoric patterning and, in particular, forms of intensification that emphasize radical commitment.

Interestingly, these literary phenomena constitute not only a continuity between Jesus and Q—so that one can say that Q's representation is "apt" for Jesus—but they also show that there is not a sharp break between the words of Jesus and human life. As Williams properly indicates, metaphoric expressions, as in Jesus' speech, embody a continuity, even while they deal with the Other. In regard to intensification, he rightly points out that this phenomenon describes the metaphoric process in parables on the whole more adequately than does paradox. The notion of paradox too readily sets the divine in opposition to the human, an outlook which does not harmonize well with a certain wisdom quality of Jesus' teaching.[6] While Jesus' words do not express a comfortable acceptance of ordinary social life and underscore a divine operation that is different from the human, they are at the same time not irrational, for it stands to reason that the infinite transcends the finite.

One can observe the presence of different levels of speech. Jesus' speech is primary here. Q's representation is secondary, talking about Jesus. Williams' analysis is tertiary, discussing Q. The present reflection, responding to Williams, represents a fourth step. It is my judgment that the three preceding levels of speech are to a large extent, at least, apt— that of Jesus, in regard to existence; that of Q, in regard to Jesus; that of Williams, in regard to Q.

The notion of aptness allows for a variety of religious, philosophical, and scholarly perspectives, but it goes beyond a purely atomistic, conventional, or fideistic outlook on reality. It is a better standard than that of accuracy, which is externally descriptive. Many may hold that a judgment concerning aptness or appropriateness belongs to neither an academic nor a theological context. It is time, however, for an opinion which accepts the significance of one of the concepts used by ancient rhetorical thought in regard to chreiai.

NOTES

[1] One cannot begin with just one aspect, for a preliminary judgment about both form and history is necessary for any literary examination. After such a preliminary judgment, one can specialize. A number of historical conclusions can be reached without prior intensive formal analysis, and the reverse holds true for formal observations. The first specialization need not reflect the primary interest, for one may want to begin with one side (such as history) in order to be able to end with the other.

[2] His reconstruction of the opening line which he thinks is presupposed by the passage fails to include a justification for the statement that "you taught in our streets" (v. 26). The hypothetical form thus creates, rather than removes, a tension in the text. It is quite possible that behind the text—known to the audience—there stood an image of a householder who closes a door at a certain time of night; but it is also possible that the Lukan passage adapts part of a parable of Jesus (cf. Matt 25:10–12).

[3] The following, it seems, stand near or beyond the border of what the term "chreia" might cover: Luke 3:7–9 (John the Baptist's exhortation—considering that it is no longer than vss. 15–17, not so classified, is it more apt or effective?); Luke 7:24–35 (Jesus' witness to John—assuming that this is apt, is it short?), Luke 11:14–26 (on exorcism—this qualifies well on the whole, but is not exactly short), and Luke 11:45–52 (against lawyers—it may be apt, but is it effective or short?). Depending on where one draws the line, one might also raise questions about passages not identified as chreiai by Williams. Among these, why is Luke 10:1–12 (commissioning the Seventy) not classified as one, or at least as much chreia-like as other texts listed? (Is it because Luke 10:13–16, following this, makes the text too long? But Luke 11:45–52, against lawyers, is preceded by Luke 11:37–44, so that this chreia is even less an independent text.) Why is Luke 10:21–24 (Son thanks Father, blessedness of disciples) not a chreia, or, better, two such? Similar questions can be raised in regard to the rest of the Q materials, except for the longer discourse of Luke 6:20b–49. (Incidentally, large parts of the remaining gospel materials are, at least loosely, chreiai, since a chreia can report simply an action.) Part of the problem may lie in the fact that Williams has used Tannehill's survey of pronouncement stories for deriving his list of chreiai. According to Tannehill, this category "overlaps with the chreia", presumably it is not identical with it. As far as the length of a saying is concerned, Theon mentions an exercise of expanding a chreia; thus longer words attributed to Jesus may be considered expanded chreiai.

[4] Williams relates Q chreiai to different subtypes of pronouncement stories as developed by Tannehill. These subtypes bear a resemblance to the subtypes of chreiai as outlined by Theon and others (see Hock and O'Neil), they give, however, more attention to content (such as correction or commendation) than do the others. Not all of Williams' classifications are indisputable. Luke 7:1–10 (the centurion's dying slave) is hardly a correction story, and Luke 9:57–58 (the seriousness of following Jesus—first part of 9.57–62) is more a warning than a correction. Yet, again, categories may be considered fluid.

[5] In view of the reflections presented earlier, one may need to make adjustments in detail. Thus Luke 11:14–26 (return of the unclean spirit) and Luke 13:25–27 (householder shutting the

door), which Williams regards as parables contained in chreiai, probably are not parables, at least in their present form. On the other hand, many of the reports of parables may need to be classified as chreiai depending on one's standards of brevity and aptness, since one has to distinguish between the report of a parable (in Q and Gospels) and the parable spoken by Jesus.

[6] In a recent work on aphorisms in Proverbs, Williams (1981) rightly points out that Israelite wisdom includes a recognition both of (significant) order and of (relative) disorder. The latter is not to be disregarded, even for wisdom, but a one-sided emphasis on paradox hardly does justice to Jesus' words.

WORKS CITED

Williams, James
    1981   *Those Who Ponder Proverbs*. Sheffield: Almond.

APHORISM IN DISCOURSE AND NARRATIVE

John Dominic Crossan
DePaul University

ABSTRACT

The article studies how a triadic aphorism, *Ask, Seek, Knock*, interacts creatively with both narrative and discourse contexts within the Jesus tradition.

The tradition began with a triadic aphorism, now visible only in Q. *Ask* could be taken literally, *Seek* could be taken either literally or metaphorically, but *Knock* could only be taken metaphorically. It was *Knock*, therefore, that dropped out most readily from the transmission. This happened everywhere after Q, except for *Gos. Thom.* 94. *Ask* and *Seek* then could easily be collapsed into one another, either as *Seek* in the *Gospel of Thomas* and *Dialogue of the Savior,* or as *Ask* in the Johannine tradition. After that preliminary diminution, the expansion could begin. In those Nag Hammadi gospels the *Seek* saying was enlarged as *Seek, Find, Marvel, Reign, Rest* into, respectively, a theological program and a structural outline. In the Johannine tradition the *Ask* saying was developed theologically over several versions in the Farewell Discourse of John's Gospel, but this was later sharply counterbalanced by the cautionary warnings it received in John's First Epistle.

This powerful heremeneutical creativity stems not only from the triadic serenity of its unconditional assertion but possibly also from its origins with Jesus himself.

INTRODUCTION

The purpose of this paper is to observe the creative interaction within the Jesus tradition between an aphorism and, on the one hand, a narrative context, and, on the other, diverse discourse contexts. The chosen example is the *Ask, Seek, Knock* saying which appears within the following text sets: (1) Mark 11:24 = Matt 21:22; (2) Q/Luke 11:9–10 = Q/Matt

7:7–8; (3) *Gos. Thom.* 2,92,94; P Oxy 654.5–9; *Gos. Heb.* 4; *Dial. Sav.* 9–10; (4) John 14:13–14; 15:7, 16; 16: 23, 24, 26; 1 John 3:21–22; 5:14–15 (Crossan, 1983: 95–104). To facilitate the discussion I have given all those texts in Appendix 1.

Obviously, the present case is but one instance from the large repertoire of the Jesus tradition and is hardly a broad enough data-base from which to derive conclusions. I consider it, however, to be a preliminary probe, a first sighting shot at a problem. As such it can only propose conclusions to be tested on further and fuller materials.

There are two major distinctions and two main conclusions which appear from studying the above text sets. A first distinction is that between aphoristic narratives or discourses and dialectical narratives or discourses. In the former case, the saying preceded the setting, the aphorism generated its narratival and/or discursive context. In the latter case, saying and setting were always a unit in the transmission. The present paper will not be able to compare two such situations but I would suggest, for example, that we are dealing with a dialectical rather than an aphoristic narrative in the *Caesar and God* unit in (1) Mark 12:13–17 = Matt 22:15–22c = Luke 20:20–26; (2) Papyrus Egerton 2, fragment 2, lines 43–59; (3) *Gos. Thom.* 100. Nevertheless, although this paper will be concerned only with an aphoristic situation, that distinction is presumed throughout the discussion. A second distinction is that between an aphoristic narrative and an aphoristic discourse. In the latter case, the aphorism generates a dialogue or discussion, a context of question and answer, of comment and response, of request and reaction. In the former case, which may also, of course, contain dialogue, there is at least some minimal connection with historical or geographical situation, some minimal localization upon this earth. Thus, for example, while aphoristic discourse could take place in heaven or on earth, aphoristic narrative must take place on earth.

After those distinctions, there are also two conclusions. A first conclusion is that a narrative context or a discursive context can each supply a clear and definite hermeneutical reading of the aphorism encapsulated by them. That appears in comparing those twin processes as they work on the *Ask, Seek, Knock* saying. A second conclusion is more tentative and requires much more discussion. In the present instance, at least, the aphoristic narrative trajectory is much less developed than is the aphoristic discourse one. For the former line there is only the one case in Mark 11:24 = Matt 21:22. But the latter line proliferates like a luxuriant vine. Is this difference just accidental or idiosyncratic? Or does the narrative setting inhibit further and diverse interpretations in a way that the discourse setting does not? If that were to prove correct, it might help explain why the catholic tradition chose only narrative gospels as a way to control what appeared to it as the excessive hermeneutical freedom of the gnostic tradition's discourse gospels.

A. APHORISM AND NARRATIVE

The first example is the presence of the aphorism in Mark 11:24 = Matt 21:22

1. Markan Context.

(a) Wider Context.
The wider Markan context is given in Table 1. What is most significant is how Mark deliberately framed the *Temple's Symbolic Destruction* with the divided parts of the *Cursed Fig Tree* unit. He put the cursing before it and the withering afterwards and he signalled the importance of those frames by concluding the former one with "and his disciples heard it" in 11:14b and beginning the latter one with "and Peter remembered" in 11:21a. "In the context of Mark's framing design the fig tree stands for the temple, and the disaster which befell the tree illustrates what occurred to the temple" (Kelber: 102). One would also conclude that there are things about the Temple that the disciples need to "hear" and "remember." This becomes clearer by Mark 13 where Mark carefully distinguishes between Jesus' prophecy of the Temple's physical destruction in 13:14–23 and his own parousiac presence in 13:24–28. Jesus did not say, Mark insists, that he himself would physically destroy the Temple. Or, in other words, there should have been no expected conjunction between destruction and parousia. Such claims belong to false Christs and false prophets, as in 13:5–6, 21–23, to perjured witnesses, as in 14:56–59, and to mocking unbelievers, as in 15:29–30.

Mark's Temple theology and Mark's framing technique are not of concern to either Matthew or Luke. The former has the withering follow immediately on the cursing, and the latter simply omits the entire incident.

Table 1

	Mark	Matthew	Luke
Cursed Fig Tree	11:12–14, 20–21	21:18–19	
Temple's Symbolic Destruction	11:15–17	21:12–13	19:45–46
Opposition from Authorities	11:18–19		19:47–48
The Children's Confession		21:14–17	
Aphoristic Cluster	11:20–25	21:21–22	

Table 2

			πίστιν	
11:22				
11:23	ἀμὴν λέγω ὑμῖν		πιστεύῃ ὅτι	ἔσται
11:24	λέγω ὑμῖν	προσεύχεσθε	πιστεύετε ὅτι	ἔσται
11:25		προσευχόμενοι		

(b) Narrower Context.

The narrower Markan context is within the aphoristic cluster of 11:22–25. There are four units linked together verbally in this cluster, as indicated in Table 2. That word linkage was inserted by Mark himself in the process of creating this unified cluster. (1) In 11:22, he prefaced the cluster with his own "Have faith in God," thereby inaugurally underlining the dominant theme of "faith" and he may possibly have intended a verbal frame between the ἔχετε of 11:22 and 11:25. (2) In 11:23, the conjunction of "faith" and "moving a mountain" may have been already present, if a version of this saying lies behind Paul's comment about having "all faith, so as to move mountains" in 1 Cor 13:2 (correcting Crossan, 1983: 157–58). Mark's contribution was to double this emphasis into "does not doubt in his heart but believes," which is a characteristically Markan "double statement: negative-positive" (Neirynck: 89–94). He also took the given phrase λέγω ὑμῖν without ὅτι from 11:24 and added it into 11:23 but now rephrased in Markan fashion as ἀμὴν λέγω ὑμῖν with ὅτι (Pryke: 73–74). (3) In 11:24, he added in the theme of "prayer" from its given position in 11:25.

Matt 21:22–22 drastically curtailed his linkage by having no parallel to Mark 11:15 here, a single inaugural ἀμὴν λέγω ὑμῖν in 21:21, and a double rather than a triple mention of "faith" as frames in in 21:21a and 21:21b.

2. Markan Text.

When the Markan redactional mentions of "faith" and "prayer" from the preceding and succeeding 11:22–23 and 11:25 are removed, the pre-Markan content of 11:24 would be "I tell you, whatever you ask, it will be yours." This is a version of the *Ask, Seek, Knock* aphorism but with only the first of the three stichs present. Those redactional additions, however, tell us exactly how Mark reads the aphorism. It concerns asking in prayer and asking with faith.

This version of the aphorism in Mark 11:24 has been well integrated into its immediate discursive context in 11:22–25 but also into the narrative context of the cursed Fig/Temple. In this context the proverbial expression about moving a mountain, known in terms of peace and unity from *Gos. Thom.* 48 and 106 and in terms of faith from 1 Cor 13:2, is specified directly as "*this* mountain" (Mark 11:23) that is, the Temple mount within sight of Jesus and his disciples as "they came from Bethany" (Mark 11: 12, 20). In this narrative context the *Ask [Seek, Knock]* aphorism, already discursively interpreted towards prayer and faith, is pointed against the Temple. It is not just Jesus who can destroy the Fig/Temple but any believer who *asks* with faith in prayer.

The narrative of the cursed Fig and destroyed Temple in Mark 11:11–17 is not a simple aphoristic narrative, that is, a narrative built up as hermeneutical development of the *Ask, Seek, Knock* aphorism. Rather the reverse. The aphorism has been taken into a context which both changes it and in return changes that context.

B. APHORISM AND DISCOURSE

That first case involved an interaction between the *Ask, Seek, Knock* aphorism and a narrative context. All the other cases involve interaction between the *Ask, Seek, Knock* saying and divergent discourse contexts.

1. Q/Luke 11:9–19 = Q/Matt 7:7–8.

In this instance the aphorism must be seen not only within its immediate Q context but also against the background of several similar complexes in Q.

(a) Q Complexes.

The *Ask, Seek, Knock* saying has its immediate context in Q/Luke 11:9–13 = Q/Matt 7:7–12 and this has a tripartite structure common to several such Q complexes (see also Piper), as indicated in Table 3.

(1) Form. I have kept the adjective "aphoristic" for all three parts of this structure because the aphoristic mode of the opening saying(s) is maintained throughout each complex. I distinguish, in other words, between an *aphoristic commentary* and a *commentary on an aphorism*. Each is commentary but the former is in aphoristic style while the latter

Table 3

TEXTS ELEMENTS	LOVE [sun, rain]	PRAYER [bread/stone] [fish/serpent] [egg/scorpion]	FEAR [sparrows]	ANXIETY [birds, lilies]
APHORISTIC SAYING(S)	Luke 6:27b-31 = Matt 5:44b, 39b-42; 7:12	Luke 11:2-4, 9-10 = Matt 6:9-13; 7:7-8	Luke 12:2-5 = Matt 10:26-28	Luke 12:22 = Matt 6:25a
APHORISTIC COMMENTARY	Luke 6:32-35 = Matt 5:45-47	Luke 11:11-12 = Matt 7:9-10	Luke 12:6-7 Matt 10:29-30	Luke 12:23-28 = Matt 6:25b-30
APHORISTIC CONCLUSION	Luke 6:36 = Matt 5:48	Luke 11:13 = Matt 7:11	Luke 12:8-9 = Matt 10:32-33	Luke 12:29-31 = Matt 6:31-33

is not. The distinction may be graphically illustrated by comparing *Gos. Thom.* 22 with *2 Clem.* 12:2–5. The former reads (Robinson: 121):
(a) "Jesus saw infants being suckled.
(b) He said to his disciples, 'These infants being suckled are like those who enter the Kingdom.'
(c) They said to Him, 'Shall we then, as children, enter the Kingdom?'
(d) Jesus said to them, 'When you make the two one, and when you make the inside like the outside, and the outside like the inside, and the above like the below, and when you make the male and the female one and the same, so that the male not be male nor the female female; and when you fashion eyes in place of an eye, and a hand in place of a hand, and a foot in place of a foot and a likeness in place of a likeness; then will you enter [the Kingdom].''

I consider (d) to be an *aphoristic commentary* on (b) since it retains the same aphoristic style and could be cited all by itself as a separate aphorism of Jesus. Indeed, this is exactly what happens to it in *2 Clem.* 12:2–5, which reads (Lake: 1. 148–49):
"For when the Lord himself was asked by someone when his kingdom would come, he said: 'When the two shall be one, and the outside as the inside, and the male with the female neither male nor female.' Now 'the two are one' when we speak with one another in truth, and there is but one soul in two bodies without dissimulation. And by 'the outside as the inside' he means this, that the inside is the soul, and the outside is the body. Therefore, just as your body is visible, so let your soul be apparent in your good works. And by 'the male with the female neither male nor female' he means this, that when a brother sees a sister he should have no thought of her as female, nor she of him as male. When you do this, he says, the kingdom of my Father will come."

This is *commentary on an aphorism* and it is a masterly job of defusing a potentially troublesome saying. It does not, however make any attempt to maintain the aphoristic modality of the saying itself. On the other hand, all the Q complexes noted above keep within aphoristic style. This of course makes it much more difficult to decide how much Q itself has added to these complexes. We cannot automatically presume that Q simply created the aphoristic commentaries and aphoristic conclusions in those clusters. For example, the aphoristic commentary in Q/Luke 12:23–28 = Q/Matt 6:25b–30 is also found in P Oxy 655.i.1–17 although not in the corresponding *Gos. Thom.* 36, and the aphoristic conclusion in Q/Luke 12:8–9 = Q/Matt 10:32–33 is also known from Mark 8:38 = Luke 9:26; 2 Tim 2:12b; Rev 3:5b.

(2) Content. First, each complex begins with one or more aphoristic sayings which serve as opening admonition. Second, there is an aphoristic commentary or supporting argument composed of rhetorical

questions and examples from natural or human experience. The logic of these arguments is as follows:

LOVE: as God does in nature, so should you do.
PRAYER: as you do, how much more will God do.
FEAR: as God does for nature, how much more for you.
ANXIETY: as God does for nature, how much more for you.

It should be noted that the heart of this second element is not just an argument from nature but an argument from *how God operates* in nature and, in the last three cases, it follows a "how much more" logic. Third, there is an aphoristic conclusion or intensified recapitulation. God is always mentioned in this conclusion and apparently as "Father": so, certainly, in Luke 6:36 = Matt 5:48; Luke 11:13 = Matt 7:11, Luke 12:30 = Matt 6:32, and, possibly, in Luke 12: 8–9 ("angels of God") = Matt 10:32–33 ("Father").

(b) Q Context.

In Luke 11:1–13 the sequence of units is as follows:
The Lord's Prayer in Q/Luke 11:2–4 = Matt 6:9–13,
Friend at Midnight in Luke 11:5–8 alone,
Ask, Seek, Knock in Q/Luke 11:9–10 = Q/Matt 7:7–8,
Good Gifts in Q/Luke 11:11–13 = Q/Matt 7:9–11.

Jacobson (215–22) has proposed that Luke 11:2–4 and 9–13 was a consecutive unit in Q. He noted that Luke 11:11–13 is somewhat remarkable since it seems to defend against the idea that the Father might give bad things to petitioners. But such an idea could well arise from the last petition of *The Lord's Prayer* which requests the Father not to lead us into temptation. So, for example, the epistle of James warns "Let no one say when he is tempted, 'I am tempted by God'; for God cannot be tempted by evil and he himself tempts no one" (1:13). Instead "every good endowment and every perfect gift is from above, coming down from the Father of lights with whom there is no variation or shadow due to change" (1:17). This seems very plausible and it means that the aphoristic commentary and aphoristic conclusion in Q/Luke 11:11–13 extends backwards not only to the *Ask, Seek, Knock* saying in Q/Luke but also to *The Lords' Prayer* in Q/Luke 11:2–4.

One can be relatively certain that the Q context extends to Q/Luke 11:2–4, 9–13 = Q/Matt 6:9–13; 7:7–11. But *The Lord's Prayer* in Luke 11:2–4 is followed by the metaphorical saying about the importunate *Friend at Midnight* in 11:5–8. Although there is no Matthean parallel for this unit one could still ask if it might have been in Q.

In terms of form, Luke 11:5–8, which precedes the *Ask, Seek, Knock* saying, is a rhetorical question beginning with "which of you" just like those in Q/Luke 11:11–12 = Q/Matt 7:9–10 which follow it. But it is also a much more awkward syntactical construction, as if the second-person question was added not too smoothly to an original third-person saying.

In terms of content it implicitly presumes a situation of knocking and opening ("the door is now shut") and it explicitly speaks of obtaining bread. That is, in terms of context, it continues the theme of bread from Q/Luke 11:4 and exemplifies the theme of knocking/opening to follow in Q/Luke 11:9c, 10c.

It seems most likely, therefore, that Luke and not Q located the *Friend at Midnight* metaphor in this most appropriate situation. He adapted its opening format to the following rhetorical questions albeit not with total success. Such a Lukan addition might also explain a minor difference between the Q versions of Matthew and Luke for the *Good Gifts* section. In Luke 11: 11–12 the food is fish/serpent and egg/scorpion but in Matt 7:9-10 it is bread/stone and fish/serpent. After he added another mention of bread in 11:5–8, Luke could have changed the Q sequence of bread/stone and fish/serpent, as in Matt 7:9–10, into that of fish/serpent and egg/scorpion just to vary the emphasis on bread.

(c) Q Text.

The *Ask, Seek, Knock* aphorism has: (1) exactly the same 24 Greek words in Luke 11: 9–10 and Matt 7:7–8; (2) a three-stich saying repeated twice in Luke 11:9 = Matt 7:7 and Luke 11:10 = Matt 7:8; (3) the first triad in the plural but the second in the singular; (4) the former with the imperative ("ask . . . seek . . . knock") followed by two future passives and one future active ("it will be given . . . you will find . . . it will be opened") but the latter with the participle followed by two present actives and one future passive ("receives . . . finds . . . it will be opened") so that both triads end with the same verbal form ("it will be opened"); (5) the first triad with second-person emphasis and the latter one with third-person emphasis; (6) the only content change in that the first stich uses "given" in the former triad but "receives" in the latter one.

It is possible to argue that Q knew one version of this aphorism from received tradition and created a second one for present emphasis. The second version would presumably be that Q creation because it has the Q preference for participial openings in aphorisms (Crossan, 1983: 173–77). But the presence, to be seen below, of both imperative and participial, singular and plural formats elsewhere in this unit's transmission makes it even more likely that the twin versions represent the separate records of two performancially different oral versions combined here by Q.

Q placed the two performancially varied versions of the *Ask, Seek, Knock* aphorism in Luke 11:9–10 at the conclusion of *The Lord's Prayer* in Luke 11:2–4 as an almost ecstatic assurance on its efficacy. This was followed by the commentary and conclusion on *Good Gifts* in Luke 11:11–13 which reflected back on all that preceding complex. Later Luke himself inserted the *Friend at Midnight*, appropriate in both form an content, into the cluster at 11:5–8.

2. *Gos. Thom.* 2,92,94; *Gos. Heb.* 4; *Dial. Sav.* 19–20.

(a) *Gospel of Thomas* (CG 11, 2).

Davies has noted, concerning this Nag Hammdi tractate, that "the theme of seeking and finding underlies much of Thomas and constitutes one of its most obvious unifying themes," that "the theme of seeking and finding is also one of the most common of all motifs in Wisdom literature," so that the theme has "a background which is solidly within the Wisdom tradition" (37).

This theme is found not only as the combination of "seeking" and "finding" in *Gos. Thom.* 2,92,94, and 38 and 107, but also as "finding" alone in 1,27,49,58,76,80,90.

(b) *Gos. Thom.* 94.

All three verbs of the *Ask, Seek, Knock* aphorism were present twice in Q, but only the first verb, *Ask*, was present in Mark. In *Gos. Thom.* 94 it is the last two verbs that are present: "Jesus [said], 'He who seeks will find, and [he who knocks] will be let in.'"

Behind those changes one begins to sense two separate dynamics at work: (1) on the one hand, the elimination of *Knock* presumably because it is the most metaphorical of the three verbs; (2) on the other, the collapsing of *Ask* and *Seek* into each other with the concomitant choice of either *Ask* or *Seek* as the only verb left in the aphorism. Both factors were at work behind Mark 11:24, so that *Ask, See, Knock* becomes *Ask*, but only the second factor was at work behind *Gos. Thom.* 94, so that *Ask, Seek, Knock* becomes *Seek* and *Knock*. This was probably facilitated in Coptic where the same verb means both "to ask" and "to seek" (Crum: 569a).

It should also be noted that the version of the aphorism in *Gos. Thom.* 94 is relatival and singular rather than imperative and plural.

(c) *Gos. Thom.* 92.

This version of the aphorism combines both the transmissional tendencies just mentioned in omitting the *Knock* section and collapsing *Ask* and *Seek* into *Seek*. But it then expands with an aphoristic commentary: "Jesus said, 'Seek and you will find. Yet, what you asked Me about in former times and which I did not tell you then, now I do desire to tell, but you do not inquire about it.'"

The aphorism takes on negative connotations here just as it does in *Gos. Thom.* 38: "Jesus said, 'Many times have you desired to hear these words which I am saying to you, and you have no one else to hear them from. There will be days when you will look for Me and will not find Me.'"

The background for both *Gos. Thom.* 38 and 92 is the two-stage situation in Proverbs 1:20–28. First, says Wisdom in 1:24, "I have called and you refused to listen," just as in *Gos. Thom.* 38. Second, says Wisdom in 1:28, "Then they will call upon me, but I will not answer; they will seek me diligently but will not find me," just as in *Gos. Thom.* 92. One must listen to Wisdom-Jesus when she speaks because, if one does not, it will be too late to seek her later.

(d) Gos. Thom. 2; P Oxy 654.5–9; *Gos. Heb.* 4.

The Coptic text of *Gos. Thom.* 2 has: "Jesus said: 'Let him who seeks continue seeking until he finds. When he finds, he will become troubled. When he becomes troubled, he will be astonished, and he will rule over the All." This is an incomplete four-stich saying in climactic sequence:

(1) seeking-finds
(2)   finds-be troubled,
(3)   be troubled-be astonished
(4)   [be astonished]-rule.

The Greek version of this saying in P Oxy 654.5–9 is badly damaged and lacks the second half of each line (Grenfell & Hunt, 1904a:3–5, 1904b:11–14). Fitzmyer's (371) restoration and translation reads: "[Jesus says,] 'Let him who see[ks] not cease [seeking until] he finds and when he finds, [he will be astounded, and] having been [astoun]ded, he will reign an[d having reigned], he will re[st].'"

The restoration is assisted by two quotations from Clement of Alexandria (Fitzmyer: 372–73). The first one in *Stromateis* 2.9.45 reads: "As also it stands written in the Gospel of the Hebrews: He that marvels shall reign, and he that has reigned shall rest." The second one in *Stromateis* 5.14.96 reads: "He that seeks will not rest until he finds; and he that has found shall marvel; and he that has marvelled shall reign; and he that has reigned shall rest" (Hennecke & Schneemelcher: 1.164). That gives a complete and satisfactory four-stich climactic saying:

(1) seek-find
(2)   find-marvel
(3)   marvel-reign
(4)   reign-rest.

It also fits with the emphasis on "rest" as one's goal in *Gos. Thom.* 50,51, 60,86,90 (Vielhauer). Clearly, then, that is the correct four-step climax for this aphorism. The best explanation for the Coptic's doubling of the "marvel" element as "be troubled" and "be astounded" is some sort of translational misunderstanding (Marcovich: 56–58).

In *Gos. Thom.* 2, and thus at the start of that gospel, the *Ask, Seek, Knock* aphorism is both reduced to its *Seek* element and then expanded climactically from *Seek* to *Find* to *Marvel* to *Reign* to *Rest*. Several of those themes reappear like musical motifs throughout the gospel: *Seek/Find* in 38,92,94,107; *Find* in 1,27,49,58,76,80,90; and *Rest* in 50,51,60,86,90.

(e) *Dialogue of the Savior* (CG 111,5).

Helmut Koester and Elaine Pagels have proposed for this Nag Hammadi tractate that: (1) the basic source of the document is a sequence of brief but seried dialogues between Jesus and three disciples, Judas, Mariam, and Matthew, which constitutes about two thirds of the text and into which other sections have been inserted; (2) the tradition of the sayings in the basic source resembles that in the *Gospel of Thomas* but at a later stage of that tradition's development; (3) the formation of the dialogues in the basic source resembles that in the Gospel of John but at an earlier stage of such a formation's development (Pagels: 66–68; Emmel: 1–16).

More important for my present concern is their suggestion that the saying, from *Gos. Thom.* 2, about seeking/finding/marvelling/ruling/resting, represents the structural *ordo salutis* for the entire *Dialogue of the Savior* (Pagels: 68, 71, 74; Emmel: 7).

The original or basic source comprises, in Emmel's numbering, *Dial. Sav.* 4–24, 19–20, 25–34a, 41–104a. One of the sections inserted into that sequence is an apocalyptic vision in 36–40 (Emmel: 2). The *ordo salutis* appears in those units as follows: *seek* in 9–10; *seek/find* in 19–20; *marvel* ("were amazed") in 37; *rule* in 49–50; *rest* in 64–68. It thus appears that the function of the inserted apocalyptic vision is to allow for the mention of *marvel* ("were amazed").

It is against that total background that the quotation of the abbreviated *Ask,Seek,Knock* aphorism in *Dial. Sav.* must be taken. The text reads (Emmel: 58–59): "And [let] him who [. . .] seek and find and [rejoice]," with possibilities for restoring the "[. . .]" given as either "[knows]" or "[is chosen]"

In the *Gospel of Thomas* the sequence of *seeking/finding/marvelling/ruling/resting* was announced in an inaugural position as *Gos. Thom.* 2. Thereafter, several of those themes reappeared throughout the document. But they were never elevated to the status of a sequential and structural outline. This is what happens in the *Dialogue of the Savior.* "As a commentary on *Gos. Thom.* 2, the dialogue explains the disciples' place in the eschatological timetable: although they have sought and found and marvelled, their rule and their rest will only come in the future. At present they still bear the burden of the body and of earthly labor; Mary, who recognizes this, received the highest praise" (Emmel: 7).

3. John 14:13–14; 15:7,16; 16: 23,24, 26; 1 John 3:21–22; 5:14–15.

In the Johannine tradition the triadic *Ask, Seek, Knock* aphorism is reduced to one stich by omitting the *Knock* element and collapsing the first two elements into *Ask*. The aphorism appears with different forms and contents in the Farewell Discourse of John 13–17 and also in the First Epistle (see Brown, 1970:633–636).

(a) John 14:13–14.

"*Whatever you ask in my name, I will do it*, that the Father may be glorified in the Son; *if you ask anything in my name, I will do it*." In form, this is a doubled version, once with relative and once with conditional opening. In content, it is clearly Jesus that responds to the asking, but for the glory of the Father. The emphatic doubling recalls, of course, that found in Q for the entire triad.

(b) John 15:7.

Within the image of Jesus as the true vine, this version appears: "If you abide in me, and my words abide in you, *ask whatever you will, and it shall be done for you*." In form, this has an imperative opening for the aphorism. In content, it leaves the respondent hidden within the passive "it shall be done" (by God?), but also mentions the glory of the Father in the next verse: "By this my Father is glorified, that you bear much fruit, and so prove to be my disciples" (15:8).

(c) John 15:16.

"You did not choose me, but I chose you and appointed you that you should go and bear fruit and that your fruit should abide; so that *whatever you ask the Father in my name, he may give it to you*" In form, we are back to the relative opening as in 14:13. In content, it is the Father who is asked in Jesus' name and it is the Father who responds.

(d) John 16:23–27a.

"In that day you will ask nothing of me. Truly, truly, I say to you, *if you ask anything of the Father, he will give it to you in my name*. Hitherto you have asked nothing in my name; *ask, and you will receive*, that your joy may be full. I have said this to you in figures; the hour is coming when I shall no longer speak to you in figures but tell you plainly of the Father. In that day you will *ask in my name*, and I do not say to you that I shall pray to the Father for you; for the Father himself loves you . . ." In form, this gives a conditional and imperative opening for two versions of the saying in 16:23b,24b, and then concludes with an incomplete version in 16:26a.

In terms of formal openings, therefore, and whether by design or accident, we have a triadic sequence of relatival, conditional, and imperative openings in 14:13,14; 15:7 and the same triadic sequence again in 15:16; 16:23–24. In terms of content, there is a deliberate progression, not from asking in Jesus' name to asking without Jesus' name, but from asking Jesus and so the Father indirectly, to asking the Father directly. In 14:13–14, it is apparently Jesus who must respond to the disciples' request but by 16:23–27 it is the Father who responds directly.

(e) 1 John 3:21–22.
"Beloved, if our hearts do not condemn us, we have confidence before God; and *we receive from him whatever we ask*, because we keep his commandments and do what pleases him." In form, this is relatival. In content, however, it is quite different from any of the versions in John's gospel. There is no mention of Jesus or his name. And, although there was already a warning "if" present in John 15:7, there is much more basic one here: "because we keep his commandments and do what pleases him." I interpret this precisely as a caution against a too ecstatic understanding of the *Ask* sayings in the Gospel. Brown has proposed that the secessionists from the Johannine community against whom 1 John was written "gave *no salvific importance to ethical behavior* and that this stance flowed from their christology" (1979:128–129; see also 1982:80–81). This version of the *Ask* aphorism insists that any guaranteed response is dependent on fundamental ethical obedience.

(f) 1 John 5:14–15.
"And this is the confidence which we have in him, that *if we ask anything* according to his will *he hears us*. And if we know that *he hears us* in *whatever we ask*, we know that *we have obtained the requests made of him*." In form, this version, moving from ask to hear to obtain, combines both conditional and relatival elements. In content, once again, it has a warning phrase, "according to his will," just as did the preceding 3:21–22. And, although, the Son of God is mentioned in 5:13, "there is little doubt that the 'him' is God," in 3:21 (Brown, 1982:609). It is God, the God of will and commandment, who answers those who ask. The rhapsodic assurance of response in the Gospel receives another cautionary condition in the Epistle.

In summary, then, the tradition began with a triadic aphorism, *Ask, Seek, Knock*, now visible only in Q. *Ask* could be taken literally, *Seek* could be taken either literally or metaphorically, but *Knock* could only be taken metaphorically. It was *Knock*, therefore, that dropped out most readily from the transmission. This happened everywhere after Q, except for *Gos. Thom.* 94. *Ask* and *Seek* could then easily be collapsed into one another, either as *Seek* in the *Gospel of Thomas* and *Dialogue of the Savior*, or as *Ask* in the Johannine tradition. In those Nag Hammadi gospels the *Seek* saying was expanded as *Seek,Find,Marvel,Reign,Rest* into, respectively, a theological program and a structural outline. In the Johannine tradition the *Ask* saying was developed theologically over several versions in the Farewell Discourse of John's Gospel but this was later sharply counterbalanced by the cautionary warnings it received in John's First Epistle.

CONCLUSION

There is one final question. Why was this aphorism so generatively powerful and so powerfully popular in early Christianity? Sieber (81) has cited parallels to the *Seek* element from Epictetus ("Seek and you shall find") and to the *Knock* element from the Rabbis ("When he knocks, the door is opened to him"). It is not that the content is so clearly profound. The elements in themselves could be taken as rather bland proverbs. They are simple injunctions to effort, to the action necessary as prelude to success. And if each element could be a bland proverb, their triadic assertion simply establishes a triply bland complex. What, then, so grasped the early Christian imagination that it generated the tremendous richness and diversity of this saying's transmission? Put another way, did that saying so express the enabling vision of Jesus himself that it flared like lightning across the tradition?

In a forthcoming article in another *Semeia* volume I argue the following position, a position which can only be summarized here (Crossan, 1988). I note that diversity in interpreting the historical Jesus seems to increase not only among contemporary scholars but also the farther back we go into the early sources and traditions themselves. I therefore propose that the first principle for historical Jesus research should be the criterion of adequacy: that is originally from Jesus which best explains this earliest and latest hermeneutical multiplicity. My conclusion is that Jesus proclaimed the unmediated presence of the divine to the human and as a direct, immediate, and concomitant result, the unmediated presence of the human to the human. In that forthcoming article my interpretation is tested through the aphorisms in Q/Luke 6:29– 30 = Matt 5:39b-42 and *Gos. Thom.* 95, as well as their dependent versions in *Did.* 1:3–4 and Justin, *1 Apol.* 15;10; 16: 1–2. These are seen as aphorisms of the historical Jesus, as metaphors for the unmediated presence of human beings to one another. Their paradoxical nature reflects the paradoxicality of the divine and human immediacy which is the Kingdom envisaged by Jesus.

I understand the transmissional fecundity of the *Ask, Seek, Knock* saying against that same background. It was not a bland proverbial trilogy because it expressed the central vision of Jesus himself. It challenged the hearers to accept something far from banality, something which was theologically paradoxical, institutionally provocative, and politically subversive, namely, the immediacy of the divine to the human.

WORKS CONSULTED

Brown, Raymond E.
    1966   *The Gospel according to John I–XII*. AB 29. Garden City, NY: Doubleday.
    1970   *The Gospel according to John XIII–XXI*. AB 29A. Garden City, NY: Doubleday.
    1979   *The Community of the Beloved Disciple*. New York: Paulist Press.
    1982   *The Epistles of John*. AB 30. Garden City, NY: Doubleday.

Crossan, John Dominic
    1983   *In Fragments. The Aphorisms of Jesus*. San Francisco, CA: Harper & Row.
    1988   "Divine Immediacy and Human Immediacy: Towards a New First Principle in Historical Jesus Research." In the *Semeia* volume on *Jesus and the Rejected Gospels*, ed. Charles W. Hedrick.

Crum, W. E.
    1939   *A Coptic Dictionary*. Oxford: Clarendon Press.

Davies, Stevan L.
    1983   *The Gospel of Thomas and Christian Wisdom*. New York: Seabury Press.

Emmel, Stephen, Helmut Koester, Elaine Pagels
    1984   *Nag Hammadi Codex III,5: The Dialogue of the Savior*. NHS 26. Leiden: Brill.

Fitzmyer, Joseph A.
    1974   "The Oxyrhynchus Logoi of Jesus and the Coptic Gospel according to Thomas." Pp. 355–433, in his *Essays on the Semitic Background of the New Testament*. SBLSBS 5. Missoula, MT: Scholars Press (= London: Chapman, 1971). [Updated revision of article in *TS* 20 (1959) 505–560].

Grenfell, Bernard Pyne, & Arthur Surridge Hunt
    1904a   *The Oxyrhynchus Papyri*. Part IV. London: Oxford University Press.
    1904b   *New Sayings of Jesus and Fragment of a Lost Gospel from Oxyrhynchus*. London: Frowde.

Hennecke, E., & W. Schneemelcher, eds.
    1963–65   *New Testament Apocrypha*. 2 vols. Philadelphia: Westminster Press.

Jacobson, Arland Dean
    1978   *Wisdom Christology in Q*. Ph.D. dissertation, Claremont Graduate School. Ann Arbor, MI: University Microfilms International.

Kelber, Werner H.
    1974   *The Kingdom in Mark*. Philadelphia: Fortress Press.

Lake, Kirsopp, trans. and ed.
    1912–13   *The Apostolic Fathers*. LCL 24–25. 2 vols. Cambridge, MA: Harvard University Press.

Marcovich, M.
    1969   "Textual Criticism on the Gospel of Thomas." *JTS* 20:53–74.

Neirynck, Frans
    1972   *Duality in Mark*. Contributions to the Study of the Markan Redaction. BETL 31. Leuven: Leuven University Press.

Pagels, Elaine, & Helmut Koester
    1978   "Report on the Dialogue of the Savior." Pp. 66–74 in *Nag Hammadi and Gnosis*. Papers read at the First International Congress on Coptology (Cairo, December 1976). Ed. R. McL. Wilson. NHS 14. Leiden: Brill.

Piper, Ronald A.
    1982   "Matthew 7,7–11 par. Luke 11,9–13. Evidence of Design and Argument in the Collection of Jesus' Sayings": Pp. 411–18 in *Logia. Les paroles de Jésus—The Sayings of Jesus*. Mémorial Joseph Coppens. BETL 59. Leuven: Leuven University Press [Colloquium Biblicum Lovaniense, 19–21 August 1981].

Pryke, E. J.
    1978   *Redactional Style in the Marcan Gospel*. A Study of Syntax and Vocabulary as Guides to Redaction in Mark. SNTSMS 33. New York: Cambridge University Press.

Robinson, James M., gen. ed.
    1977   *The Nag Hammadi Library in English*. Ed. Marvin W. Meyer. New York: Harper & Row.

Sieber, John H.
    1966   *A Redactional Analysis of the Synoptic Gospels with regard to the Question of the Sources of the Gospel according to Thomas*. Ph.D. dissertation, Claremont Graduate School. Ann Arbor, MI: University Microfilms International.

Vielhauer, P.
    1964   "ANΠAYCIC: Zum gnostischen Hintergrund des Thomasevangeliums." Pp. 281–299 in *Apophoreta*. Festschrift für Ernst Haenchen zu seinem siebzigsten Geburtstag am 10. Dezember 1964. BZNW 30. Eds. W. Eltester & F. H. Kettler. Berlin: Töpelmann.

APPENDIX 1.
TEXTS & CONTEXTS OF *ASK, SEEK, KNOCK* APHORISM USED IN THE ARTICLE.

(1) **Matt 7:7–8**
    7 "Ask, and it will be given you; seek, and you will find; knock, and it will be opened to you. 8For every one who asks receives, and he who seeks finds, and to him who knocks it will be opened."

(2) **Matt 21:20–22**
    20 When the disciples saw it they marveled, saying, "How did the fig tree wither at once?" 21And Jesus answered them, "Truly, I say to you, if you have faith and never doubt, you will not only do what has been done to the fig tree, but even if you say to this mountain, 'Be taken up and cast into the sea,' it will be done. 22And whatever you ask in prayer, you will receive, if you have faith."

(3) **Mark 11:20–25**
    20 As they passed by in the morning, they saw the fig tree withered away to its roots. 21And Peter remembered and said to him, "Master, look! The fig tree which you cursed has withered." 22And Jesus answered them, "Have faith in God. 23Truly, I say to you, whoever says to this mountain, 'Be taken up and cast into the sea,' and does not doubt in his heart, but believes that what he says will come to pass, it will be done for him. 24Therefore I tell you, whatever you ask in prayer, believe that you have received it, and it will be yours. 25And whenever you stand praying, forgive, if you have anything against any one; so that your Father also who is in heaven may forgive you your trespasses."

(4) **Luke 11:9–10**
    9 "And I tell you, Ask, and it will be given you; seek, and you will find; knock, and it will be opened to you. 10For every one who asks receives, and he who seeks finds, and to him who knocks it will be opened."

(5) **John 14:12-14**
12"Truly, truly, I say to you, he who believes in me will also do the works that I do; and greater works than these will he do, because I go to the Father. 13Whatever you ask in my name, I will do it, that the Father may be glorified in the Son; 14if you ask anything in my name, I will do it."

(6) **John 15:1-7**
1"I am the true vine, and my Father is the vinedresser. 2Every branch of mine that bears no fruit, he takes away, and every branch that does bear fruit he prunes, that it may bear more fruit. 3You are already made clean by the word which I have spoken to you. 4Abide in me, and I in you. As the branch cannot bear fruit by itself, unless it abides in the vine, neither can you, unless you abide in me. 5I am the vine, you are the branches. He who abides in me, and I in him, he it is that bears much fruit, for apart from me you can do nothing. 6If a man does not abide in me, he is cast forth as a branch and withers; and the branches are gathered, thrown into the fire and burned. 7If you abide in me, and my words abide in you, ask whatever you will, and it shall be done for you."

(7) **John 15:12-17**
12"This is my commandment, that you love one another as I have loved you. 13Greater love has no man than this, that a man lay down his life for his friends. 14You are my friends if you do what I command you. 15No longer do I call you servants, for the servant does not know what his master is doing; but I have called you friends, for all that I have heard from my Father I have made known to you. 16You did not choose me, but I chose you and appointed you that you should go and bear fruit and that your fruit should abide; so that whatever you ask the Father in my name, he may give it to you. 17This I command you, to love one another."

(8) **John 16:20-28**
20"Truly, truly, I say to you, you will weep and lament, but the world will rejoice; you will be sorrowful, but your sorrow will turn into joy. 21When a woman is in travail she has sorrow, because her hour has come; but when she is delivered of the child, she no longer remembers the anguish, for you that a child is born into the world. 22So you have sorrow now, but I will see you again and your hearts will rejoice, and no one will take your joy from you. 23In that day you will ask nothing of me. Truly, truly, I say to you, if you ask anything of the Father, he will give it to you in my name. 24Hitherto you have

asked nothing in my name; ask, and you will receive, that your joy may be full.

25 "I have said this to you in figures; the hour is coming when I shall no longer speak to you in figures but tell you plainly of the Father. 26In that day you will ask in my name; and I do not say to you that I shall pray the Father for you; 27for the Father himself loves you, because you have loved me and have believed that I came from the Father. 28I came from the Father and have come into the world; again, I am leaving the world and going to the Father."

(9) 1 John 3:21–22

21 Beloved, if our consciences have nothing to charge us with, we can be sure that God is with us

22and that we will receive at his hands whatever we ask. Why? Because we are keeping his commandments and doing what is pleasing in his sight.

(10) 1 John 5:14–15

14 We have this confidence in God; that he hears us whenever we ask for anything according to his will. 15And since we know that he hears us whenever we ask, we know that what we have asked him for is ours.

(11) POxy654 2

(2) [Jesus said], "Let him who seeks continue [seeking until] he finds. When he finds, [he will be amazed. And] when he becomes [amazed], he will rule. And [once he has ruled], he will [attain rest]."

(12) GThom 2

(2) Jesus said, "Let him who seeks continue seeking until he finds. When he finds, he will become troubled. When he becomes troubled, he will be astonished, and he will rule over the All."

(13) GThom 92

(92) 1Jesus said, "Seek and you will find. 2Yet, what you asked Me about in former times and which I did not tell you then, now I do desire to tell, but you do not inquire after it."

(14) GThom 94

(94) Jesus [said], "He who seeks will find, and [he who knocks] will be let in."

140   Semeia

(15) **DialSav 9–12**
(9) His [disciples said, "Lord], who is it who seeks, and [. . .] reveals?"
(10) [The Lord said . . .], "He who seeks [. . .] reveals . . . [. . .]."
(11) [Matthew said, "Lord, when] I [. . .] and [when] I speak, who is it who . . . [. . .] . . . who listens?"
(12) [The Lord] said, "It is the one who speaks who also [listens], and it is the one who can see who also reveals."

(16) **DialSav 19–20**
(19) And Matthew [asked him] "[. . .] . . . took . . . [. . .] . . . it is he who . . . [. . .]."
(20) The Lord [said], "[. . . stronger] than . . . [. . .] . . . you . . . [. . .] . . . [. . .] . . . to follow [you] and all the works [. . .] your hearts. For just as your hearts [. . .], so [. . .] the means to overcome the powers [above] as well as those below [. . .]. I say to you, let him [who possesses] power renounce [it and repent]. And [let] him who [. . .] seek and find and [rejoice]."

(17) **GHeb 4a**
(4a) As also it stands written in the Gospel of the Hebrews:
He that marvels shall reign, and he that has reigned shall rest.
(Clement, *Stromateis* 2.9.45).

(18) **GHeb 4b**
(4b) To those words (from Plato, *Timaeus* 90) this is equivalent:
He that seeks will not rest until he finds; and he that has found shall marvel; and he that has marvelled shall reign; and he that has reigned shall rest. (Clement, *Stromateis* 5.14.96).

APHORISM AND NARRATIVE: A RESPONSE TO JOHN DOMINIC CROSSAN

by Robert C. Tannehill
Methodist Theological School in Ohio

In his article "Aphorism in Discourse and Narrative," John Dominic Crossan presents a detailed analysis of the aphorism *Ask, Seek, Knock* through its various transformations both inside and outside the canon. His analysis includes a number of keen observations. At the edge of his discussion are some references to the relation between this aphorism and narrative. I would like to carry this discussion further, even though my comments must be tentative.

In his conclusion Crossan asks, "Why was this aphorism so generatively powerful and so powerfully popular in early Christianity?" Its power is puzzling, for the elements of this triple aphorism seem to be "rather bland proverbs." Crossan attributes its power not to its content or form but to the fact that it expresses "the enabling vision of Jesus," a vision of the "unmediated presence" of the divine to the human and the human to the human.

The question of why this aphorism was so powerful could have been addressed by discussing the socio-historical context of those who used it. Crossan does not choose this route. However, he feels that it is necessary to appeal to something beyond the "rather bland" aphorism itself. He places the aphorism in a larger context, the context of "the enabling vision of Jesus." It would be good to be more specific, provided we have some data to guide us. The attempt to be more specific may also enable us to say something about this aphorism's relation to narrative.

Crossan believes that the context of the aphorism in Q is preserved in Luke 11:2–4, 9–13 (the saying about the friend at midnight in 11:5–8 being a Lukan addition). If this is so, the aphorism *Ask, Seek, Knock* immediately followed the Lord's Prayer in Q. This is not the only indication of a connection between this aphorism and the Lord's Prayer. Crossan asserts that Mark 11:24 is another version of the aphorism, to which the evangelist has added references to faith and prayer. We should note that Mark 11:24 is immediately followed by an indication of the kind of petition to which a favorable answer is promised: "Whenever you stand praying, forgive if you have anything against someone, in order that your Father in the heavens might also forgive you your trespasses." This is a hortatory version of the prayer for forgiveness in the Lord's Prayer, and its relation to 11:24 suggests that forgiveness is one of the most important things one should ask for. The connection of 11:25 with the Lord's Prayer is indicated not only by the tie between forgiving others and being forgiven but also by the reference to God as the disciples' father, which is rare in Mark (this is the only clear instance). Matt 6:14–15, an instruction that comes directly after the Lord's Prayer and resembles Mark 11:25, also supports the connection of the Markan verse with this prayer.

Thus there seems to be some evidence in both Q (according to Luke) and Mark that the promise of a favorable response to the one who asks was connected to the Lord's Prayer, perhaps especially to the petition for forgiveness. Thus the petition of the prayer that suggests a requirement—receiving forgiveness requires forgiveness of others—would have been supported by an exhortation and a promise: "Ask, and it will be given you." This connection would explain why it was not necessary at first to add cautionary conditions to the promise, as we find later in I John 3:21–22 and 5:14–15. The content of the asking is being guided by the content of the Lord's Prayer.

At the end of his introduction, Crossan tentatively suggests that a narrative setting may inhibit diverse interpretations in a way that a discourse setting does not and that narrative gospels serve to control what the catholic tradition regarded as excessive hermeneutical freedom. Since Crossan prizes the "fecundity" demonstrated by diverse uses of a saying, I take his remarks to express a negative attitude toward narrative settings. However, discourse contexts also control interpretation (e.g., the Q context in Luke 11:2–4, 9–13 applies the aphorism to prayer); it is not clear that discourse contexts are less inhibiting than narrative contexts. Furthermore, "control" can increase rather than limit hermeneutical power. Especially if the elements of the aphorism themselves are "rather bland proverbs," a controlling context may be useful in guiding interpretation away from superficial applications to applications that are more profound, with a resulting increase in the saying's power. In the case of *Ask, Seek, Knock*, the power of the aphorism depends on the importance of what one is seeking and the lack of obviousness to the promise that one will indeed receive it. There is also the danger of turning God into the servant of human selfishness, which a controlling context may help the aphorism to avoid.

The aphorism *Ask, Seek, Knock* may have a closer connection with narrative than Crossan recognizes. In studying a different genre, Norman

Petersen made this interesting observation: "While letters are not narratives they nevertheless refer to narrative worlds" (Petersen: 9). Indeed, events of a narrative world "are re-emplotted in the composition of letters, usually with clear rhetorical significance" (Petersen: ix). Petersen has discovered a way of relating letter to narrative. It might also be possible to relate aphorism to narrative.

Note, first of all, that "ask and it will be given you" links two events, asking and being given, and implies that the first leads to the second. When converted from potential to actual events, this sequence is the abstract core of a multitude of plots which move from expressed desire to fulfillment of that desire. Everything from love stories to heroic adventures can be plotted on this core. It is abstract, but not completely abstract, for one possibility has been eliminated: the non-fulfillment of the desire. At least one choice in determining the outcome of events has been made, which is sufficient to establish a minimal plot.

Since this plot is so abstract, the asking and seeking are easily trivialized. This contributes to the blandness that Crossan notes. In an earlier work Crossan made a suggestion that may lead us further. He said, "If a proverbial expression is recalled and remembered in the tradition, it may well be that its continuance is due to contextual or circumstantial data that render it memorable" (Crossan: 35–36). These contextual or circumstantial data may imply a narrative. It may be possible to escape the trivial if we can discover significant narratives into which the aphorism fits. Since Crossan is not primarily concerned with the narratives of Matthew and Luke, I also will ignore these narrative contexts and seek a narrative context behind the gospels.

We might first ask some general questions: 1) In what narrative context would it be useful to speak this aphorism? 2) In what narrative context could one say this with conviction? Note that Q presents a triple aphorism using the second person plural imperative (αἰτεῖτε, etc.), followed by a triple aphorism using singular participles (ὁ αἰτῶν, etc.). This trebling provides more rhetorical emphasis than would be necessary if the speaker were not working against resistance. This remains true even if we assume that Luke 11:9 and 10 are originally separate versions of the same aphorism. The phrase "everyone who asks" seems particularly emphatic. It evidently intends to completely eliminate the possibility of a negative response. Such a statement is not supported by ordinary experience, for many people ask and do not receive. A special context seems to be assumed.

To return to the two questions: the repetitive emphasis on asking, seeking, and knocking would be most useful when told to people who are the victims of stories that lead to resignation and constricted hopes. These promises could be stated with greatest conviction in a narrative context supporting faith in an untapped reservoir of benevolent power that is now available, though previously hidden, i.e., in the context of a narrative concerning the coming of God's reign.

Finally, these observations must be combined with my previous remarks concerning the relation of this aphorism to the Lord's Prayer. If this connection is original, we can be more specific about the narrative context of this urgent exhortation and promise. Its context is a story that leads one to trust in a redeeming power, now manifest in the release of sins. Its use would be to address persons who do not fully share the speaker's conviction that this blessing is available for the asking.

WORKS CONSULTED

Crossan, John Dominic
    1983   *In Fragments: The Aphorisms of Jesus*. San Francisco: Harper & Row.

Petersen, Norman R.
    1985   *Rediscovering Paul: Philemon and the Sociology of Paul's Narrative World*. Philadelphia: Fortress Press.

NARRATIVE, HISTORY, AND GOSPEL

Adela Yarbro Collins
University of Notre Dame

In their correspondence with contributors, the editors formulated a series of questions to stimulate thinking on the topic of this volume. One of the questions raised concerned the ways in which generic analysis may assist the reader in arriving at a critical interpretation of the Bible in general and the gospels in particular. A recurring issue in the history of the generic analysis of the Bible has been the problem of myth and history. The editors, in explicating their second question for contributors (see Preface), asked whether these are fundamentally genre terms and whether they presuppose the same or different sociocultural contexts, experiences and structures of meaning. Another question raised was whether gospel is a genre representing a form or modification of biography in late classical antiquity or whether it is a completely new form. The editors went on to ask, if it is not history in any conventional sense, why it has been read as such (and continues to be).

My reading of the essays in this volume and the questions raised by the editors have led me to reflect on the origin of the Gospel of Mark. Why did its author choose the narrative mode and what is the genre of this particular narrative? How did the author's choice of the narrative mode relate to the choices of other writers, such as the authors of the Sayings Source (Q) and the Gospel of Thomas? What are the theological implications of these choices?

A tentative conclusion drawn by J.D. Crossan in his essay is that the narrative setting of the aphorism inhibits further and diverse interpretations, whereas the discourse setting fosters the growth of variants and new interpretations (Introduction). Crossan suggests that this may explain why "the catholic tradition" granted authority only to narrative gospels. The representatives of this tradition wished to control what they saw as the excessive hermeneutical freedom of the "gnostic tradition's" gospels in discourse form. Crossan does not claim in this essay that this explanation applies also to the actual composition of the narrative gospels. If it could be shown that the intention of the author of Mark in choosing narrative was something else, then the question would arise whether the reason for that choice was a major factor in the preference for that mode in the emerging catholic tradition.

The intention of the (at least implied) author of Mark may be addressed by returning to the issue of myth and history. History may be seen as one type of a larger mode of expression, namely, narrative. The shift from chronicle to history is generally seen to coincide with the move from list to narrative. Myth is also a narrative genre. The distinction between myth and history is not always an easy one to make. Both seem to be highly perspectival and relative terms. Originally, the Greek word *mythos* meant simply a word or speech, like *logos*, without any distinction of truth or falsehood. According to Liddell-Scott-Jones, some writers began to use *mythos* in the sense of fiction as opposed to historic truth, for which the term *logos* was then reserved, as early as the fifth century B.C.E. (e.g., Pindar). The underlying questions are what is real and what is true. Another issue is the status of fiction. Is it less true and real than history, or does it simply have different kinds of truth and reality? Does not historiography involve fiction or at least bias in the selection and interpretation of data? It is clear that individuals and intellectual traditions have disagreed over what is *mythos* (fiction, legend, myth) and what is *logos* (historical or ontological truth or fact). How the distinction is made depends on the world-view of the individual or intellectual tradition involved. My working hypothesis is that some individuals and intellectual traditions, ancient and modern, will include some elements under the rubric of history which other individuals and intellectual traditions, ancient and modern, would consider to be mythic. Thus, the modern interpreter must be very careful in categorizing ancient texts as myth or history to keep point of view in mind. The presence of elements in a text which a particular modern interpreter would call mythic does not exclude the possibility that the author of the text intended to write history.

Related to this discussion of myth and history is the distinction made by Charles Talbert in his essay between ancient history and biography: "whereas history focuses on the distinguished and significant acts of great men in the political and social spheres, biography is concerned with the essence of the individual" (55). Talbert's highlighting of the variety in ancient "lives" is very important, especially his observation that they need not cover the individual's entire life, be in chronological order or show development, may or may not use myth (reference to the divine or supernatural world and extraordinary deeds), and may have any one of a variety of social functions.

Talbert concludes that some of the Christian gospels either belong to the genre ancient biography or at least are very similar to it, namely, the four canonical gospels, the Gospel of Peter, and the Childhood Gospel of

Thomas. The basis for this conclusion is that their aim is to set forth the essence of their subject, a significant person, Jesus Christ. All employ myth as do some of the non-Christian lives. The reason for the use of myth in both the Christian and non-Christian texts is, according to Talbert, that the subject is a hero or founder. Myth is used to characterize the events which brought the community into being as sacred time.

Taking the Gospel of Mark as an example, one may question whether the main purpose of the work is to depict the essence or character of Jesus Christ. This may be seen as a secondary aim: the identity of Jesus and the proper understanding of that identity is a major theme in the gospel. But it is doubtful that this is the primary or controlling aim of the work. Similarly, Jesus as one who suffers and dies serves as a model for the readers who live threatened by persecution. The theme of the true tradition is also implicitly present: the true followers of Jesus are those, for example, who interpret properly both the parables (chapter 4) and the prophecy of Jesus (chapter 13). At most, however, these are secondary aims or functions of the gospel.

This discussion leads to the question why Mark utilized narrative in general and ancient biography in particular in producing his text. Talbert, following Achtemeier, concludes that "the canonical gospels were written to give a controlling context to individual Jesus traditions so they could not be misinterpreted as easily as was possible without such a context" (63). This explanation is grounded in a similar way to that of Crossan, mentioned above, with the addition of evidence from Paul.

Talbert elaborates this point by arguing that the canonical gospels were written in connection with a sort of synthetic compromise to resolve the diversity among early Christians, some of whom emphasized the presence of God in Jesus as miracle-worker, others as teacher of morality, etc. The canonical gospels in his view then are not so much kerygma as the result of a conscious and deliberate attempt to gather up the various insights into the presence of God in Jesus and into discipleship in a comprehensive and balanced composition, including miracles, teaching, and death on the cross. Since the major aim of the evangelists was to avoid misunderstanding and reductionism in the presentation of the significance of Jesus, no great theological weight should be placed on the choice of genre.

This thesis is plausible to the extent that it accurately reflects the fact that the genre of the canonical gospels is complex (it should probably be called a *host genre;* see Aune: 80). It also credibly describes one of the functions of these gospels.

But one must question whether the main purpose of the Gospel of Mark, for example, is to depict the essence or character of Jesus Christ. I would like to suggest that the primary intention of the author of Mark *was to write history.* The objection could be raised that Mark is not history because Jesus was not generally recognized as a great man in the first century C.E. E. Auerbach, however, in his book *Mimesis,* has shown that part of the novelty of the Gospel of Mark is that it writes of ordinary (i.e., non-elite) people as if they were great and thus fit subjects of literature. The presence of miracles and other mythic elements in the narrative do not refute the hypothesis, since for the author of Mark these elements were simply true and real, i.e., they were part of his worldview. It is true that Mark focuses on the person of Jesus. In light of that focus, it is instructive to review what Talbert has said about works in which history and biography approach one another. In Sallust's *Catiline,* the aim is not to set forth the character of Catiline, but to narrate political events with which he was associated. This work is historical even though it concentrates on an individual. My hypothesis is that Mark is analogous. Mark focuses on Jesus and his identity, not in the interest of establishing his character or essence, but in order to write a particular kind of history, which may be called a narration of the course of the eschatological events, which are yet to be completed (thus the open-endedness of the ending). The gospel is not only "the good news that God was present in Jesus for our salvation"; it is the good news that God has acted and is acting in history to fulfill the promises of Scripture and to inaugurate the new age. The gospel begins with a reference to Jesus Christ [the Son of God], not out of interest in his character, but to present him as God's agent. This interpretation is supported by the presentation of John the Baptist as the fulfillment of prophecy (1:2–4; also cf. 9:13 with Malachi 4:5–6 [MT 3:23–24]). Although the Gospel of Mark is not history in the rational, empirical Greek sense or in the modern critical sense, it seems to have been such in an eschatological or apocalyptic sense and in the intention of the author.

Thus Mark was written, not only to avoid reductionism or to provide a controlling context for the Jesus tradition, but to place the various genres of the Jesus tradition into a historical framework. The genres of this tradition were integrated into a historical narrative of a particular type which became a host-genre to those smaller forms. The result was that the various insights into "the presence of God in Jesus" were incorporated into a vision of the significance of God's activity in Jesus for history and the world. If this hypothesis is correct, the question is still open why "the catholic tradition" granted authority only to the narrative gospels (see the reference to Crossan above). It may be that the representatives of this tradition shared with Mark the conviction that Christian faith is deeply related to history and that the non-narrative gospels were perceived as lacking that relation.

If the author of Mark intended to write a historical work, this intention is rightly perceived by those who today continue to read Mark as history. The problem of interpretation is acute for those who are self-conscious about the fact that they do not share the world-view presupposed by Mark. What is the significance of the hypothesis stated above for such people? The theological significance of the hypothesis is the implication that a modern interpretation of Mark ought to aim at achieving the broad scope of the vision of the gospel which is expressed in the choice of the historical genre in its apocalyptic mode. This scope may be achieved by focusing on an aesthetic experience of Mark as parabolic narrative if the implications of the "parable" are conceived broadly in keeping with the roots of narrativity. Crites (cited by Talbert) has suggested "that narrativity has it roots in the fact that the individual self has a developmental history, that the individual is part of multiple communities that have histories, and that both individuals and communities are intertwined with an environment that also has a developmental history."

The broad scope of the vision of Mark may be resymbolized by interpreting Mark as the foundation document of a particular community, if it is seen as a community with a message and purpose of cosmic and universal significance. In other words, the apocalyptic-historical vision of Mark is best expressed through a theological perspective which attempts to embrace the universe as God's creation with a "developmental history" and a destiny.

A number of other interesting issues have been raised by the essays. In her discussion of Segovia's review of recent research on 1 John, Mary Gerhart states with approval that Segovia did not make contemporaneity with historical context a decisive factor in his conclusion about the genre of 1 John. The decisive factors were rather novelty and "the power that the genric designation has for illuminating the text" (38). These remarks raise the question of what criteria are appropriate for determining the genres of ancient works. It is clear that one should not simply adopt ancient designations of genre, because often the same designation is used for texts of widely differing types or genres. The issue seems to be whether one should start with, take seriously, and as far as possible remain within the thought-world and intention of the ancient designations. The underlying question is, of course, the aim of the interpreter. One must ask *for whom* is a genric designation illuminating and *what* does it illuminate? It would seem that more than one approach is legitimate. If the focus is on the interaction between the text and the interpreter, the historical context need not set limits to the range of possible designations of genre or meanings. Such a focus may be taken by a literary critic or by a historical critic. A historical critic may take such a view in the effort to complement what the ancients said about their genres with the modern scholar's inductive and analytical study of the extant texts. Alternatively, the focus may be on the intention of the (at least implied) author and on the response of the early generations of readers. In such a case, the ancient designations of genre and explicit reflection on genres and meaning will set the boundaries for the process of interpretation. Confusion and scholarly controversy may be minimized if interpreters are explicit and clear about their aims.

In the last section of her essay, Gerhart takes a position which I find congenial. She argues that theological language should not *substitute* itself for the Biblical text. On the other hand, genric analysis and the language of the various Biblical genres, such as narrative, should not *replace* theological language and genres, such as argument, analogy and the treatise. I agree that Biblical theologians should understand themselves to mediate between genres. Gerhart goes on to say that "the historical is a constructed configuration of elements and, like authorial intention, is not normative for an adequate understanding of the text" (41). The underlying question is what constitutes an adequate understanding of the text. As a historical critic, I am inclined to give more weight to the original historical context of the text. This context cannot and should not totally determine all subsequent meaning and use of the text. But if, as I am convinced, all meaning is context-bound, the original context and meaning have a certain normative character. I suggest that Biblical theologians are not only mediators between genres. They are also mediators between historical periods.

Werner Kelber's conclusion, that the identity secrets in the Gospel of Mark exert pressure on the narrative by enhancing the momentum toward revelation, is insightful. His argument that the Gospel of Mark presents itself not "as a patron of secrecy, but rather as an ardent demythologizer of the myth of esoteric secrecy" (11) is ingenious but ultimately unconvincing. In spite of the tension between secrecy and proclamation in Mark, secrecy is never totally repudiated and the disciples never become total outsiders. The theme of secret revelation to a few is taken up again and presented positively in chapter 13. In spite of Jesus' foreknowledge (within the narrative) of Peter's denial and the flight of the disciples, he promises to go before them to Galilee (14:27–31). This promise is repeated even after the narration of the disciples' failure (16:7).

Kelber's hypothesis, that the identity secrets and esoteric secrecy converge "in order to make room for a rather different epiphany inside narrative," namely the cross (13), is intriguing. But the deferral of the "luminous Christ" beyond narrative time may be explained as a pointed way of expressing an intense expectation of the coming of the risen Christ as Son of Man (13:24–27).

Kelber is certainly right in highlighting the first passion-resurrection prediction (8:31) and the confession of the centurion (15:39). But the interpretation of the crucifixion scene is problematic. It is not obvious that the cry of Jesus on the cross (15:34) implies that he dies forsaken by God or that he suffers the absence of God. On the contrary, as a citation of Psalm 22:1, the cry is not an expression of despair, but a prayer, a plea for help. The question "Why have you forsaken me?" is a narratively plausible intensification of the earlier prayer, "remove this cup from me" (14:36). It is important to note that Psalm 22 expresses a bitter lament, but one in the context of an ongoing trust and confidence in God. Thus it is doubtful that the climactic epiphany of Mark is "epiphany as the darkness of God's absence" (17). Kelber is right in saying that this epiphany does not imply that revelation is transparent, but not in the way that he means. Strangely, he makes no comment on 15:38. This description of the tearing of the curtain of the temple is intercalated between Jesus' death and the centurion's response to it. The tearing of the curtain is clearly symbolic, but its meaning is not transparent. The unveiling of the Holy of Holies is an epiphanic commentary on the death of Jesus whose significance is veiled.

I find Talbert's view of genre as "a literary grouping tied to a particular time, place, and cultural milieu" (54) appropriate and illuminating for the function of the gospels in their earliest historical contexts. His method, which combines sensitivity to what the ancients said about their genres with the modern scholar's inductive study of the extant texts, is also appropriate to a historical study of genres. A problem that has to be faced, however, is that explicit reflection on genre by early Jewish and early Christian writers is very rare. Thus, the theories on genre of Greco-Roman writers must be used with caution in the analysis of the genres of early Jewish and early Christian texts.

The task James Williams has set himself in his essay is an interesting and important one, the investigation of the relation of the pronouncement story and the parable in Q as a way of understanding how the sayings tradition of Jesus came to be framed in a biographical narrative. The study would be more helpful if it had greater conceptual clarity about parables and related forms of speech. Williams seems to imply that every use of figurative language is a parable, a near-parable, or parabolic. If the study aims to examine two specific genres and their significance, it needs to distinguish clearly between one of these (the parable) and genres related to it (the similitude, the metaphorical aphorism, etc.). If clear genre distinctions are not important for the study, the terminology should make this clear.

The method employed is synchronic. Synchronic studies of the individual gospels have demonstrated the fruitfulness of such an approach. The existence of the Sayings Source may be taken as given for exploratory purposes. One may then attempt to demonstrate the fruitfulness of a synchronic study of this hypothetical text. The aim of this essay, however, to understand how the sayings tradition of Jesus *came to be* framed in a biographical narrative, seems to require that the synchronic approach be complemented by diachronic methods. Form-critical studies show a process taking place on the micro-level which is similar to the process which Williams argues for on the macro-level.

From a form-critical point of view, two of the passages listed as pronouncement stories seem to be secondary accommodations to that genre. In other words, they seem not to have originated as pronouncement stories, but as small sayings collections which were given a narrative setting at a relatively late stage (3:7–8 and 7:24–35). This phenomenon seems to be different from the one in which additional sayings material is attached to an earlier pronouncement story (e.g., 11:29–32). In the former process, sayings which originally had no narrative or historical context were provided with such. This diachronic analysis provides support for Williams' thesis.

I agree with Williams' criticism of Kloppenborg's thesis that Q's formative stratum was an instructional genre. It is unnecessary to conclude that clusters of an identifiable genre or mode (wisdom material) represent a different stratum of redaction from clusters of another genre or mode (prophetic and apocalyptic material). By the first century C.E., indeed long before, the use of wisdom and prophetic/apocalyptic forms or genres in the same document was commonplace (see Yarbro Collins).

Williams' criticism of Boring's thesis is also well taken. The evidence about the historical and social context of much of the sayings tradition is insufficient to support it.

Williams is right in saying that Q contained both pronouncement stories and parables. It is not correct to conclude that Q is therefore a parable-chreia collection. This designation ignores the fact that Q contained other material as well, notably prophetic and apocalyptic sayings (see Yarbro Collins).

Williams argues that Q, at least in the form in which it was taken over by the communities in which the gospels of Matthew and Luke were written, did have a significant narrative element. This observation is a welcome complement to recent work on the Sayings Source. This narrative element is manifest in the pronouncement stories, in the tendency to give small sayings collections a narrative setting, and in the temptation narrative. The sequence of teaching of John the Baptist, temptation of Jesus by Satan, and teaching of Jesus (with allusions to healing activity) is, one might say, on the verge of being a plot. How one weighs this observation depends on whether one is looking at Q as a still photograph or as a moving picture. If one looks at Q as a moving picture, one can say that, before it was incorporated into Matthew and Luke, it had moved closer to the literary form of Mark than the Gospel of Thomas ever did in its developmental history. If one looks at Q as a still photograph, however, the claim that Q is "considerably closer to . . . Mark, than to the Gospel of Thomas (110)" is less persuasive. Thomas, after all, has some dialogues, which provide a modicum of a narrative setting for some of the sayings material. More importantly, Q, as far as we know, did not yet have an actual narrative framework. Thus it still must be seen generically as a collection of individual units. In that sense it is closer to Thomas in genre than to Mark. The view of Q as a moving picture, is however, the more adequate one historically speaking. It did become part of narrative gospels in its developmental history.

The questions and suggestive answers offered by the editors and other contributors to this volume amply show both the accomplishments and promise of generic/genric studies of the gospels. This response has attempted to show that, whatever tension there may appear to be between literary- and historical-critical methods, the two approaches are complementary.

WORKS CITED

Aune, D.
    1986   "The Apocalypse of John and the Problem of Genre." *Semeia* 36: 65–96.

Auerbach, E.
    1953   *Mimesis: The Representation of Reality in Western Literature*. Princeton: Princeton University Press.

Yarbro Collins, A.
    forthcoming   "The Son of Man Sayings in the Sayings Source." Festschrift for Joseph A. Fitzmyer. Edited by Maurya P. Horgan and Paul J. Kobelski. New York: Crossroad.

ANTERIORITY, AUTHORITY, AND SECRECY: A GENERAL COMMENT

Frank Kermode

It will surprise no one that my remarks begin with a discussion of secrecy, primarily with reference to Werner Kelber's paper on "Narrative and Disclosure." However, these topics appear to be quite intimately related to the investigations of Charles H. Talbert, Mary Gerhart and James Williams (especially in his earlier study of Mark (Williams, 1985)) and to the whole matter of genre, on which I shall say something towards the end of this paper.

Revealing and Reveiling
Kelber claims that narrative is more concerned with overcoming secrecy than with enforcing or increasing it, though he allows that the very business of revealing entails the possibility of "reveiling." Still, it is intuitively acceptable that a narrative of which at least part of the purpose is to affirm the authority of a particular version of events and teachings, and the authority of a particular person, will as far as possible be produced *en clair*. The real difficulty (to which the extremely various interpretations of the gospel narratives testify) is that narrative as a cure for secrecy has inevitable side effects that may be as troublesome as the ailment.

I think this is the point at which I swerve away from a very persuasive paper. "It is well to remember," says Kelber, "that in the history of story there was no such thing as narrative reticence before we knew what narrative plenum was." We might possibly amend this to read "before we imagined we knew . . ." (3). But even that is not enough, for it is not the case that the discovery of narrative reticence had to wait upon the development of even a myth of full closure. The *not saying* of something (or the pretending not to say it) is an ancient rhetorical device, and it has always had its reflection at the higher level of narrative rhetoric. Modern analysts of the David narratives like to speculate about the exact motive of the King in urging Uriah to go home to bed with Bathsheba; the author is reticent. Vergil gets a famous effect by not explicitly telling the reader why *tu Marcellus eris* is a pathetic prophecy, though it would take a very dull reader to miss the point. And so on.

It is a consideration of some importance that such reticences are a long-established part of the repertoire of narrative. Often enough the reticence is intended to increase the impact of what it purports to conceal while making it inevitable that a properly informed reader will at once, and with the added emotion attendant on discovery, recognize what is really meant. But sometimes this very activity of the reader, whether under authorial direction or not, may cause him to be deceived. The whole genre of detective fiction (as distinct from crime novel) depends upon an assumption that readers are capable of making both correct and incorrect inferences. Hence the presence in such stories (though not only there) of what Barthes called *leurres*—lures or traps for the reader (Barthes: 82). Since the text certainly contains *leurres* of all sorts, some meant to be concealed from all but the cleverest, the reader may very well invent them even when they are not intended. He will discover enigmas; he cannot be prevented from doing so. This is a characteristic given specialized development in detective stories, but it is also a characteristic of narrative in general; so it will also be exploited by writers who advertize some enigmatic features and not others, leaving a large area of indeterminacy, of uncontrolled enigmatic potential. Hence it may be to a greater degree than Kelber suggests that the very activity of revealing entails what he calls reveiling. Narrative may confer authority on what is narrated, but it may also substitute one sort of obscurity or enigma for another.

Anteriority

I shall return to this point, but first it is necessary to make an obvious remark about Kelber's inescapable presumption of a prenarrative stuff which is inherently secret; it is what the revelatory function of narrative exposes. There is a sense in which this is always so, though it may not be quite the sense Kelber intends. The primordial stuff may not be a body of doctrine which, however figurative or aphoristic in expression, is in principle capable of exposition *en clair;* it may be fugitive, elusive, dispersed, rather than secret.

Bakhtin tells us that the writer is dependent on another's voice, and that his word comes from another context which is already involved in other interpretations. The point, which has lately impressed itself as one of real importance, was made slightly differently by Barthes in his treatment of narrative codes. Also by Todorov, who distinguishes between what he calls monovalent and polyvalent discourse: the first invokes "no anterior 'way of speaking'," the second invokes "an anterior discourse more or less explicitly." The distinction is not as clear as it might be, for he also holds that reference to an anterior discourse, that is, "an anonymous ensemble of discursive properties" is unavoidable (Todorov: 23–24). But Todorov means that the text sometimes calls for some recourse to anterior texts (and so is polyvalent) and sometimes doesn't (and so may be called "monovalent," although it presumably cannot escape evoking that "anonymous ensemble"). The polyvalent text may be parody, plagiarism, allusion, imitation, etc.; it clearly refers to a conscious practice on the part of the writer. But even when he intends no such thing there is still, inevitably, reference to anterior texts.

In polyvalent texts, then, the reference to what is anterior is explicitly part of the project, and may have, perhaps must have, an influence on its meaning: that is, the sense of the text under analysis is in some measure controlled by an absent text. Take, as an obvious example, *Paradise Lost* i.84: "If thou beest he; but O how fallen!" is polyvalent in terms of Todorov's distinction; it alludes to Isa. xiv:12, "How art thou fallen from heaven, O Lucifer," and also to *Aeneid* ii.274, *quantum mutatus ab illo/ Hectore . . .*

Clearly the double reference to Isaiah and Vergil is relevant to an informed reading of the poem as a whole. It mediates between the Hebrew and Greek languages, myths and cultures; it comments on or exposes a disputed issue between religion and poetry (the Greek stories were after all false, yet the epic machinery could be revalidated by applying its principles to the true biblical stories; there was a biblical heroism more authentic than Hector's, the highest achievements of the muse—of the heavenly muse—were to be found in the Bible and not in the classics, etc.). This line could generate much comment and interpretation, but only if readers were aware of the pressure of the anterior texts. They were certainly more likely to do so in the 1660s than now, but even then the fit audience was few, and we can suppose some people saw only one of the anterior references, and many neither of them, reading the text as perfectly plausible in its narrative context: that is, monovalent.

Now, as I have suggested, the Kelber reading of the narrative must always be polyvalent, since it presupposes an anterior text of which the mysteries are to be fully explained. The gospel, in so far as it aspires to simple explanation, may need to sound as monovalent as possible; but what it illuminates is what is absent from it, and must be so, since by the premiss the anterior text resisted explanation to the world at large. Milton's absent texts were accessible to (and the need for such access was understood by) contemporaries of the right formation; they would derive from them further knowledge of Milton's poem, and the pleasure of that knowledge. But we—even if we have the means of access—understand the classical world, and the world of Isaiah, very differently.

Milton was heir to a system of knowing about the ancient world that has completely disappeared from the view of educated people, except for those who concern themselves with Renaissance and post-Renaissance conceptions of antiquity. Consider such ideas as *sapientia veterum, prisca theologica*. We are no longer under the impression that Greek philosophy derived from patriarchs of Israel, that Plato had access to the teachings of Moses, and that certain Greek works, such as the *Hermetica*, were of very great antiquity. We know they belong to the early centuries of the present era (Walker). Consequently there is a great deal of Renaissance and seventeenth-century literature which presupposes anterior texts of a character we know they did not possess, and a whole map of ancient esoteric knowledge and interrelations between languages and cultures we know to be false. Anteriorities, that is to say, can, though eternally absent, be abolished or discredited. Of course it is not the purposes of scholars like Walker merely to demonstrate that the Renaissance had wrong ideas about the *Hermetica* and the Egyptian god Thoth, or about Orpheus as poet and theologian; he is interested rather in restoring to our attention polyvalencies in the philosophies and theologies of the period, for example in the anteriorities which helped to shape their thought on the creation, the Trinity, and monotheism. It is one of the consequences of what Kelber calls the "hermeneutical dynamic" that absent anterior texts change, sometimes quite radically. Nobody would consider risking a martyrdom like that of Servetus for the sake of a belief, in part inspired by the *Hermetica*, that the one God was *polysōmatos*. (Walker: 190). Our interest in the Hermetic and Neo-Platonic studies of Servetus has to be different from his own; moreover we should do well to remember that if anybody in future is interested in ours, their interests will be just as different. In the case of absent texts, it is interest that determines their content and nature.

More about anteriority

My interest in the nature of anterior texts is of course related to a desire to understand what it is that the narrative, on Kelber's view, is revealing. But I shall continue for a moment to look at aspects of the general problematic of anteriority. The original Formalist distinction between *fabula* and *sjuzhet* now has wide currency and a diversity of formulations and terminologies which need not concern us. The distinction depends on the assumption, which is similar to Kelber's, that there is always something outside narrative which is absent or concealed, and which is in part revealed or made present by any particular narrative.

A characteristically sophisticated development of the idea is proposed by Jonathan Culler. He believes in two conflicting narrative logics. One is of the Formalist kind and presupposes a "non-textual substratum" which pre-exists the text but is absent from it. The other is a "tropological logic" by means of which the fable is generated by the discourse of the text. The two logics give different accounts of the story, for the second is not concerned with selection from something pre-existent, but with the invention or generation of the events which constitute the *fabula*. Thus in the first logic the non-textual substratum simply contains events of importance in the text—say, in *Oedipus Rex*, the killing of Laius—which take their place among many others. But according to the second logic the killing of Laius is an event generated by the text, a tropological product. Oedipus' recognition is an event compelled by the logic of the drama, not by pretextual events. He becomes the murderer of his father not by having committed a violent act later brought to light, but by deeming (in the text) that such an event had taken place. In the first logic the deed produces the guilt, in the second, the guilt produces the deed, and so the event—the murder—is not a cause but an effect.

As in many deconstructionist arguments, the happy ending is an aporia. The narratologist Shlomith Rimmon-Kenan, finding herself rather unhappily betwixt and between her own poetic and the temptations of deconstruction, observed of Culler's argument that "if the absent story motivates the narration, then it logically precedes it; if, on the other hand, narration tells an absent story, then there is no story to tell" (Rimmon-Kenan).

But this is a pseudo-problem, for there are not two logics. Where there is no narration there is no *fabula*. In fact the *fabula* is a heuristic fiction of which the purpose is to facilitate narratological investigations, and it is simply wrong to hypostasize it in this way. It is always "tropologically generated"; to speak of a pretextual substratum in which the killing of Laius takes its place with a chronicle of other events is to confuse the Oedipus myth with the *fabula* of Sophocles' play. When you take the figurative liberty of speaking as if Sophocles selected events from a pre-existent fable you are really doing exactly the same thing as saying that the events are tropologically generated by the text of the play. There are not two processes but only one. To say that in the second "logic," the guilt generates the deed is valuable as a reminder that we risk naive confusions if we suppose that cause operates in fictional worlds exactly as it does in life. But this doesn't mean that the second logic isn't a fiction, or simply another way of talking about the "first logic." The absent, pre-existing *fabula* can be deduced only from the text of the play. We are not, as Culler suggests, being asked to read the work in two registers, and to reconcile two contradictory accounts, one affirming the priority of the guilt and the other of the murder.

It seems to follow that absences, pretextual materials *outside* the narrative, are also produced by narrative tropes, and that Kelber's "mechanisms of disclosure" should be thought of as the attempts of the text to explicate *itself*, and to reduce our ability to infer the existence of tropologically generated events that do not suit the conscious ideological purpose of the narrative. The power of this conscious purpose is probably rather limited, so that tropological inference enjoys a considerable measure of freedom.

I believe that a tacit understanding of this fact was granted to novelists before it occurred to the critics to consider it. They eventually discovered what Allon White calls "the uses of obscurity." I myself have argued that it is impossible to distinguish, in Conrad's *Under Western Eyes*, between enigmas prescribed or inserted by the author, and others which, detected by the eye of the reader, may subvert the ostensible ideological purpose of the work, or suggest covert ideologies of a quite different sort (Kermode). These enigmas or clues are, in Culler's expression, tropological constructs. Nothing we might discover about intention, and nothing the narrative itself can do by way of emphasizing one purpose and suppressing tropes that seem to conflict with it, can alter the situation.

White, in a discussion which may remind one of Todorov's words on monovalency and polyvalency, maintains that a fictional event can belong to "the code of the real" yet simultaneously be what, following Althusser, he calls a symptom, requiring "symptomatic reading," and related to what Macherey, in his literary application of Althusser, calls the "determining absent centre." Such symptoms can be identified in various ways, for example by verbal, thematic or figural repetitions: Henry James repeats the figure or fictive event of the turned back over and over again (in the preface to *The Tragic Muse* the author's back is turned "*in triumph*,") and all the backs are emblems of the ways in which the novels themselves make "reference to things unimparted," like Densher's back as presented to Kate Croy—"links still missing and that she must ever miss, try to make them out as she would" (*The Wings of the Dove*, cap. xxxvi; White, 1981; 160, citing Beebe).

Hina versus hoti again

It seems to me that when Kelber and Williams, each in his way, read Mark parabolically they are allowing for this "symptomatic" aspect of narrative. Williams describes Mark as "a gospel informed by parabolic hermeneutics," adding that Matthew and Luke attenuated Mark's "parabolic dimension" by extending his narrative realism, making up for it by including more narrative parables than Mark used (Williams: 205). He bases this insight on a perception of Kelber's, which bore directly on the problem of the relationship between the narration and what was supposed to be in process of narration, namely the absent mystery (Kelber). Crossan treats gospel and parable as different levels of the same genre; he too, it seems, is working out the relation between narrative in its modes as disclosure and as trope (Crossan, *apud* Williams, loc. cit.). They all rightly assume that the relation between these two modes or functions can vary; they assume also that the absent referent is generated by the text. There is agreement, then, that narrative, in Kelber's words, both unlocks and creates secrecy. In my shorthand we are dealing with the *hina/hoti* problem again; the slash defines the shifting border between revealing and concealing.

Kelber supposes the absent *hina* material (actually an imaginative projection from the text) to be along the lines of sayings-gospels like Thomas, gnomic stuff with an audience of the fit few, lacking in narrative explanation. He fruitfully associates the choice of secrecy with the traditions of the craft guilds that regulate printing (extensible, one supposes, to pseudo-craft guilds such as freemasonry). Insofar as secrecy and the parabolic persist in the gospel they are survivals of an absent orality. And he ingeniously develops a dialectic of loss and gain, of absence and presence. In the end the insiders lose out; "interpretation begins to prevail over orality's urgent needs for preservation and secrecy " (10). However, one still needs to remember that the oral secrets are all tropologically inferred from the public script. Moreover it is important to qualify the claim that script enabled writers to pretend to omniscience. It may be so; but the assumption of omniscience does not require the writer to be *omnicommunicative*. In the present context this distinction of Meir Sternberg's may have peculiar importance, for the withholding of information by omniscient authors is a fertile source of mystery. Not everything is *parrhesia* (Mk. 8:32), *en clair,* and so the story may, in this as well as in other ways, acquire "parabolic mystery," and leave us, like the disciples, outside.

Genre: Gospel and Novel

I have already encroached on the issue of genre, and must now approach it more directly. Secular literary criticism has been actively engaged on the topic for some time, and we see from the present collection that it has had an impact on biblical criticism. Investigation has, however, reached a new level in Michael McKeon's book *The Origins of the English Novel, 1600–1740*. McKeon is concerned with the claim that the novel has unique status as "the *modern* genre" (11). Is it, as the "archetypalist" argument (mostly associated with Northrop Frye) maintains, a relatively anarchic displacement of existing forms? Or was Bakhtin right in making an analogy between genres and languages, saying that the study of the novel was like the study of a modern language, while other genres were like dead languages? It is admitted that the new genre incorporates precursors. In fact on a Formalist view its effectiveness depends upon its being seen against the ground of earlier forms; it is the defamiliarizing device which allows a new representation of the world. But McKeon's own subtle argument holds that "the persistence of the traditional categories is . . . an optical illusion, since the categories themselves [whether the literary category 'romance' or the social category 'aristocracy'], and the crucial 'traditionality' that determines our sense of their persistence, are conceptual products of the same centuries in which 'the novel' and 'the middle class' come into being" (19). He himself sees the novel as "a deceptively monolithic category that encloses a complex historical process" (19). It reflects and also formulates and explains modern "problems of categorial instability," both generic and social.

McKeon explores the relation between these generic and social instabilities, the one having to do with the signifying of "truth," and the other with the signifying of "virtue," terms which he uses in a special sense too refined to expound here. Such survivals as "romance idealism," "naive empiricism," "aristocratic ideology," "progressive ideology," and "conservative ideology" are treated not as atavisms but as newly abstracted and constituted categories "incorporated within the very process of the emergent genre" (21) with which they are, in a sense, in tension. This tension between the historical modes of discourse, which are as it were paradoxically generated by the new genre, reminds one of Kelber's similarly generated oral-secret ideology, in tension with the script-public gospel.

Moreover, McKeon is clear that a central issue is the establishment of authority, in his case the authority to answer questions relating to "truth" and "virtue." And it is clear that considered on similar lines the tension between gospel and the oral-secret is also a conflict about authority. Again, McKeon—who also follows Eisenstein—sees print as "framing" and "periodizing" romance, so that the technology which gave its birth is simultaneously the agent of its obsolescence. If we transfer this point from the manuscript/print threshold to the oral/script threshold we can see that on Kelber's view that which gives wide circulation to what was formerly oral is equivalently that which causes its obsolescence.

Finally, McKeon argues that the seventeenth-century distrust of figurative language was related to an "empirical-capitalist alienation of creativity," the consequence of which was the notion, now so firmly grounded among us as to seem quite natural, that "an idea does not really belong to you until you alienate it through publication. Before the existence of patents and copyrights, the value of ideas was preserved by the maintenance of secrecy and by strictly private and elitist consumption. But once ideas can be owned their value lies in disowning them by making them public . . . the very meaning of conceptual ownership depends upon the knowledge of others of your ownership. . ." (123). If we translate this back to the oral/script threshold we find a similarly paradoxical situation. To keep possession of ideas formerly preserved by secrecy it was necessary to "publish" them; or so it seemed to some. A certain secrecy of course remains, insofar as the proclamation is not wholly plain, and tends toward parable; but the continued possession of the secret, the mystery, is all the same dependent henceforth on its proclamation. Henceforth also our knowledge of the secret version arises from the exoteric gospel, as product of the emergent genre whose authority supersedes it.

Authority
If we now ask in what the authority of that genre consists, we can easily see that it differs greatly from the authority inherent in the anterior and "secret" doctrine, in which the secrets were fully available only to an elite and at best in dilute and distorted form to the many (a form which, in the eyes of the elite, would be that of a canonical gospel). The new authority depends not on the limited transmission of secrets but on the combination of narrative realism with a repeated appeal to another anterior source of authority, "the Scriptures"; hence the unique blend of "reality effect" and typology in the Passion narratives. Among the things that had been secret from the beginning of the world was the structure of the Passion. "For nothing is hidden, except to be revealed; nor has anything been secret, but that it should come to light," says Kelber's first epigraph; "A 'gospel' is a narrative of a son of god who appears among men as a riddle inviting misunderstanding," says his last. As Kelber knew when he chose them, these observations are perfectly compatible. The double claim to authority ("It happened this way"; "it happened according to the Scriptures") requires from the outset to be validated by interpretation, and this validation can only be given by the power of an institution, or by schismatic confidence in a personal contract with the deity: the magisterium, or *sola scriptura*. Kelber's gospel banishes one sort of mystery (so far as it can) and at once introduces another.

Consequences of metacritical reflection
If we think of the text of Mark as containing two different and conflicting traditions, one aphoristic, figurative, deriving its authority from secrecy yet the locus of an attempt to oust it, and the other more public, deriving its authority from narrative, we have created a recognisable genre, somewhat analogous to McKeon's novel. We could say with the Formalists that the relation of one to the other—say, *chreia* to parable—is the relation of figure to ground; the secret versions of Mark foregrounding parable (in a wide sense) and the public version foregrounding *chreia*.

Gerhart raises the question of competence, which is clearly relevant here, for to make such discriminations we have to claim competence in what Bakhtin would call a dead language, and I take it that we can't have anything analogous to Chomskyan competence outside a living language community. In what sense are we competent to analyse the conditions of genre in the first century C.E.? Our investigations are raids within the horizon of the contemporary, and require a different sort of effort from that demanded by the letter-example of John Barton. Only his imaginary Martian is baffled by the "Dear" in "Dear Sir" (13) but in respect of the gospels we are all Martians, more or less. However, even Martians, in their day-to-day lives on Mars, must have to deal with extra-linguistic conditions that help to determine interpretation, and the solution to our hermeneutic problems is likely to be dictated by our understanding of modern genres to which our response is as intuitive as our first naive response to gospel; the novel is the obvious instance. By a conscious effort we may, like McKeon, experience novels non-intuitively, for example by considering them as forming a category in which many preexisting categories, now belatedly identified as such, co-exist, whether in conflict or in reconciliation. Our ability to do this is what makes it possible for Williams to observe *chreia* interacting with parable in a manner characteristic of the genre known as "gospel." So it seems that a characteristically modern metacritical reflection may enable us, though with a good deal of historical effort, to see what is going on inside a genre that in our more naive view of it seems so much itself, so totally authoritative, that its four members would never, if we were not critics or historians, strike us as requiring this kind of reflection at all. We simply accept the mixture of exclusive mystery and authoritative public narrative as constitutive of gospel.

Talbert makes the interesting point that patristic polemic includes the charge that the Gnostics interfered with the narrative order of the gospels. A consecutive and plausible narrative has its own authority. His quotation from Achtemeier is particularly suggestive: narrative can act as a positive control on the wild interpretation of individual logia, subordinating them to a larger interpretandum, a whole. Yet the combination of the narrative with other non-narrative material has the beneficial effect, Talbert suggests, of limiting a certain reductiveness; it prevents the foregrounding of one type of discourse, for instance the Passion narrative, at the expense of the others. He is skeptical of the Kelber-Williams parable-theory, largely because other elements are present that may have the provocative function credited to parable without aspiring to be anything like parable. The point is well taken, especially since it is clearly one of the functions of *narrative* to shock or provoke. But the difference between his view and those he criticizes is not great; the relation of figure and ground is what lies behind all these theories.

Another way of expressing this relation is to say that one type of discourse tends to melt into another. This is Crossan's point: aphorism can generate narrative. Another piece of evidence is provided by the semantics of *mashal* and *parabole*. For instance, the *mashal* may be virtually an aphorism, it may be a narrative adapted to some fairly strict scheme like the "king-*meshalim*," or it may open out into an anecdote in free form, or even a short story like The Prodigal Son. It is only as a convenience to schematic thinking that we may regard these generic constituents as strictly confined. The view of Williams that there was already in Q an interaction between *chreia* and parable is very plausible—if there indeed was a Q, with a more or less exoteric orientation, that is what we ought to expect of it. Leaving the defence of secrecy to the rival tradition of Thomas-like gospels, it would be committed to authoritative exposition *en clair*, which, as we have seen, tends towards narrative.

Not of course that it wouldn't, if we had a copy, seem mysterious. For consider the trajectory of parable; it might start off being gnomic, but then it is asked to serve a rhetorical purpose, as illustration and example; whereupon its point seems, on investigation, obscure; and so it is once more a mystery of the sort that creates such turbulence in our readings of Mark 4.

Conclusion

I have tried to explore some of the implications of these essays, starting with Kelber's. The main problem seems to be that of anteriority—we tend to regard the traces of secrecy in our text as traces of an absent text, perhaps without sufficiently considering that it is the text itself—despite its desire to present everything in the full light of day—that generates the secrets we explain by hypotheses of anteriority. We ought to consider what it is we are doing when we invent texts on the basis of tropological "traces." And however gratifying it may be to speak of the narrative *plenum*, it is necessary to remember that there is really no such thing, and that, in a sense, the narrative cannot avoid turning its back on us, whether or not to do so is part of the conscious purpose. Or, to put it another way, *hina* is the inescapable shadow of *hoti*.

Another suggestion, derived from McKeon, is that the constituent elements of a genre are identified as it were *après coup*, by metacritical reflection on the emergent genre. Of course this does not mean that they had no anterior existence, only that the *forms* of their anteriority are established by reflection on their successor. Thus the characteristics of parable and of *chreia* are perfectly adapted to discussion of the relations held to exist between them in the gospels; for they are shaped to fit those relations.

There is an important issue of authority, and the most interesting question of all may be this: why does the publication of what was oral and secret have most authority when it introduces narrative into what was mostly aphoristic and figurative? And how does it come about that the attempt to be authoritatively plain creates more secrets and demands more interpretation, including the variety that postulates, in some detail, the existence of anterior secrets?

WORKS CONSULTED

Bakhtin, Mikhail
    1984   *Problems of Dostoevsky's Poetics*, Ed. and Trans. Caryl Emerson. Manchester; Manchester U.P.

Barthes, Roland
    1971   S/Z, Paris: Seuil.

Barton, John
    1984   *Reading the Old Testament*. London: Darton Longman and Todd.

Beebe, Maurice
    1954   "The turned back of Henry James," *South Atlantic Quarterly*, reprinted in T. Tanner, ed., *Henry James: Modern Judgements*. London: Methuen, 1969.

Culler, Jonathan
    1980   "Fabula and Sjuzhet in the analysis of narrative." *Poetics Today*, I:27–37.

Kelber, Werner
    1983   *The Oral and the Written Gospel*. Philadelphia, Fortress.

Kermode, Frank
    1983   "Secrets and Narrative Sequence." Pp 133–55 in *The Art of Telling*. Cambridge, Mass.: Harvard University Press.

McKeon, Michael
    1987   *The Origins of the English Novel*. Baltimore: Johns Hopkins.

Rimmon-Kenan, S.
    1986   "Absence, repetition, and the status of narration" (unpublished paper).

Sternberg, Meir
    1978   *Expositional Modes and Temporal Ordering in Fiction*. Baltimore: Johns Hopkins.

Todorov, Tzvetan
    1981   *Introduction to Poetics*, trans. Richard Howard, Minneapolis; Minnesota U.P.

Walter, D.P.
    1972   *The Ancient Theology*. London: Duckworth

White, Allon
  1981   *The Uses of Obscurity*. London: Routledge and Kegan Paul.
Williams, James G.
  1985   *Gospel against Parable*, Sheffield: Almond.

www.ingramcontent.com/pod-product-compliance
Lightning Source LLC
Chambersburg PA
CBHW021811220426
43662CB00006B/267